STRICTLY PROHIBITED

NO RUNN

45

6

Caroline Clements
Dillon Seitchik-Reardon

PLACES WE SWIM

Exploring Australia's best beaches, pools,
waterfalls, lakes, hot springs and gorges

EXPLORE
AUSTRALIA

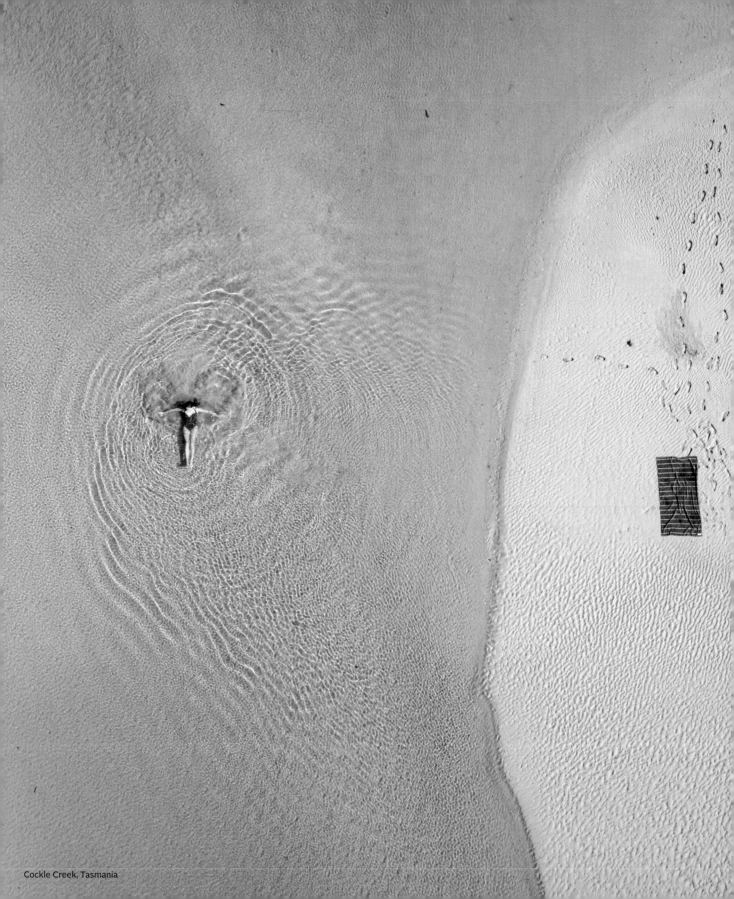

Cockle Creek, Tasmania

Foreword	v
Introduction	ix
Top 5s	xii
Honourable Mentions	xiv

New South Wales — 1

Cabarita Beach	2
Whites Beach	4
Yamba Main Beach	7
Lightning Ridge Bore Bath	10
Merewether Ocean Baths	12
North Curl Curl Beach	15
Andrew 'Boy' Charlton Pool	18
Bondi Icebergs	20
Clovelly Beach	23
Wattamolla Beach	26
Clarence Dam	29
Yarrangobilly Thermal Pool	32
Bermagui Blue Pool	34
PROFILE: Volunteer Life Saver, Emma Finnerty	36

Victoria — 39

Turpins Falls	40
Childers Cove	42
Addiscot Beach	44
Fitzroy Pool	47
Half Moon Bay	50
Bushrangers Bay	53
Little Waterloo Bay	57
PROFILE: Chef, Matt Germanchis	60

South Australia — 63

Dalhousie Springs	65
Blinman Pools	68
Shell Beach Rock Pool	70
Port Lincoln Swimming Enclosure	72
Second Valley	74
Little Blue Lake	77
PROFILE: Photographer and Travel Writer, Jackson Groves	80

Western Australia — 83

Emma Gorge	85
El Questro Gorge	88
Cape Leveque	90
Bell Gorge	92
Hamersley Gorge	95
Turquoise Bay	99
Cottesloe Beach	102
The Basin	104
Castle Rock	106
Greens Pool and Elephant Cove	109
West Beach	112
PROFILE: Remote Pools, Royal Life Saving Society WA	114

Northern Territory — 117

Alice Springs Aquatic and Leisure Centre	118
Glen Helen Gorge	120
Bitter Springs	122
Leliyn (Edith Falls)	125
Gunlom Falls	129
Maguk	132
Wangi Falls	134
Tjaynera (Sandy Creek) Falls	136
Nightcliff Pool	138
PROFILE: Senior Ranger, Stuart Woerle	140

Queensland — 145

Lawn Hill Gorge	146
Josephine Falls	149
Arthur Bay	153
Whitehaven Beach	156
Lake Wabby	158
Granite Bay	160
Tangalooma Wrecks	162
Centenary Pool	164
Twin Falls	166
PROFILE: Aqua English Instructor, Sarah Scarce	168

Tasmania — 171

Bay of Fires	173
First Basin	176
Wineglass Bay	179
Cockle Creek	182
Maria Island National Park	184
PROFILE: Olympian and Ocean Swimmer, Shane Gould	186

Index	188
Acknowledgements	191

Bondi Beach, Sydney, New South Wales

Foreword

Benjamin Law

Grow up in Australia and you're just meant to *know* how to swim. It makes sense: most Australians live within easy walking or driving distance to the coastline; our national anthem proclaims a country 'girt by sea' (even if the phrase still confuses most of us); and even now people across the world still refer to freestyle as the 'Australian crawl'. We're a country synonymous with our relationship to water. As Australian writer Anna Funder once wrote of the inhabitants of the driest continent on Earth: 'We cling to the edge of the continent, and we swim from a very early age.'

All true. Yet, I hated swimming as a kid. My parents migrated from Hong Kong to Queensland's Sunshine Coast – home to some of the country's most beautiful beaches – which was a strange match considering neither of my parents could swim. Water compelled and horrified my entire family. While other people saw stunning coastlines, we just saw a picturesque way to die. Rips could kill you, people said. Sharks could kill you. Skin cancer could kill you. Weirdly, it was always white people who told us these things, the same white people who seemed to *keep going to the beach*. Were we missing something? Did they *want* to die?

What made things worse was that in Queensland – a sun-saturated tropical paradise – the main exports seemed to be sugar, coal and championship swimmers. You weren't just expected to know how to swim here; you were expected to be good at it too. While white friends at school took to swimming laps like a birthright, carving through water like porpoises, I was the skinny kid from the migrant family, flailing and windmilling in the water uselessly, holding onto the sides of the pool every few metres like a capsize survivor clinging onto debris, spluttering and gasping for life.

It was only much later in adulthood – away from the ritual humiliations of mandatory school swimming classes and competitions – that I slowly fell in love with swimming. A back specialist told me to swim for my twisted spine, and I reluctantly signed up to my local Olympic pool in Brisbane. Gradually I improved my stroke; eventually I started swimming regularly for exercise; in several years I'd be swimming kilometres – plural! – every week.

It wasn't simply the act of swimming I fell in love with. It helped that no matter what Australian town or city I found myself in for work, there would be a world-class municipal – often Olympic-sized – pool nearby. It was easy to fall in love with swimming when I was doing it in pristine beaches and freshwater lakes, or ocean pools carved into rock walls.

And every body of water in this country has a compelling story behind it. Australian swimming spots tell this country's social and political history. Indigenous Australians – whose First Nations far outnumber those of modern Europe – harvested and swam in these waters for 60,000 years, far longer than any other human civilisation on this planet. The Freedom Ride of 1965 – led by activist Charles Perkins – was staged to protest the fact that the local Moree pool in northern New South Wales banned Aboriginal ('quarter caste, half-caste or full blood') swimmers. Aboriginal protestors picked up children from the local mission, escorted the kids into the pools personally and not only changed the pool's policy, but set the stage for the successful referendum on Indigenous rights two years later.

Pools still set the scene for our nation's stories, from Fitzroy Pool in Helen Garner's 1977 novel *Monkey Grip*, to the Cronulla beaches of Gabrielle Carey and Kathy Lette's *Puberty Blues*, to the Olympic pools of Christos Tsiolkas's *Barracuda*. These places where we swim remind us of the values to which Australians aspire: egalitarianism and fairness. What form of leisure is more accessible and democratic than dipping into a shared stretch of beach or a suburban pool on a baking summer's day? You don't need money to access the best spots this country has to offer.

Some of my favourite Australian memories are now imprinted with water. Many of those swimming spots are in this book. It was outside Brisbane's Centenary Pool that I discovered my best friend was pregnant. The first time I ever skinny-dipped was at Alexandria Bay (another story for another time). I've swum alongside schools of fish at Wylie's Baths, swum restorative laps at the chapel-like sanctuary of Melbourne's City Baths, and felt close to baptised at Bondi Icebergs.

Some other tips: it's impossible to take a bad photo of North Sydney Olympic Pool, where the Sydney Harbour Bridge towers above the pool like a CGI hallucination. Andrew 'Boy' Charlton Pool – nestled into Sydney's Botanical Gardens – will make you reassess your expectations of what a public pool can be. Hopping into the freezing freshwater pools in the Northern Territory is close to a religious experience. And for the best hangover cure on New Years Day, join locals and wash the previous year off at Clovelly – my annual tradition.

Is it too far to say swimming is the Australian version of baptism? To me, these places feel sacred; to swim in them veers towards sacrament. When I get writer's block now, I swim. When I need space, I swim. When I need company, I swim. When I'm depressed, I swim. When I'm happy, I swim.

It's not until Australians travel outside our own country that we realise ours is the best country for swimming. To know this country is to know it by its bodies of water into which we can plunge. Use this book not just as a guide but as an important reminder that whenever you find yourself anywhere in Australia, have your swimsuit and towel handy. Goggles too, preferably.

Benjamin Law is an Australian author, journalist, radio host and TV personality. In the book world he is best known for his memoir *The Family Law*, which became an award-winning TV series, as well as *Gaysia: Adventures in the Queer East* and the *Quarterly Essay Moral Panic 101*. Benjamin co-hosts ABC RN's weekly pop culture show *Stop Everything*, and is part of the 2018 SBS series *Filthy Rich & Homeless*.

Parts of this introduction were first published in *The Guardian*

Centenary Pool, Brisbane, Queensland

Dillon and Caroline deep in research mode in south-west Tasmania (top left), Lucky Bay Western Australia (top right), and with the beloved Troopy

Introduction

This is a book of our favourite places to swim in Australia, and the people and cultures that are shaped by them. We are not hardcore swimmers. In some ways, this book is hardly even about swimming. It should really be thought of as a celebration of Australia's incredible landscape, both natural and built. It should also be thought of as a celebration of the Australian experience. 'Places' and 'We' are the most important words here. Swimming is simply a mechanism to access it all.

The idea of documenting our swims is something that we had been indirectly working on through years of road trips and exploration. However, it was only when our far-fetched pitch was accepted by our publisher that it coalesced into a book. We had always talked about driving a big lap around the country, and suddenly had found the perfect excuse to do so. We quit our jobs and hit the road.

One year was not enough time: we weren't ready, and our car was far from roadworthy (at one point we traded a surfboard to a mechanic in lieu of payment). Quite simply, we were in over our heads. It was a naively ambitious project. Do you realise how big this country is? We sure didn't. Yet, it all came together thanks to the help of friends and kind-hearted strangers.

This book is the result of many hundreds of people who contributed their own experiences and advice to help guide our adventures. It is also a collaboration with some of our favourite photographers, who generously shared pictures of the places they love.

We have tried our hardest to capture the very best possible representation of the country, and wanted it to be as democratic as possible. Swimming cuts through age, class, gender, religion and ethnicity. After all, what is more equalising than being outdoors in near nakedness among strangers? We have endeavoured to research every corner of every state, but we are sure that we will have missed a few gems. Indeed, we had to cut a few gems just to fit what we have into this book. In our selection, we were guided by some core ideas – that places should be eye-poppingly beautiful, be enjoyable for all types of people, be reasonably safe in good conditions, and not be prohibitively difficult or expensive to access (sorry, Lord Howe Island). In this process, we found ourselves repeatedly asking: Is this place special or unique to the region? Would we want to spend all day here? If a friend was visiting from overseas, would we want to show this off?

We have included a balance of beloved favourites that are popular for good reason, as well as lesser known places that you may have all to yourself. The result is 60 beautiful places to swim that will change your life (for the better). It was our great joy to research this book and we put a lot of ourselves into it. It gave us a deeper understanding and love of our country, as well as one another. Things didn't always turn out as expected, but we always woke up with a sense of wonder and awe for the next adventure around the corner. We hope this book inspires you to get out and explore, even if it is in your own backyard. All it takes is the courage to dive in.

Important Ideas

Acknowledgement of Countries

Caroline Clements and Dillon Seitchik-Reardon acknowledge the Traditional Owners of the various countries we have visited, and pay our respects to Elders past, present and emerging. We thank all Traditional Owners for sharing their swimming places with us.

Although we have only included swims that are open for public use, many of the places have long been significant sites to local Indigenous people and form an important part of customary law, tradition, spirituality, history, knowledge, belief, language and practices. All swim sites should be visited with respect, appreciation and acknowledgement of Traditional Owners. It is their country, and all visitors have an obligation to be considerate of the land, plants and animals.

We hope that visiting these places will allow you to better understand not only the land, but also its people and any requests they make in relation to the area.

General etiquette

Each swimming spot has its own unique culture and it is incumbent upon everyone to gauge the situation and act accordingly. Be respectful and considerate of these shared spaces and the locals who love them. Clean up after yourself (and even collect rubbish that isn't yours). It's everyone's responsibility to maintain a good vibe, which can mean different things in different places. Some swims are quiet, peaceful escapes; some are nudie spots; while others may be rowdy social spaces. No matter where you are, what you are doing, and who you are with, don't be a dickhead. Enjoy!

Please Note

Every effort has been made to provide clear and correct information throughout this book. Nevertheless, some information is subject to change depending on seasons and various other conditions. *Places We Swim* is intended as a guide to swimming spots, but is by no means comprehensive or authoritative. Please check all official websites before visiting these places to get the most up-to-date information you need for your own visit. We wish you the best of luck and all the enjoyment in the world swimming at these incredible spots.

Swimming safety

Swimming can mean a lot of things to a lot of people – from traditional horizontal stroke swimming, to what is known as 'teabagging' (a vertical bobbing up and down), to virtual swimming from the edge of the water. No matter your style, swimming is a great way to experience beautiful places and it's this sentiment that has taken us to some of the most wild and pristine landscapes in Australia. As a result, most of our recommendations in this book are unpatrolled and do not have lifesaving services. Even when there are lifesaving services, it is up to the swimmer to recognise their own abilities and identify when and where it is safe to get in the water. We made an effort to visit and shoot all of these listed locations when they were looking their friendliest, but conditions are constantly changing. Your safety is your own responsibility and a little bit of common sense goes a long way.

HERE ARE A FEW RULES WE TRY TO FOLLOW:

- If it doesn't look safe, don't swim.
- Read all nearby signs.
- Swim with a buddy.
- Ask other swimmers about warnings and local information.
- Enter water slowly and feet first on arrival.
- Check the water temperature before jumping in.
- Check the depth (often very deceptive).
- Look out for natural hazards such as snags and submerged objects.
- Identify currents and rips (*see* Beach safety, p. 37).
- Swim between the flags on patrolled beaches.
- Don't swim in fast-flowing water.
- Don't swim when impaired by alcohol or drugs.
- Don't swim during a thunderstorm.
- Always. Have. Fun.

Cliff-jumping best practices

Cliff-jumping is great fun and one of the most exciting things you can do around water. We've featured a few legendary places in this book that we know everyone will love. That said, jumping multiplies any of the normal risks that we associate with swimming and can be very dangerous. The key here is knowing your abilities. You don't have to do the highest jump to have a good day. You don't even have to jump at all. Remember, 'the man' will only turn a blind eye to popular jumping spots so long as people act responsibly.

- Swim around the landing zone to inspect depth and hazards before jumping (even if you have done the jump before).
- Always bring a friend or make sure there are other people around.
- Watch others jump first.
- Ask others if there are any hazards (we usually ask a few people).
- Wear shoes to protect your feet and assist with climbing.
- Start small.
- Jump feet first with your arms tucked in.
- Quickly swim away from the landing zone.
- Don't let people pressure you; it's okay to just watch.

4WD advice

Some places in this book require a four-wheel drive (4WD) vehicle to access them. We are not 4WD enthusiasts and didn't have any such experience prior to setting out across the country. We learned a lot through trial and error, as well as by asking lots of questions (usually after we got something wrong). Sometimes it was bloody fun, while other times we were counting down the time until we could get away from corrugated roads. In general, we found that people treat off-road travel as if they are on a pioneering expedition. People love their gear, and you really get a good show of it in the outback. While we believe it is always good to be prepared, we tried to remain balanced in our approach. There is usually someone else around if you really get stuck and they are probably dying to show off their equipment. Nothing in this book is too far, remote, or obscure that you can't flag down some help if you find yourself in a tough spot.

We've put together a list of a few things we learned. We are not professionals and this shouldn't be taken as gospel. All vehicles are different and it is important to learn how your car works before putting it to the test. Practise getting in and out of the 4WD setting (this may include manually locking hubs) and understand how to change between high- and low-range gearing.

GENERAL TIPS:

- Ask others about road conditions ahead.
- Normal traffic rules apply.
- Avoid driving during, or immediately after, wet weather.
- When in doubt, drive slowly (a good way to avoid punctures).
- Don't drive at night.
- High clearance is 90% of the battle.
- Always engage 4WD in sand.
- High range is good for cruising and almost all situations.
- Low range is for going really slowly across gnarly terrain – some water crossings, driving up or down really steep ground, getting unstuck in sand, etc.
- Slow down and be prepared to stop for oncoming vehicles.

IF YOU GET BOGGED:

- Do not spin your wheels; this just sinks you in deeper.
- Ensure that the underbody is clear of sand or other obstacles.
- Try to reverse out over your tracks (try low-range).
- If that doesn't work, reduce tyre pressure a little and try to back out.
- If that doesn't work, it's time to start digging.

Tyre pressure

This is probably the biggest topic of conversation among people on the road but there is a lack of any clear consensus. Everyone agrees that lowering pressure is important, but how much is up for debate. In our opinion, running tyre pressure too low can make you more prone to sidewall punctures. We generally let out about 10psi to 12psi from our highway pressure. Which leaves room to go lower if we need to.

THINGS TO NOTE:

- It's best practice to drop your air pressure before driving, while tyres are still cool, to get an accurate reading.
- Lower pressure over corrugated terrain can make for a softer ride.
- Running a low tyre pressure when driving in soft sand increases surface area and improves traction (we aimed for about 20psi).
- Slower driving speeds are imperative when running low pressure.
- Remember to inflate tyres when returning to 2WD roads or whenever conditions change.

Water crossings

This is another topic with multiple theories. Important to know are your air intake height and exhaust manifold height. Air intake will keep you driving, which is why a lot of people have snorkels. You should never turn your car off mid-crossing because if the exhaust manifold is submerged it can send water back into the engine, even if the air intake is clear.

Assess the conditions: depth, water flow and type of bottom (if it's sand, you may need to lower your tyre pressure). Our approach is to drive slowly and steadily, to displace as little water as possible. It's especially important to enter the water slowly, so that you don't aquaplane. You can accelerate a little once in. Keep the pace steady. Racing through will push water higher under the bonnet, causing it to cover more of the engine. We just drop the car into low range and let it cruise like a tractor. Once out, don't turn off the car for 10 to 15 minutes so that all components can dry.

Essential items

You could spend a king's ransom outfitting your 4WD – there are plenty of sales clerks who will happily send you off with everything from $2000 satellite navigation to solar barbecues and rapid tyre deflators. However, we like to remind ourselves that Burke and Wills didn't have any of that fancy stuff, and things worked out pretty well for them. Right?

AT ANY RATE, THESE ARE THE THINGS THAT YOU SHOULDN'T LEAVE HOME WITHOUT:

- A good map (ideally of the place you intend to visit)
- Air compressor
- Tyre pressure gauge
- At least one spare tyre
- Working jack
- Digging tool (can be improvised)
- Tow rope
- Plenty of drinking water and food

Top 5s

People often ask us which are our favourite swimming spots. It's a cruel and nearly impossible question to answer, but we do our best. We've found it is easier when we focus on a specific theme, so during our trip we kept lists of our top 5s: best meals, best roadhouses, best regional haircuts, best sunburns, most interesting people we met, and yes – best swims. Because you asked so nicely, here are the very best of the best (in no particular order). They are a great place to start your own swimming wish lists.

Best beaches

Probably the hardest list to whittle down, but also the strongest. These beaches are by far some of the most incredible places we've swum in the world. And they're the reason Australians are so hard to impress when travelling overseas.

WEST BEACH,
ESPERANCE, WA

(*see* p. 112)

WHITEHAVEN BEACH,
WHITSUNDAY ISLAND, QLD

(*see* p. 156)

Best for a nudie swim

In a country bound by so much sea, it's not hard to find somewhere to shed your clothes. But we love these spots for their unique landscape and privacy. Some are sanctioned 'clothing-optional' swims while others are places where the spirit overtakes any sense of propriety.

CAPE LEVEQUE,
DAMPIER PENINSULA, WA

(*see* p. 90)

ADDISCOT BEACH,
POINT ADDIS, VIC

(*see* p. 44)

Best for relaxing with a cold beer

It is impossible to do a trip around Australia without quenching your thirst in celebration of the country's many picturesque places. Here we raise our stubbies to five great swims.

BITTER SPRINGS,
ELSEY NATIONAL PARK, NT

(*see* p. 122)

BOODJAMULLA (LAWN HILL)
NATIONAL PARK, QLD

(*see* p. 147)

Best waterfalls

Because everyone loves chasing waterfalls.

TJAYNERA (SANDY CREEK) FALLS,
LITCHFIELD NATIONAL PARK, NT

(*see* p. 136)

LELIYN (EDITH FALLS),
NITMILUK NATIONAL PARK, NT

(*see* p. 125)

WINEGLASS BAY,
FREYCINET NATIONAL PARK, TAS

(*see* p. 179)

WHITES BEACH,
BROKEN HEAD, NSW

(*see* p. 4)

LITTLE WATERLOO BAY,
WILSONS PROMONTORY, VIC

(*see* p. 57)

BLINMAN POOLS,
FLINDERS RANGES, SA

(*see* p. 68)

MARIA ISLAND,
EAST COAST, TAS

(*see* p. 184)

ALEXANDRIA BAY,
NOOSA NATIONAL PARK, QLD

(*see* p. 160)

DALHOUSIE SPRINGS,
WITJIRA NATIONAL PARK, SA

(*see* p. 65)

TURPINS FALLS,
CENTRAL HIGHLANDS, VIC

(*see* p. 40)

CLARENCE DAM,
BLUE MOUNTAINS, NSW

(*see* p. 29)

JOSEPHINE FALLS,
WOOROONOORAN NATIONAL PARK,
QLD

(*see* p. 149)

EMMA GORGE,
THE KIMBERLEY, WA

(*see* p. 85)

TWIN FALLS,
SPRINGBROOK NATIONAL PARK, QLD

(*see* p. 166)

Honourable Mentions

Numerous places didn't make the cut – not because they aren't great, but because we decided to include something similar or nearby, factors like accessibility and/or cost were prohibitive, or we simply ran out of space in the book. We begged our publisher for extra pages, but were already well over our limit. The following are all incredible places to swim and should not be missed. Careful readers will notice that Jim Jim Falls and Babinda Boulders are briefly mentioned in their respective chapters, but we think they deserved some extra air time here and a photo to do them justice.

JIM JIM FALLS, NT

We love love Jim Jim, but it was pushed aside by other incredible spots in Kakadu (Maguk, *see* p. 132, and Gunlom Falls, *see* p. 129) and requires some technical 4WD-ing to get there. It's one of the most dramatic landscapes we've visited, in terms of both scale and quality of swim. The main plunge pool is found along a boulder-strewn riverbed, and near the base of the falls there is a succession of outstandingly beautiful, white, sandy beaches. For the more adventurous, an exposed walk will take you to the top of the falls where you can swim in more pools and peer over the edge from 200-plus metres. If you look closely you may even spot some rock-art sites – a very special place.

BABINDA BOULDERS, QLD

This neighbour to Josephine Falls (*see* p. 149) is set in a region home to mystical landscapes, where deep, cold water rushes through lush, wet rainforest. There are several elements to Babinda Boulders, but the main swim here is a large natural pool at the intersection of three streams. Up- and downriver, the waterways are dotted with groups of giant granite boulders that create natural pools, many of them wildly unswimmable. The water wraps around these huge rocks, buffing them into large, soft creatures dotted along the river. At the meeting point of the rivers, warm and cool currents mingle under the canopy of the rainforest. It feels like a scene from *The Jungle Book* in here.

SEAL ROCKS, NSW

We first visited the tiny coastal town of Seal Rocks on a summer road trip up the east coast, and it has since become a favourite stop on our route. Number One beach is the first stretch as you come into town. Cliffs frame the bay on one side, and gentle swell rolls at the point, where swimmers splash around between longboarders. One of the best things about this area is the shape and orientation of the coastline; given any combination of wind and swell, you'll find a protected place for a swim and opportunities to surf. If you follow the road up over the hill, you'll find more epic beaches: Sugarloaf Point, Treachery and Submarine. Outside of holiday periods, Seal Rocks is a sleepy place with little more than beach life to offer.

VIVONNE BAY, KANGAROO ISLAND, SA

The one that got away... Sheer limestone cliffs and brilliant semicircles of white sand dominate Kangaroo Island's 540 kilometres of coastline. It's one of South Australia's most celebrated tourist destinations, rich in fertile land, great cheese and remote sandy beaches. Vivonne Bay is a protected cove on the southern side of the island, with cracking blue water and the ideal mix of accessibility and seclusion. Kangaroo Island is a surfing, swimming and grazing paradise.

FLINDERS ISLAND, TAS

This extremely remote island halfway between Wilson's Prom (*see* p. 57) and Tassie's northeast coast appears to be left over from an ancient continental divorce settlement. Because we've covered the region extensively (*see* Bay of Fires, p. 173; Wineglass Bay, p. 179; and Maria Island, p. 184), we felt it would be a little too indulgent to write about yet more granite mountains, crystal-clear water and white sand, but we couldn't resist a nod of appreciation here. Flights to Flinders Island depart from Melbourne and Launceston.

Babinda Boulders, Queensland

Jim Jim Falls, Northern Territory

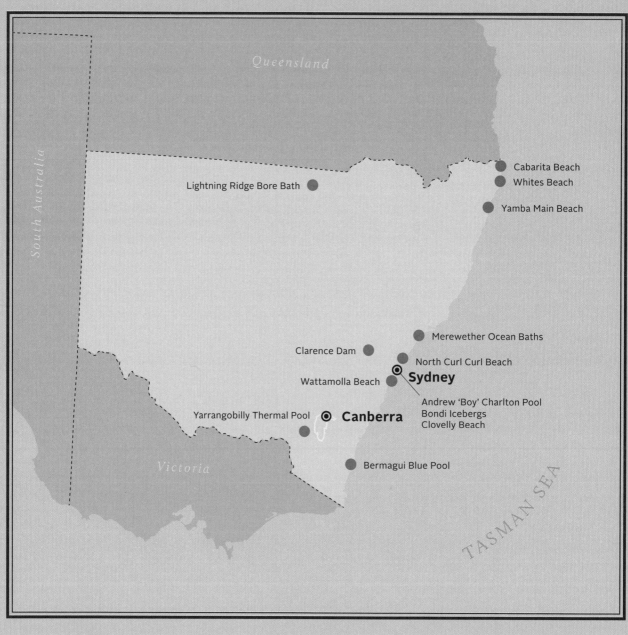

Queensland

South Australia

Lightning Ridge Bore Bath

Cabarita Beach
Whites Beach

Yamba Main Beach

Merewether Ocean Baths

Clarence Dam

North Curl Curl Beach

Sydney

Wattamolla Beach

Andrew 'Boy' Charlton Pool
Bondi Icebergs
Clovelly Beach

Yarrangobilly Thermal Pool

Canberra

Victoria

Bermagui Blue Pool

TASMAN SEA

When to visit

Year-round. However, the South
Coast and mountain areas are
warmest from November to March.

Favourite swim

CLOVELLY
(see p. 23)

Best meal

SHUK
(see p. 21)

Road-trip advice

With so much focus on Sydney and
northern NSW, there are still plenty
of quiet places to discover. Make an
effort to explore the Central Coast
from Newcastle to Coffs Harbour,
as well as the South Coast from
Batemans Bay to Tathra.

New South Wales

New South Wales is the Goldilocks state.

Not too big, nor too small. Not far enough north to worry about crocs and jellyfish, yet not far enough south to be challenged by cold water. Some would say that everything here is 'just right', and we are inclined to agree. No matter the season, there is always a good swim to be found; the hardest part is choosing between excellent options.

Every year we do a winter and a summer road trip, and every year we find our new favourite place. The entire NSW coastline is profoundly hospitable. Winter brings reliable surf and we gravitate towards the wild, remote solitude of the South Coast (*see* Bermagui, p. 34). Summer, on the other hand, tends to be more social; we catch up with friends in Sydney and invariably get pulled further north. We often find ourselves in Yamba (*see* p. 7) or Cabarita (*see* p. 2), wondering where all the time went and how much of it (16 hours) we need to make one big push back home to Melbourne.

The state's most celebrated swimming places would have to be its abundant ocean pools (or baths). These are monuments to Australia's love of swimming, and rank as some of our best public spaces. There are more than 100 across the state, each of which provides a fundamental gathering place for its coastal community. They come in all shapes, sizes and depths, often built on top of existing Aboriginal 'bogey holes'. Read into this what you will.

In researching our book, we made extra effort to explore inland swims as well. Getting away from the coast reveals the different character of the regions, each bending its identity around its unique relationship to water. The Great Artesian Basin is a hard land to the naked eye, yet offers ancient healing water from deep in the earth at its bore baths (*see*. p. 10). By comparison, the Snowy Mountains (*see* p. 32) feel young and raw; water is transient as it exuberantly tumbles through every valley.

Like Goldilocks, we couldn't help but eat every meal and sleep in every bed. Thus, there are a lot more entries for this state than any other. Some will be familiar, and others will be a pleasant surprise, but we guarantee all will be enjoyable.

BEACH

◑ **Best time to visit**
Summer, but anytime is good.

◭ **How to get there**
Cabarita Beach is about 20km south of
Tweed Heads along the Tweed Coast Rd.
From the Pacific Mtwy, take the Clothiers
Creek Rd exit, following signs to Cabarita.
The best beaches are across the street
from Diamond Beach Resort (105 Tweed
Coast Rd).

⊖ **Access**
Easy. There's abundant parking along
Tweed Coast Rd, but spaces get
competitive on a hot summer's day.

⑤ **Cost of entry** Free

☺ **Kid friendly** Yes

⊗ **Dog friendly** No

◠ **Water temperature** Balmy

◷ **Open** 24 hours

⊕ **Facilities**
Toilets, outdoor showers,
picnic tables, BBQs

⊚ **Must bring**
A longboard and zinc.

LOCAL KNOWLEDGE

Cabarita is a local Bundjalung
word meaning 'by the water'.

Cabarita Beach

NORTHERN NSW

THE ULTIMATE SUN-DRENCHED, PALM-FRINGED BEACH,
WITH PERFECT SWIMMING CONDITIONS.

We sort of, like, accidentally fell in love with Cabarita, after
spending some time here over summer. This beach has all the
celebrated features that we swoon over – including pandanus trees for
shade, beach showers, and surfers even when there are no waves.

We arrived at this popular surf town during a swell drought in
the peak of summer. Cars were parked up on the hill, gazing down at
the water on both sides – the main beach and the smaller coves near
Norries Head. We pulled our van up alongside them, made some lunch
and looked hopefully out to sea, waiting for waves that never came.
The ocean may have been flatter than the sand itself, but that didn't
dull the crowds. We hardly moved for two days for fear of losing our
prime park at the top of the hill.

There are several spots you can swim in Cabarita – there's the main
beach, some small coves near Norries Head and the back beach. As
hordes of sun-seekers pour in with boards, beach brollies and bottles of
Banana Boat sunscreen under their arms, picturesque waters around
this point provide perfect conditions for swimmers.

Even though it's surrounded by shiny destinations like the Gold
Coast and Byron Bay, Cabarita still feels like a local spot. When hot
and bothered drivers catch sight of the sparkling waters, an eruption of
horns breaks out as they all vie for beachside car spots. It's all in the name
of getting to the sand as soon as possible. But if accessing the beach is the
most frustrating part of your day, that's not such a bad thing.

Breezy low-rise apartments look over the beach along Tweed Coast
Road, only a stone's throw from the water's edge, boasting prime
people-watching and surf-checking prospects from their balconies.
Along the boundary of the beach, the scenery changes as you walk
through a tunnel of remnant coastal rainforest. Down on the sand,
families erect tents and colourful umbrellas to sit under all day as
kids schnitzel themselves in the sand. Ever-hopeful longboarders haul
heavy crafts in and out of the water. Waves do get in to this popular
point break, just not today, but even when there's swell, the cove
provides protection for swimmers of all levels.

Views of this classic beachscape can be seen from the boardwalk up
to the point at Norries Head. Emblazoned on a rock in full view of the
beach below is a hand-painted sign that reads 'Locals only'. So I guess
we'll just have to move here ...

NEARBY

CABANA CABARITA
107 Tweed Coast Rd, Cabarita

A coffee cart on the headland next to the Diamond Beach Resort serving Campos coffee, acai bowls, smoothies and house-baked almond croissants. Open in summer, but closed Saturdays.

HALCYON HOUSE
21 Cypress Cres, Cabarita

This luxe, revamped 1960s Aussie beach hotel with 21 rooms features designer styling by Anna Spiro, in-house restaurant Paper Daisy, a Hamptons-style pool deck, and free bikes for guests. Even if you're not staying, visit for breakfast (order the crumpets) or come for a cocktail at sunset.

BRUNSWICK HEADS

Take a 30-minute drive south to the town of Brunswick Heads. Grab a coffee at Jones & Co (15 Tweed St), and eat at Fleet (2/16 The Terrace), a small restaurant masquerading as a bar, with a concise, ever-changing menu using local produce. Have a drink at the Hotel Brunswick (4 Mullumbimbi St).

BEACH

◑ **Best time to visit**
Summer during low to mid-tide. At high tide the water washes right up over the beach, so there's nowhere to sit.

◬ **How to get there**
Head towards Broken Head Beach and turn off at Seven Mile Beach Rd. Continue curving around the narrow forest stretch through Broken Head Nature Reserve to the third carpark. Signs read 'Whites Beach'. Follow the steep path down to the beach.

⊖ **Access**
Easy. The narrow, hilly, well-maintained unsealed road will take you to the trailhead. It's a short walk from there.

⑤ **Cost of entry** Free

☺ **Kid friendly** Yes

⊗ **Dog friendly** No

⌒ **Water temperature** Mild and refreshing

◷ **Open** 24 hours

⊕ **Facilities**
None

⟳ **Must bring**
Shade: there isn't much around if you plan to stay a while.

LOCAL KNOWLEDGE

Get here early during summer as there are only about 10 carparks.

Whites Beach   BROKEN HEAD, NORTHERN NSW

A SHELTERED, SEMI-SECRET COVE SURROUNDED BY STEEP SUBTROPICAL RAINFOREST.

The North Coast of NSW near Byron Bay is so highly travelled that it's hard to imagine there being any secret beaches left. Whites Beach might be about as close as you come to some seclusion in this area, particularly in the heart of summer. This protected bay, just out of Broken Head, has a real sense of discovery about it, taking you down through subtropical rainforest surrounds to an idyllic sheltered beach of white sand and crisp, clear water.

This beach is surrounded on three sides by palm-covered cliffs, giving visitors a big reveal walk-in down a rocky staircase overlooking the water. A trailhead at the carpark tells you the walk is 30 minutes return; this must account for a swim, because it's less than 800 metres down before you hit the sand. But just before you do that, take in the ultimate beach panorama, which comes at a steep turn on the stairs as you cut back past pandanus trees that fringe the beach – get your camera out here. At the base of the path a channel of water has created a warm, shallow pool to wash your feet in.

Visiting Whites early in January, we see young kids with their parents arriving with pristine boogie boards tucked under their arms, fresh from Christmas. With only a little bit of swell getting in, this beach seems like the perfect place to bodysurf. On a big swell, though, we're sure it can get pretty wild on this unpatrolled strip. Soon enough, some surfers come out for a wave here too.

At the south side of the beach there are some caves and rock pools to explore. Nearby, freshwater creeps over rocks from a spring, creating a sandy stream down into the ocean. At the north side, you can see a neighbouring sheltered cove, where people fish from the rocks or with spears in the shallows.

At high tide, the beach is almost completely covered with white water and beachgoers move towards the rocky backdrop to keep their towels dry. At low tide, you can wade around to the neighbouring bay, which may mean a Jane Fonda–like work-out to contend with on your return through the channel against the current.

Though our secret beach fantasies fade quickly when holidaying sun-seekers begin filling up the sand, the atmosphere is high. It's the first time we see tanning oil (rather than sunscreen) pulled out of beach bags, but with it come colourful beach umbrellas, watermelons and frisbees. People settle in for the day at Whites because this is what summer holiday dreams are made of.

NEARBY

HARVEST
18–22 Old Pacific Hwy, Newrybar Village

An airy weatherboard cottage with a deli, a bakery, a coffee cart and a restaurant for breakfast, lunch and dinner. The food is all made from local, organic produce. Try the handmade reginette (ribbon-shaped pasta) with sea lettuce and finger lime.

YELLOW FLOWER
11 Clifford St, Suffolk Park

A casual Indian eatery serving a rotation of traditional, soul-warming curries from a bain-marie (meat, vegetarian and vegan-friendly). We rarely go past a rendang, but it's hard to choose. Start with a giant samosa; end on a mango lassi. Eat in or take away.

SHELTER
41 Pacific Pde, Lennox Head

Along the beachfront in neighbouring Lennox Head is Shelter, a cafe and bar open seven days for breakfast and lunch (and dinner on weekends). Dine on charred red mullet with oyster butter, lemon and sea succulents, along with ocean views.

Yamba
Main Beach

ONE OF OUR FAVOURITE
ANNUAL STOPS, WITH A FUN
BEACH, AN OCEAN POOL AND
A PUB THAT HAS THE BEST
VIEWS IN AUSTRALIA.

BEACH   **OCEAN POOL**

◑ **Best time to visit**
Summer for swimming,
winter for surfing

⃝ **Address**
1 Marine Pde, Yamba

⊖ **Access**
Easy. The road dead-ends behind
the surf life saving club.

⑂ **Cost of entry** Free

☺ **Kid friendly** Yes

⊗ **Dog friendly** No. Off-leash areas are
nearby at Wattle Park and south end of
Pippi Beach.

⌂ **Water temperature** Warmish

◷ **Open** 24 hours

⊕ **Facilities**
Toilets, beach showers, kiosk

⊚ **Must bring**
Your wallet to buy hot chips
from the kiosk.

LOCAL KNOWLEDGE

Many NSW surf clubs claim to be the
oldest in Australia, but Yamba Surf Life
Saving Club proposes to be one of the
oldest in the world. We'll let you make
the final assessment – it's hotly debated.

There are a few places on the east coast that we just can't get enough of. Yamba is just about at the top of that list. One of our best friends, James, grew up here and we often invite ourselves to his family Christmas. Hardened by his youth of surf life saving and sibling rivalry, James is one of the most fearless water people we know. Every year he convinces us to do a deep-water ocean swim, rock-jump into a gurgling rip, or surf a sketchy river mouth at dusk. Every year we feed him excessive peanut butter and banana sandwiches and convince him to watch bad summer blockbusters at the local cinema. Traditions are traditions.

Though we are unashamedly biased, Yamba's appeal is obvious. It is essentially an island, surrounded by national parks (Yuraygir to the south and Bundjalung to the north), and further isolated by its distance from the motorway. Some would call it the perfect northern NSW coastal town: possessing warm water, a river mouth, a breakwall, open beaches, reefs and rocky points. Whether you surf, swim, fish or bushwalk, it's hard to find a better place. However, being only an hour and a half from Byron Bay, most people drive past without giving it a second thought. Hopefully most of those people never read this book.

Yamba Main Beach is the focal point of the town, set at the base of a steep hill and bounded by rocky outcrops and reefs. The lighthouse perches atop the northern hill, while the Pacific Hotel assumes prime position overlooking it all. Ancient pandanus trees and towering hoop pines complete the landscape, gathered around one of the state's most beloved surf life saving clubs. Locals take a lot of pride in this beach, and despite the small population there are always people swimming in the 33-metre ocean pool, surfing out the front, sunbaking or meeting for coffees at the kiosk.

If you stay in the water long enough, you will probably encounter dolphins, and in winter you can even hear the distant songs of migrating humpback whales. Dolphins are extraordinarily abundant and sociable here, never missing an opportunity to inspect a swimmer. Although it is momentarily unnerving to be surrounded by dorsal fins, there is no greater pleasure than sharing waves with these creatures and watching them race beneath the surface.

It is with great reluctance and no little conflict that we take the lid off this favourite spot. However, we would be hypocrites not to. All places change, but we expect that our friend James will still be here every Christmas, plotting the next cliff-jump into shallow water.

NEARBY

YAMBA CINEMA
13 Coldstream St, Yamba

It's as if this small, single-screen cinema has been frozen in time with 1990s prices: $8 tickets to see summer blockbusters, $1 bag lollies and $3 choc tops. We're not complaining. In fact, we make it an annual ritual to see the latest *Star Wars* release. Right time, right place.

ANGOURIE BLUE POOL
The Crescent, Angourie

Only 7 kilometres south of Yamba is the world-famous wave at Angourie Point, between the reserve and Spooky Beach. Less famous, but more accessible to non-surfers, is this old quarry turned waterhole, which was formed when an underground freshwater spring was disturbed and transformed into a dazzling blue aquatic heaven. Cliff-jumps aplenty.

PACIFIC HOTEL
18 Pilot St, Yamba

If Main Beach is Yamba's focal point, then the pub is its spiritual centre. Located on the cliff overlooking the water, this is the most prominent building in town and has arguably the best pub view anywhere in the country. No, the world.

Yamba's appeal is obvious.
It is essentially an island,
surrounded by national parks

THERMAL SPRING

Best time to visit
Winter, when the outside temperature is cool and mist forms on the water's surface.

Address
189 Shermans Way, Lightning Ridge

Access
Easy. The pool is at the edge of town and there is abundant parking.

Cost of entry Free

Kid friendly
Yes (but don't let them cook)

Dog friendly No

Water temperature 40°C

Open 24 hours;
cleaning from 10am–12pm

Facilities
Toilets, showers, covered picnic tables

Need to know
You should only stay in the bath for a few minutes at a time because of the high temperature; it'll make you woozy. Local pros alternate between cold showers and hot plunges. Apparently this is the secret to eternal life.

LOCAL KNOWLEDGE

Not for the first time, the spectre of *Crocodile Dundee* emerged while writing this book – this town is the birthplace of Paul Hogan.

Lightning Ridge Bore Bath WESTERN NSW

THIS THERMAL POOL IN THE MIDDLE OF COUNTRY NSW SITS AT A STEAMY 40°C LIKE A GIANT OUTDOOR BATHTUB.

After months of continuous travel through WA, NT and SA we were reluctant to give up the gentle hospitality of the coastal NSW landscape. Within a couple of hours' driving, however, that old familiar outback feeling was restored. The creased edges of the country quickly iron out as you travel west. Monuments to pineapples and lobsters give way to golden guitars and, no joke, horizontal oil drills. The landscape opens up and the sky breathes a sigh of relief, stretching itself from horizon to horizon like a dancer after a long flight. As we pushed deeper into the flatlands we were immersed once again in vivid stillness.

We are intractably drawn to the Great Artesian Basin and the contradiction of this vast parched land sitting on an underground sea. The basin underlies a fifth of Australia, stretching from Cape Yorke, to Dubbo, to Alice Springs, down to SA. Best estimates suggest that this aquifer takes about 2 million years to recharge – a very slow trickle from the tropical north to the continent's interior. If you sink a well deep enough, however, there's plentiful water to grow cotton in the desert (just because you can, does it mean that you should?), which is what you see on the road to Lightning Ridge. More to the point, the water promises to heal all ailments, from arthritis to sciatica.

Bore baths are abundant in this region, but this is in a class all to itself. The giant circular spa is a brilliant public space, free to enter. The mineralised water is an intersection for weary travellers and eccentric locals, a de facto town square. It's a welcoming place and you can't help but find yourself relaxing in the 40°C spa pool – no doubt the result of the magnesium, lithium and dehydration. Whatever the reason, it feels great.

We visited a lot of towns in western NSW, spiralling from pool to pool, but none of them pulled us in quite like Lightning Ridge. Sincere in its kitsch, its identity as the black opal capital of the world adorns every sign, wall and face. It's a masterpiece of tea-towel Australiana that unapologetically rides the line between junkyard and artist colony. People spend their lives looking for precious stones here, but the biggest gem of all boils up from the ground every day.

NEARBY

HARLIQUIN TAKEAWAY & CONVENIENCE STORE
Morilla St, Lightning Ridge

There's nothing too flash in this part of the world, so this convenience store and cafe will do. Serving fast food like egg-and-bacon sangas, it's rated by locals, who tell us that the 'Monster Burger' is the size of your head, for better or worse.

LIGHTNING RIDGE DISTRICT BOWLING CLUB
1 Agate St, Lightning Ridge

Widely acknowledged as the best pub in town, which may or may not have something to do with the cheap beer. A good towny atmosphere, with all of the usual fare, plus lawn bowls. Live music on Friday nights.

HERGOURMET GECKO
7 Opal St, Lightning Ridge

Admittedly, we're suckers for a tacky paint job and some classic signage. This town is full of colourful buildings, including this baby-blue cafe serving breakfasts and lunches of pies, pancakes and the best iced coffee in town.

People spend their lives looking for precious stones here, but the biggest gem of all boils up from the ground every day.

OCEAN POOL

◐ **Best time to visit**
You cannot beat the morning vibes around here. Water is warmest from December to May.

◎ **Address**
5 Henderson Pde, Merewether

⊖ **Access**
Easy walk, ride or drive. Free parking on Henderson Pde and Frederick St.

$ **Cost of entry** Free

☺ **Kid friendly** Yes

⊗ **Dog friendly** No, but there's an off-leash zone at nearby Dixon Park Reserve.

∿ **Water temperature**
Unheated ocean water varying with the season (cool to warm).

⏱ **Open** 24 hours; closed for cleaning mornings Mon–Thurs Oct–Mar, Thurs Apr–Sept

⊕ **Facilities**
Toilets, showers, picnic tables, wading pool

◉ **Must bring**
Goggles if you are doing laps, so you can see oncoming swimmers (there are no lane ropes here).

LOCAL KNOWLEDGE

The stairs around the pools, known as the Steps of Knowledge, are rumoured to be the place for enlightenment after a swim, or perhaps just a place to meet for a chat. People hang out here to discuss all kinds of things in the morning.

Merewether Ocean Baths   NEWCASTLE

THE LARGEST OCEAN BATHS IN THE SOUTHERN HEMISPHERE, AND FREE TO ALL.

Newcastle is the discreet, under-appreciated and under-celebrated swimming capital of Australia. It possesses all the style and flair of Sydney's coastal landscape with only a fraction of the population. Like many people, we often bypassed this once-industrial city in our hurry to get over the Hunter River and up the coast. A few years back, however, we were sent here to report on the reopening of the Bogey Hole public pool and discovered what many of the locals have long known – Newcastle is a brilliant place to live and swim. Merewether Baths is the crown jewel of the city and, in our opinion, the best ocean pool in the country.

As with many of our favourite places, there is something about this coastline that fosters a healthy lifestyle and strong community. The neighbourhood wakes up at first light, and on any day of the week, rain or shine, you can find people running, swimming, pramming, surfing, training or latte-ing. Merewether Baths is the nucleus of it all, with beaches and cafes radiating outwards. Even as a visitor you can't help but be drawn into the spirit of it. We often find ourselves swimming those extra few laps, secretly competing with the 70-year-old marathon swimmers in the next lane. They always win.

Like many NSW ocean pools, Merewether was built as part of a Depression relief scheme and opened its lanes in 1935. It was, and remains, a grand monument to Australia's vision of itself as a water-loving culture. The complex is the largest in the country and consists of two pools: the main pool is 50 metres long by 100 metres wide, with 10 unroped lap lanes. The adjacent sand-bottomed wading pool is 27 metres by 100 metres – it's mostly for kids, but you can do a sneaky 100-metre lap along the deep edge. A wide concrete walkway separates them. Most remarkably, the baths are completely free and open 24 hours a day.

This kind of access means there is almost universal community participation, and great effort (and cost) is invested to maintain the baths. Swimmers here seem to be more courteous than elsewhere, even enthusiastic to share their pool. The typical sense of urgency and entitlement found elsewhere is dropped, elevating the spirit of community. Whenever we visit, we always end up staying much longer than we planned. We find ourselves chatting with strangers and mind-surfing the waves out the front. We're enabled to become both closer to nature and to one another, which is the best outcome you could hope for in a place we swim.

NEARBY

BLUE DOOR KIOSK
corner Watkins St & John Pde, Merewether

The Blue Door Kiosk is a hub of activity on the beach. This hole-in-the-wall coffee stop sees a constant flow and hubbub in the mornings as locals meet pre, post or during their morning exercise. A great place to start your day, looking out to glassy waves and surfer babes. Coffee only comes in takeaway cups, so BYO vessel.

THE BOGEY HOLE
Shortland Espl, Newcastle

A heritage-listed site, the Bogey Hole has a long history. The pool was built by convicts and originally constructed as the Commandant of Newcastle's private bath in 1820. Come during high tide when waves crash over the sides. Bring a waterproof bag for your valuables.

SCOTTIE'S
36 Scott St, Newcastle

You might need to jump in the car; it's back towards the city in East Newcastle, but only a block from the beach, so you can still smell the sea breeze. Scottie's is a Newy favourite – a cosy neighbourhood restaurant serving fancy fish and chips under palms trees and festoon lights from Friday to Sunday. It's open as a cafe by day, but we come for dinner.

North Curl Curl Beach

SYDNEY NORTHERN BEACHES

A LOCAL SURF BEACH WITH A SHELTERED COVE, AN OCEAN POOL AND A SANDY LAGOON – ALL THE OPTIONS FOR ALL THE PEOPLE.

NEW SOUTH WALES

BEACH   **OCEAN POOL**

◐ **Best time to visit**
Summer, from November to March

◇ **Address**
Huston Pde, North Curl Curl.
There are no street numbers;
it's at the end of the road.

⊖ **Access**
Easy. Abundant parking behind the
North Curl Curl Surf Life Saving Club.

⑤ **Cost of entry** Free

☺ **Kid friendly** Yes

⊗ **Dog friendly** Yes

⌣ **Water temperature** Cool

◷ **Open** 24 hours

⊕ **Facilities**
Toilets, showers, kiosk

⊚ **Must bring**
Gold coins for the parking metre;
the inspectors are ruthless.

LOCAL KNOWLEDGE

Like many surf life saving clubs along
the coast, the North Curl Curl SLSC
spends in excess of 5000 volunteer
hours patrolling this beach. Pretty
damn impressive.

We are sure we will be stepping on a few toes by saying that North Curl Curl Beach was one of the easiest decisions we made all year. Even the name is a delight. We've literally been to all of Sydney's northern beaches, even a secret bay called Paradise. This one makes Manly look like Melbourne's St Kilda. Freshwater like a backwater. Nothing comes close. Perhaps what elevates North Curl Curl above all others is its unique combination of great elements. It has a warm lagoon (why so warm?), a dog beach, a sheltered corner, reliable surf, an ocean pool, and no tourists. It is the perfect Sydney beach.

We first came here on a recommendation from a local friend. Almost everyone in Sydney has a strong attachment to their home suburb, and the word 'best' gets thrown around pretty loosely. Much of our research has been chasing down such leads, but this was one of the rare occasions when the place was better than we ever could have hoped.

North Curl Curl is a few hundred metres from the main road and completely surrounded by parks and sea cliffs, which automatically gives it a secluded feel. Sand dunes conceal the low-rise suburb behind, to the effect that you might mistake it for Queensland's Fraser Island (if you squint). The broad lagoon further reinforces this idea, conjuring memories of Lake Wabby (*see* p. 158). This is one of a few off-leash dog beaches in Sydney and you will often see these 'good boys' herding children around the shallows.

White sandstone cliffs look like frothy waves about to crash on the north end of the beach, yet they provide shelter and shade throughout the day. This cosy corner tends to be protected in most conditions, making it an ideal place to swim when other beaches are blown out. Follow the pockmarked rocks along the reef to get to North Curl Curl's ocean pool. At 25 metres it's not the biggest on the coast, but the large boulder in the middle gives it character.

It's not Sydney's most famous beach, nor does it aspire to be. However, North Curl Curl has a humble local beauty that feels timeless and elegant; it has personality in excess; and every time you visit, you just want to get to know it better.

NEARBY

GUSTO ON THE BEACH
52/54 Carrington Pde, Curl Curl

Inside the SLSC at the southern end of the beach, with little more than sand between the cafe and the water, Gusto is often filled with barefoot customers straight off the beach after their morning swim or stroll. Order an egg-and-bacon roll with a coffee made from Belaroma Espresso beans, roasted just down the road in Manly Vale.

MRS JONES THE BAKER
6a Lawrence St, Freshwater

We're a sucker for a good bakery, because early morning swims and baked treats go hand in hand in our opinion. Croissants, doughnuts, pies, loaves of bread and even gelato are all made in-house here. So are the traditional English Eccles cakes – disks of puff pastry with spiced currants. There are a few bar seats where you can sit for a coffee too, and make sure you leave with a loaf of bread.

MUCHACHA MEXICAN KITCHEN
3/142 Pitt Rd, North Curl Curl

We were stoked to find this spicy little spot in the backstreets of North Curl Curl. A fun, colourful, lo-fi Mexican eatery serving hot and spicy Cali-Mex cuisine on colourful tabletops. Plates are piled high with corn chips and guacamole, pulled-pork tacos, cheesy quesadillas and bean burritos. The lively dining room is fun for small groups and is BYO (corkage $3 per person).

This is one of a few off-leash dog beaches in Sydney and you will often see these 'good boys' herding children around the shallows.

POOL

◐ **Best time to visit**
9am–5pm weekdays in summer

△ **Address**
1c Mrs Macquaries Rd, The Domain

⊖ **Access**
Easy. A 20-minute walk from
Sydney CBD. Metered parking
along Mrs Macquaries Rd.

$ **Cost of entry**
Adults $6.50, concession $4.90,
family (2 adults and 2 kids) $18.40

☺ **Kid friendly** Yes

⊗ **Dog friendly** No

◠ **Water temperature**
Warm (heated to around 28°C)

◷ **Open** 6am–7pm (8pm during daylight
saving) 1 Sept-30 Apr

⊕ **Facilities**
Toilets, changing rooms, cafe,
wading pool

⊘ **Must bring**
Sunscreen – there is no shade over
the pool.

LOCAL KNOWLEDGE

So who is Andrew 'Boy' Charlton,
anyway? We're glad you asked. Andrew
Murray 'Boy' Charlton was a celebrated
Australian swimmer who began
competing at a high level from the age
of 14. At 16 he won a gold medal in the
1500m freestyle at the 1924 Summer
Olympics in Paris, and set five world
records, among numerous other awards,
before he was 18. Thus, an Australian
legend was born. There is another pool
named after him in Manly.

Andrew 'Boy' Charlton Pool   SYDNEY

AN ICONIC, HEATED SALTWATER SWIMMING POOL
ON THE HARBOUR – A TRUE SYDNEY EXPERIENCE.

Andrew 'Boy' Charlton Pool (ABC) is our go-to place for an inner-city swim (though we do love the Prince Alfred Park Pool in Surry Hills too). ABC is where we have 'business meetings' with our office-worker friends and colleagues. It's an oasis of calm, overlooking the Woolloomooloo wharf and nestled into the furthest corner of Sydney's Royal Botanic Garden. Immersed among Moreton Bay fig trees and palms, with a soundtrack of tropical birds, it is hard to imagine that you are in the middle of Australia's largest city. And yet, where else but Sydney could a pool like this ever exist?

Woolloomooloo Bay has had almost as many swimming facilities over the years as it has 'O's' in its name. However, this site didn't really take off until 1901, when Sydney diverted its sewerage system from the harbour to Bondi Beach (maybe this is why the whole city still enjoys hanging shit on Bondi). Originally called Domain Baths, ABC was renamed in honour of, you guessed it, Andrew 'Boy' Charlton in 1968. Charlton was Sydney's homegrown Olympic champion who famously challenged and beat the world's top swimmer, Arne Borg, in this very pool.

Recent modifications have given a modern adaptation to this iconic site. Entering the 50-metre pool via the perforated deck feels like boarding a ship. To the left is the Poolside Cafe, where floor-to-ceiling windows and an open-air terrace overlook the lap lanes. Down the stairs we find the city's finest changing rooms; admittedly, there is little competition. Filtered light floods through the building's metallic brise-soleil, giving the rooms an open and airy atmosphere. Rather than scurrying in and out, holding our breath, we are almost tempted to linger on the wooden seats. Almost. After all, they are still changing rooms.

These days the most competitive event at the pool is sunbaking atop the lounge chairs. They are hot property, with uncompromised views of the naval fleet at the wharf behind. The eight lanes of heated saltwater fill up with pre- and post-work crowds, plus a little bump in numbers around lunchtime. But most of the day it is just us freelancers cutting slow laps between the cafe and pool.

NEARBY

SMOKING GUN BAGELS
129 Cathedral St, Woolloomooloo

Because one of us is from bagel country, we're quite partial to an interesting take on the tradition. The guys at Smoking Gun might be some of the only (or at least the first) to make Montreal-style bagels in Sydney. Boiled in honeyed water and baked in a woodfired oven, they are thinner and sweeter than New York–style bagels. We order the Not So Salmon, with smoked trout, trout caviar, cream cheese, pickles, red onion, capers and dill.

FLOUR AND STONE
53 Riley St, Woolloomooloo

The celebrated panna cotta lamington at Flour and Stone is pretty hard to pass up, if you're into that kind of thing. They sell out early, so if you do miss them, cram into this cute cafe for scones piled with jam and cream instead or a slice of date and almond cake with caramel – it's perfect with a cup of breakfast tea.

THE APOLLO RESTAURANT
44 Macleay St, Potts Point

So the Apollo is located back up in Potts Point (a 20-minute walk from the pool), but it's also one of our favourite Sydney restaurants. Its woodfired Greek food is designed to share, such as tentacles of octopus and shoulders of lamb. But it's for some of the simple dishes like the grilled saganaki with honey or the taramasalata that we keep going back.

POOL

◔ **Best time to visit**
Summertime, because nothing beats a quintessential Aussie summer's day in Bondi, as long as you don't mind crowds.

⊘ **Address**
1 Notts Ave, Bondi Beach

⊖ **Access**
Easy. Parking can be tricky if you're driving. Cycle, walk or catch the bus.

⑤ **Cost of entry** Adults $7, kids $5

☺ **Kid friendly** Yes

⊗ **Dog friendly** No

⌁ **Water temperature** Ocean temperature, 16°C–25°C, depending on season

⌚ **Open** Mon–Wed & Fri 6am–6.30pm, Sat–Sun 6.30am–6.30pm year-round; closed Thurs for cleaning and when swell is too big. Check website for weather reports.

⊕ **Facilities** Toilets, hot showers, sauna, cafe

⊚ **Must bring**
Your best swimsuit. Looking good is feeling good at Bondi.

LOCAL KNOWLEDGE

After your swim, jump into the sauna upstairs and sweat it out over colourful post-pool chats and the best sauna views in the country.

Bondi Icebergs

SYDNEY EASTERN SUBURBS

AN INTERNATIONAL SWIMMING LANDMARK AND THE MOST PHOTOGENIC POOL IN THE COUNTRY.

Is there a more photographed pool in Australia? In the world? If there is, we can't think of it. Bondi Icebergs is like no other. How could we write this book without including it? It's an icon of Aussie swimming and landscape, and one of our favourites. No one leaves Bondi without snapping a pic of this ocean pool and, we hope, jumping in for a swim.

On the south side of Bondi Beach is the famous white building, home to the Bondi Surf Life Saving Club, Icebergs Dining Room and Bar, and the landmark 50-metre pool, fed by the ocean. It's filled weekly, a feat of cleaning that closes the pool for an entire day each Thursday.

At any given time, the pool at Bondi Icebergs is abuzz with swimmers and bathers, here for a ritual dip and sauna, to catch up with friends or soak up rays on the tiered concrete steps (the best seats in the house). The water conditions vary, and so will your swim. Some days are as calm as Lake Eyre, water quietly lapping at the outer walls of the pool. At other times you might as well be out in the ocean itself, waves crashing into your mouth on every second breath, a whiff of sea sickness stirring in your belly. During winter, the pool runs a swimming club called Bondi Icebergs, which trains every Sunday from May to September to encourage fitness during the cooler months. For the kids, there's the Bondi Icecubes, on a similar training schedule. This is for the brave and wetsuits are discouraged.

Up above, diners at Icebergs Dining Room and Bar sip on spritz and graze on Mediterranean food in a slick, sunlit room. Down below, a regular crew jumps off a ledge near the steps up to the pool deck to cut laps of Australian Crawl (freestyle) across the bay (800 metres one way), or sits taking in the morning sun. Bondi photographer Eugene Tan will be out on the sand capturing this scene, and showcases beachlife in all its glory at his Aquabumps gallery down the road.

Perhaps one reason why we are so fond of this pool is because it's so familiar. A few years ago we did a short stint in Sydney, living just two blocks from Icebergs, and making it in for an early morning swim several times a week. On more than one occasion, when the swell was too big in the main pool, we'd join the swimming club and run laps in the wading pool. They'd always invite newcomers for coffee at the kiosk after, hoping to lure in a new recruit or two. Which is tempting if you need a good reason to get out of bed. Though, most people in Bondi already appear to be well into their exercise routine by 6am. It's widely acknowledged that as soon as you move to the suburb you automatically become 30 per cent fitter – it must be all the swimming.

Icebergs is a place we never get sick of. In fact, we moved back to Sydney this year with the intention to make it our local once again.

NEARBY

SHUK
2 Mitchell St, North Bondi

We've been known to stop here on the way to or from various swims for the $9.50 egg-and-bacon rolls that will keep you going well past lunch. This Middle Eastern cafe and bakery has been setting hearts and stomachs alight for years now in the backstreets of North Bondi. If you're dining in, it's hard to go past a traditional shukshuka, followed by a rugalch (a bite-sized hazelnut croissant). But everything at Shuk is delicious.

SOY
3/38 Campbell Pde, Bondi Beach

It took us a while to realise that the perfect swim snack is a sushi handroll. It has changed our life – that and finding Soy right on the main drag just across from the beach and pool. This is no ordinary sushi cabinet. We're talking super-fresh tuna and salmon in crispy nori, seaweed salads and other flavourful Japanese dishes to tide you over during a day in the water.

DA ORAZIO PIZZA + PORCHETTA
75–79 Halls St, Bondi

For us, Da Orazio is like a snapshot of the Bondi scene – casual, beachy and fun. Everything in here is white: the walls, the tables, the uniforms and the pizza oven. Thin bubbling pizzas land on tables, alongside bowl of olives, caprese salads and carafes of wine, as waiters zip around the restaurant with the music turned up.

Clovelly Beach

SYDNEY EASTERN SUBURBS

THE LARGEST NATURALLY
OCCURRING SWIMMING POOL
ON THE NSW COAST, WITH A
UNIQUE CONCRETE BEACH.

BEACH **OCEAN POOL**

◐ **Best time to visit**
Summer. Locals often say they prefer winter when crowds subside and the water is crisp and clear; however, Clovelly is unpatrolled April to September.

⊘ **How to get there**
Follow Clovelly Rd around the coast to the beach. You can't miss it.

⊖ **Access**
Easy. Accessible parking and public transport.

$ **Cost of entry** Free

☺ **Kid friendly** Yes

⊗ **Dog friendly** No

◠ **Water temperature** Ocean temps, usually quite refreshing, but never icy cold.

◷ **Open** 24 hours

⊕ **Facilities**
Toilets, changing rooms, kiosk

※ **Must bring**
A towel – you don't want to be lying on the hot concrete.

LOCAL KNOWLEDGE

Though this whole bay is protected by a breakwall and a rocky reef at the ocean end, be careful of tides and currents.

We found deciding which pools and swims would make the cut in Sydney a very hard task. Between ocean pools, harbour pools, public pools and beaches, it's a tough list to whittle down.

When it comes to the eastern suburbs of Sydney, and particularly this strip of coast south of Bondi, people are often strongly from one of two camps: the Gordons Bay camp, or the Clovelly Bay camp. For many of us, summertime memories are inseparable from the smell of sunscreen and the feel of sandy feet. But favourite swimming places come with their own set of personal experiences, and some people just don't like sand. There's something about the strange, post-apocalyptic concrete job at Clovelly that really floats our boat. Seriously, is this a wharf or a pool? Whatever it is, we love it.

If you think all this concrete is unnecessary, you're probably right. It was originally poured by the Randwick council during the Great Depression to create jobs for local men and easier access to swimming for the community. This is essentially a concrete beach. On a real humdinger of a day, this scene feels reminiscent of the Amalfi Coast – hundreds of people sprawled on colourful towels and banana loungers or jumping joyfully from the banks into the deep water below – an epic view from the sky.

It's a little-known fact that Clovelly is also the largest coastal swimming pool in the state. The inlet is enclosed by a naturally occurring rock shelf that protects the bay from open sea, creating an ocean pool that's 60 metres wide and 350 metres long. And if a giant bay between concrete esplanades wasn't enough, at one end is a sandy beach and on the southern side of the inlet is a 25-metre saltwater pool known as Geoff James. Like most pools in Sydney's coastal suburbs, this one is home to a winter swim club, the Clovelly Eskimos. These cold-water advocates swim competitively against the South Maroubra Dolphins, the Cronulla Polar Bears, the Maroubra Seals, the Coogee Penguins, and other neighbouring sea colonies.

Clovelly is a major stop on the Bondi to Coogee coastal walk, appearing over the hill just after the Waverley Cemetery when you really need a dip. Sometimes it's easier to swim across the inlet than to walk the iconic bright yellow line around its perimeter. Whichever way you go, you'll always find an international cross-section of people in their swimsuits – Italian and Portuguese mixes with strong Aussie twangs, and more than a few pairs of bright-coloured budgie smugglers are on show. There's a lot to love here.

NEARBY

TOPHAT COFFEE MERCHANTS
315 Clovelly Rd, Clovelly

When we think of early morning swims, we think of the coffee that follows. This is your best post-swim coffee stop, a 10-minute walk from the beach. With house-blend single origin coffee, cold drip and Aeropress, these guys know their brews. Enjoy yours with an egg-and-bacon jaffle.

SWEET KISS CAKE SHOP
345 Clovelly Rd, Clovelly

A nostalgic Hungarian bakery making strudels stuffed with cheese and sour cherries, classic esterhazy, a hazelnut sponge with brandy mousse, and traditional Easter bejgli – brioche with walnut paste and poppyseeds. They also make sourdough bread, pies and chorizo sausage rolls. Post-swim isn't just about the coffee.

WYLIE'S BATHS
4b Neptune St, Coogee

The final destination of the Bondi to Coogee walk, Wylie's Baths is another true Sydney icon. You're probably familiar with this beautiful, heritage-listed tidal pool from images, even if you haven't visited. The stilted entry, with kiosk and changing rooms, looks out to the Pacific, while the rocky, oceanic pool sits below, filled with swimmers and sunbakers.

Is this a wharf or a pool?
Whatever it is, we love it.

BEACH   LAGOON

◐ **Best time to visit**
The weekend summer scene has to be witnessed. Winter is great if you are crowd-averse.

◬ **How to get there**
Royal National Park is between Sydney and Wollongong. Turn off the A1 at Farnell Ave, following signs to Royal National Park. Follow the road for 13km as it changes name from Farnell Ave to Audley Rd and then to Sir Bertram Stevens Dr. A well-signed turn-off leads to Wattamolla Beach; follow Wattamolla Rd about 4km until the carpark.

⊖ **Access**
Easy. Very well signed. Abundant parking.

⑤ **Cost of entry** Park entry $12 per vehicle. Cash only.

☺ **Kid friendly** Yes

⊗ **Dog friendly** No

⌁ **Water temperature** Balmy in the lagoon, cool at the beach

◷ **Open** 7am–8.30pm

⊕ **Facilities**
Toilets, showers, BBQs, picnic tables

🐾 **Must bring**
Snags for the BBQ or kofte if you are feeling classy.

LOCAL KNOWLEDGE

Wattamolla is derived from a Dharawal word meaning 'place near running water'.

Wattamolla Beach

ROYAL NATIONAL PARK

A COVE, LAGOON AND BEACH, ALL CELEBRATED BY THE MASSES.

This place must be human-built. Nothing else can explain the absurd combination of so many epic swimming elements in one location. A 10-metre waterfall doubles as a cliff-jump into a deep lagoon. In one direction that lagoon stretches into tranquil native bush; in the other, it dead-ends at a white-sand beach. Follow the sand to a calm bay where the water is impossibly clear. If we hadn't seen it all for ourselves, we wouldn't believe it was real.

Wattamolla is the golden child of Royal National Park, a family-friendly hotspot within easy striking distance of Sydney. For better or worse, it is on most people's radar and crowds swell on hot summer days and weekends – nothing like the scale of Bondi or Cronulla, but you are guaranteed to make a few friends while swimming. We are of the opinion that not every experience needs to be solitary. Not every beautiful place has to be a secret. Wattamolla is vast and diverse enough to accommodate the needs of every visitor. Each section offers a different experience.

The cliff-jump* is the first thing that most people encounter and it is almost exclusively the territory of males aged 12 to 32 (though everyone is warmly welcomed and strongly encouraged). This is where we find our friend James teaching the younger generations his reckless swan dive. Down below is a mixed-use area. Partners and family members of jumpers stand transfixed and slightly horrified. Children fill a natural wading pool, floating among a thriving ecosystem of inflatable animals. Groups laze about in the forest, pumping music from their cellphones and analysing their hangovers – past, future and present.

Upstream we join the explorers – knots of couples, families and friends leaving behind the crowds to colonise pristine beaches and flat rocks. This is where we take a visiting parent who wants to enjoy the national park but isn't up for a long bushwalk. A quick meander or swim and you can be fully immersed in nature, out of ear- and eyeshot of the masses.

The beach has its own culture, and even without the rest of the landscape it would be a top destination. A group of weekenders bypass the freshwater crowds, taking the stairs directly to the soft sand. With gazes fixed firmly on the horizon they move back and forth from the water to their towels; umbrellas mark the time as their shadows trace a slow ellipse. Our favourite swims are along the fringing reefs and boulder-filled edges of the bay. Clear, deep water offers prime fishing and snorkelling and even on the hottest, busiest day you feel like the only person here.

---

* Cliff-jumping is prohibited here and penalties apply. We didn't do it. It's not fun. We definitely don't recommend it.

NEARBY

GIRO OSTERIA
1 McDonald St, Cronulla

On your way in, or out, of Royal National Park, you'll likely pass through the coastal suburb of Cronulla, the best option for dining nearby. There's a growing food scene here and Giro is at the top of our list. This simple, contemporary Italian trattoria is a modern take on traditional European dining, with a small, seasonal menu – think plates of salumi (cured meats), deep-fried zucchini flowers, whole flounder and bowls of pasta.

FIGURE EIGHT POOLS
Burning Palms, Royal National Park

An incredible series of small, round, conjoined plunge pools on a rocky platform that has become Instagram famous. Figure Eight Pools is located south of Burning Palms Beach in Royal National Park. It's a 3-kilometre walk in from Garrawarra Farm, where you park. Follow the Burgh Ridge Track to the Coast Track and continue towards Burning Palms Beach, then hop over rocks around to the tip of the second headland where the pools are accessible at low tide. Take care here: more than one selfie-stick has been lost due to big tides crashing over the platform.

SRI VENKATESWARA CANTEEN
348 Temple Rd, Helensburgh

We love driving through the outer suburbs of Sydney heading south to explore the city's diverse cuisines and communities. SVT Canteen at the Helensburgh Hindu temple serves up a vegetarian selection of dosa, biryani, deep-fried flat breads, Indian sweets and masala tea. It's on the south side of the national park (near Stanwell Park), and only open weekends, but is a lot of fun and well worth the journey.

Clarence Dam

DARGANS CREEK RESERVE,
BLUE MOUNTAINS

THE BEST DAM SWIMMING
SPOT IN THE BOOK, WITH A
CLIFF-JUMP AND SOME FUN
ROPE SWINGS INTO DEEP,
COOL WATER.

DAM

Best time to visit
Late summer and autumn – it takes
a few months for the winter chill to
leave the water.

How to get there
Located just off Bells Line of Road
near Clarence. Turn off Chifley Rd just
before a bridge over the railway line.
Drive alongside the train tracks for 1.7km
before turning left to the dam. The 1km
dirt track is suitable for 2WD (provided
you drive with caution) and leads to a
large clearing where you can park. Walk
200m down to the water.

Access
Moderate. Can be a bit tricky to find. It's
a bumpy dirt road in, but fine for 2WD.
Take it slow.

Cost of entry Free

Kid friendly Yes, for tweens and above.
This isn't somewhere you learn to swim
and there are some exposed cliff lines.

Dog friendly No

Water temperature Cold enough to cool
your beers in.

Open 24 hours

Facilities
None

Must bring
A tinnie to crack open after (or during)
your swim.

LOCAL KNOWLEDGE

The rock-climbing community calls this
reserve the 'Cosmic County Area' and it
has some of the best climbing, abseiling
and canyoneering in the Blue Mountains.
Climbers can be found in the valley
beneath the pool.

In the early days of our trip, on a bumpy road in the South Australian desert, we happened upon two dusty architects riding across the country – Owen and Bobbie (see Dalhousie Springs, p. 65). Like a few of the lovely people we've met on our travels, these guys invited us to stay with them when we passed through Owen's hometown in the Blue Mountains, where his parents still live. They probably didn't think we'd take them up on their offer, but eight months later we arrived on their doorstep and they handed us the keys to their kingdom.

Owen and his father, Wayne, the ultimate one-two punch father-son team, were eager to show us a few of their favourite swimming spots – one of which was Clarence Dam. At first we were reluctant at the idea of an artificial swimming hole in such a natural setting, but this magnificent location soon impressed itself upon us as we pulled into the rugged track. Signs pointed us in the direction of the big dam; 'The small one is for the kids', Owen said from the driver's seat like a tour guide.

From the carpark we made our way on foot into the reserve, alongside a P-plated camo-coloured Landcruiser, which was slowly manoeuvring over huge rocks into the dry, shrubby, bushland. Dressed in native gumtrees, the landscape here feels like true blue Australiana. Around Christmas time, the tea-tree near the waterline turns white, like it's somehow snow-covered in the middle of summer. The reserve is home to two disused railway dams (that feel like lakes) built to supply water for steam engines, and is still bordered at the north side by a functioning western railway corridor. But the Crown Land area is now used mostly for public recreation such as bushwalking, rock climbing, canyoning and swimming.

Swimmers are in for a treat. Huge pieces of ironstone protrude out of the water in soft shapes of all sizes, like artful, abstract sculptures. It's not the water that makes this swimming hole great, it's the rock. Some have an architectural quality, which starts to make a lot of sense when we remember we were brought here by an architect. The water is cool and deep, and we swim from a low entry point over to a large 10-metre high wall. The drop is sheer; it's also a rite of passage for local teenagers. We're about 20 years older than most, but we take the deep plunge into the cool freshwater below, slapping the water with our feet first.

In other sections there are rope swings tied to tree branches at different heights, but this is no amateur set-up. There are various jumps that range from your standard rope swing to full-on carnival trapeze, none of which should be taken lightly. If jumping isn't your thing, floating down the river in an inflatable ring might be. Soak up this stunning landscape before you get whisked off to the next location by some local tour guides.

NEARBY

ART IS AN OPTION
22 Chiffley Rd, Dargan

A gallery space by local artist Henryk Topolnicki, a sculptor and furniture maker who works principally in steel, stone and wood. His work ranges from large outdoor sculptures to home furniture, gates and balustrades and can be seen on private properties and in public commissions around the Blue Mountains. His creative studio in Dargan is open for public viewing.

MOUNT VIC FLICKS
2a Harley Ave, Mount Victoria

A famous theatre in an old dance hall in the Blue Mountains' highest town. This cinema is a much-loved local haunt screening mainstream and art-house movies for $12, as well as filmed performances by the National Theatre and the Metropolitan Opera. Baked goods, tea, soup and choc tops are available to enjoy with the show.

BILLS OLD-FASHIONED CAKES AND PIES
70 Main St, Lithgow

Bills Cake Shop (formerly Allens) is a classic old bakery serving sweets and cakes, iced and stuffed, from a bygone era. Favourites include pastry mushrooms with jam and nutmeg, cream-filled honey rolls, neenish tarts and – our host Wayne's pick – pineapple tart with passionfruit icing. A real (sugar) high.

POOL

◐ **Best time to visit**
Summer, when the weather is at its warmest in the mountains.

◍ **How to get there**
Turn off to Yarrangobilly Caves Entrance Rd, about 3km south of Yarrangobilly township on Snowy Mountains Hwy. It's very well signed. Follow the well-maintained unsealed road 3.7km, past the visitor centre, to the Thermal Pool carpark. It's a 1km walk in.

⊖ **Access**
Easy. Roads are well marked and well maintained. Winter brings a lot of snow to this area, so 4WD may be required.

⑤ **Cost of entry**
$4 per car to access the national park. Additional fees apply for cave access.

☺ **Kid friendly** Yes

⊗ **Dog friendly** No

◠ **Water temperature** 27°C year-round

◷ **Open** 9am–5pm daily

⊕ **Facilities**
Toilets, showers

◍ **Must bring**
A container to carry your berries home in.

LOCAL KNOWLEDGE

Hike the tracks around the pool and caves to find delicious wild blackberries.

Yarrangobilly Thermal Pool

KOSCIUSZKO NATIONAL PARK, SNOWY MOUNTAINS

AN UNEXPECTEDLY WARM AND GLISTENING GREEN THERMAL POOL IN THE SNOWY MOUNTAINS.

Just when you think you have seen it all, Australia unveils a karst landscape in the middle of the Snowy Mountains. Limestone monoliths loom above river valleys like hulking grey castles straddling deep caves. It's the kind of scene you expect to see in Southern China or Vietnam. There should be groves of bamboo shrouded in fog, or else the ribbed sails of junk ships gliding across the rivers. Instead, it is quintessentially Australian, a who's who of eucalypts: ribbon, mountain, peppermint and snow gums mingle with alpine ash and candlebarks. A generous supply of wild blackberries ensures you never stray too far from the walking tracks. Nestled among all of this wild beauty is a crystal-clear 20-metre thermal pool. There is no other place like this in the entire country.

There is an undeniable feeling of lightness up here, a slow stability that you don't get on the coast. Where the ocean is heavy and volatile, amplifying our highs and lows, the mountains are grounding. Walking down the gentle track to bathe, there is an easy predictability. No matter the weather or time of year, the pool will always be 27°C. Just enough to cool you in summer or to warm you in winter.

The first thing you will notice is that the water is extraordinarily clean. This is because the spring-fed pool is constantly replenished at a rate of 100,000 litres per hour. The water overflows into a small wading pool below, before flowing out to the river, forming a natural swimming hole. The second thing you will notice are the signs to Glory Hole Ranch. You cannot imagine our excitement as we walked the short track to the old homestead. Unfortunately, little more than a shabby chimney remains. No obvious glory holes upon close inspection. South Glory Cave, on the other hand, did not let us down. It opens to the sky like a James Turrell artwork, an enormous cavern with a collapsed roof.

Yarrangobilly thermal pool is a great place to be alone with your thoughts, to step away from an urban or coastal context, to sit, and watch, and listen. The sun comes and goes. Clouds swirl overhead, racing from peak to peak. The joy of the Snowy Mountains is its juxtaposition of familiar and foreign. Driving across the alpine plains of Kosciuszko National Park you could just as easily be in the European Alps or North American Rockies. In the evening, long shadows cling to treeless frost hollows, dancing through a cool palette. Here we find the unlikely partnership of kangaroos and wild horses, two animals unified only in their abilities to graze and write-off your car. Fortunately, we passed through unscathed.

NEARBY

BLUE WATERHOLES
Clarke Gorge, High Plains

The drive to get here is a pleasure in itself, taking you through alpine frost hollows and past the old Cooleman Homestead. At the end of Long Plain Road, about 30 kilometres off Snowy Mountains Highway, is the Blue Waterholes Campground, from where a 5-kilometre trail weaves downstream through Clarke Gorge. Calcium-rich blue water runs through the gorge, carving out deep waterholes, ideal for swimming from October to June (it's way too cold in winter).

THE ALPINE HOTEL
170 Sharp St, Cooma

We love the rounded exteriors of some of these classic old Australian pubs. Though the Alpine has been refurbished to freshen things up inside, there's nothing fancy about this place. But it does have a big island bar with friendly staff and hearty pub fare, and that's enough to get us in the door on our way up to the Snowy Mountains.

MT KOSCIUSZKO SUMMIT HIKE
Thredbo

Yes, it's a 2-hour drive to the trailhead. Yes, this really stretches the notion of 'nearby'. However, when you are so close (a mere 64 kilometres, as a kookaburra flies) to Australia's highest mountain, you should make that trip every time. This iconic day-walk track starts at the top of the Kosciuszko Express Chairlift in Thredbo, and will have you conquering the summit of Mt Kosciuszko in a couple of hours. Epic.

POOL

Best time to visit
During summer, from December
to February.

How to get there
Drive east through the town of Bermagui
to Pacific Dr, which runs along the cliff
on the southern side of the headland.
The road to the Blue Pool carpark is
well marked.

Access
Easy. A short walk from Bermagui's main
street, or drive to the carpark on the cliff.
Stairs lead down to the pool.

Cost of entry Free

Kid friendly Yes

Dog friendly No

Water temperature Cool

Open 24 hours

Facilities
Toilets, outdoor showers, picnic tables

Must bring
Goggles to glimpse the sea life

LOCAL KNOWLEDGE

Swim in the mornings when the sun is on
the pool. The ocean breeze can pick up
here in the afternoons. If you are lucky
you'll run into the Blue Balls, the local
swimming group.

Bermagui Blue Pool

SAPPHIRE COAST

A NATURAL OCEAN POOL TUCKED SNUGGLY INTO THE
BASE OF A SEA CLIFF.

The first time we visited Bermagui was on a return journey home to Melbourne after a month-long east-coast summer road trip. There was a dog show on in town, and every primed and puffed pooch from the area had convened at the local sports oval. The day was hot, and while the dogs remained as obedient as ever, we slipped away to cool off in the cliff-side Blue Pool. It was a memorable and perfect afternoon and we became enamoured by the town of Bermagui.

Since then, we've stopped here every summer. Spending cooler days pitched up in our car on the cliff-top, long mornings drinking coffee and eating sweet pastries at our favourite local cafe, and trips further down the coast to find waves at Mimosa Rocks National Park. But we always find time to enjoy the apple of the town's eye – a swim in the iconic natural rock pool.

The Blue Pool may be one of the best-known ocean pools on the south coast of NSW – but its distance from both Melbourne and Sydney means that it never sees too much traffic. No matter how many times you visit, every trip is filled with a sense of discovery. This swimming spot is slow to reveal itself and your first glimpse will likely be from above, via a viewing platform. The natural rock pool is tucked snugly into the base of the sea cliffs, surrounded by exposed reef. Follow a set of stairs to the base, stopping at the changing rooms halfway down, before reaching the water.

The pool was originally named the Blue Hole, for its deep blue water, but in the 1930s a redevelopment was publicly funded to expand the site. As with many of the sea pools on this coastline, workers used dynamite to blast through nearby rocks, creating a more accessible swimming spot with a shallow wading pool. The location then became known as the Blue Pool.

The main pool is about 50 metres long, curving around the honey-coloured rocks at the bottom of the cliff, where sunbakers spread out their towels. For snorkellers, the conditions here are ideal. The uneven, rocky bottom is oceanic, so you will find fish, crabs and other sea fauna right below you. Put your goggles on and dive down to search for underwater treasure.

Being an ocean-fed pool, the water temperature can be quite cool, but the wall is high and shelters you from too much tidal movement. Waves sometimes crash over the side at high tide, but it doesn't stop locals doing laps year-round.

NEARBY

MISTER JONES & HONORBREAD
4 & 8 Bunga St, Bermagui

A cute, neighbourhood coffee shop with mid-century furniture, great music and good vibes. Come here for a coffee after your morning swim (but before midday when they close). They also sell sweet pastries from local sourdough bakery Honorbread, two doors down. Poke your head in the hole-in-the-wall to try the cardamom buns (kardemummabullar) and take home a warm loaf of bread.

GULAGA ORGANICS
2 Lamont St

Eating well on the road is an important part of travelling for us – it's easy to get caught up jumping from the local bakery to the fish and chip shop. Gulaga is an organic, wholefood grocer selling bulk dry goods and fresh, local produce. We always stock up on good eggs and pantry items to keep us going on the road. Everything comes from big tubs to minimise waste, and you buy your rice, beans and nuts by the kilo. It's a rare treat to find nourishing, quality food stores like this in small towns. Go easy on the chocolate covered strawberries.

ARAGUNNU
Aragunnu Rd, Wapengo

Located in Mimosa Rocks National Park, Aragunnu is a popular spot for fishing and surfing and has a couple of lo-fi beachside campgrounds. We've spend more than a few lazy summer days pitched up here, enjoying the remote bushy surrounds, swimming, playing cards and cooking pizza on the public barbecues with friends. Campsites tend to book out during school holidays, but it is reliably quiet all other times of the year.

Volunteer Lifesaver

EMMA FINNERTY

We've found common characteristics in swimmers we've met during our travels. One thing is that they can be extremely parochial about the places they swim. The other is that they are early risers and often want to meet before 7am, which is actually the best time to tap into a swimming community.

What is striking when you arrive at Bronte first thing in the morning is how many different people have come together. There are literally hundreds of people running along the boardwalk, walking dogs, swimming in the ocean or the pool, training on the sand and exercising on the grass – active people old and young. It's a real melting pot and has a contagious energy.

Emma Finnerty is one of these people. She's been a volunteer lifesaver at Bronte Beach for five years. We meet her on the sand after a training session with other lifesavers. She's wearing a pink cap and bib, with 'Bronte' emblazoned across her bottom. She's dragging a pink lifesaving board behind her in the sand, which we sit on to chat with her out the front of the oldest surf life saving club in Australia.

Q. You're a lifesaver, not a lifeguard. What's the difference?
A. Lifesavers are the volunteers in yellow and red - we just patrol on weekends and public holidays. Lifeguards are employed by the council and their colours are different depending on the region. In Waverley it's blue. Watch *Bondi Rescue*!

Q. Why do you think people are so passionate about their surf life saving club?
A. It's a community organisation and there is an opportunity to be involved at any age. You can go through the club from under-five to life-member status. The surf club is an important way for people to feel a sense of belonging and ownership of a beach. We all walk around with our beach on our backside. It's very tribal, but in a good way.

Q. Is Bronte the first surf life saving club in Australia?
A. Yes, but it's fiercely contested with Bondi. Bondi started in 1908 and we were 1903, so we're clearly older (laughs). What constituted the first surf life saving meeting still comes up for debate – it's just as contested as the oldest pub in Australia. 'Bronte First' is on our club flag though...

Q. How different is the culture at each club?
A. The same. You've got older groups, nippers, nipper parents, competitors, the rubber ducky team. You have ocean swimmers, and people who literally come down at the same time every day, dive in, get out and go home. You've got people who hang out; you've got the people who run the club and never seem to go home.

Q. What about the pool and swim club?
A. There are at least four clubs. I am in the Bronte Splashers Winter Swimming Club, we only swim in winter. There is also a Summer Swimming Club, an RSL Swimming Club and Doctor Bronte, a group of older men who meet because swimming heals their ailments.

Q. Why do you choose the winter swimming club?
A. Winter swimming started as a way for the summer lifesavers to keep fit over winter. Winter is actually nicer at the beach – it's quieter; the water is better.

Q. Why do think people are so connected to swimming in Australia?
A. Something amazing happens in the water and it's a feeling people want to share with each other, even strangers. The beach is a place of joy and acceptance, and where you come to get away from your private life.

Q. How much of your personal community comes from this beach culture and lifesaving?
A. A big proportion. It's so easy, you turn up and your friends are there. It's such a privilege to live here. That's part of the payback for volunteer lifesavers – we donate our time so others can be safe at the beach.

Beach Safety

Going to the beach is a pastime for many of us in Australia, but it can be a dangerous place. Rips, currents, waves, sudden drop-offs, sandbars, marine life, submerged objects, other people and surfboards all pose risk of potential injury and drowning.

Rips are one of the most dangerous hazards; they occur where strong, narrow currents move water back out to sea. It's easy to get caught in this fast-flowing movement and be swept out deep and into surf. Not everyone knows how to identify a rip, and sometimes they can be hard to see. Enter the water where waves are breaking in a regular pattern. This is the safer place to swim.

General beach safety

- Learn how to swim and understand your ability in the water.
- If in doubt, don't go out.
- Swim between the flags.
- If you're not a competent swimmer, don't swim at unpatrolled beaches.
- Never swim alone.
- Look for rips before you get in.
- Swim parallel to the beach.
- Put your hand up if you need assistance; signal to lifesavers and wait to be rescued.

How to identify a rip

- Look for discoloured water where sand is being stirred up.
- Look for a ripple appearance when the surrounding water is generally calm.
- Look for a calm area of water with waves breaking larger and further out on both sides – the calm water is a rip.
- Look for signs of foam on the surface that extend beyond the breaking waves.

If you get caught in a rip

- Don't panic. Try to remain calm; panicking will wear you out.
- Swim parallel to the beach, not against the rip.
- If you are not a competent swimmer, go with the rip (don't fight it).
- Stay afloat and signal to lifesavers or others on the beach for help.
- Try to angle your body across the current and return to shore through the breaking waves.

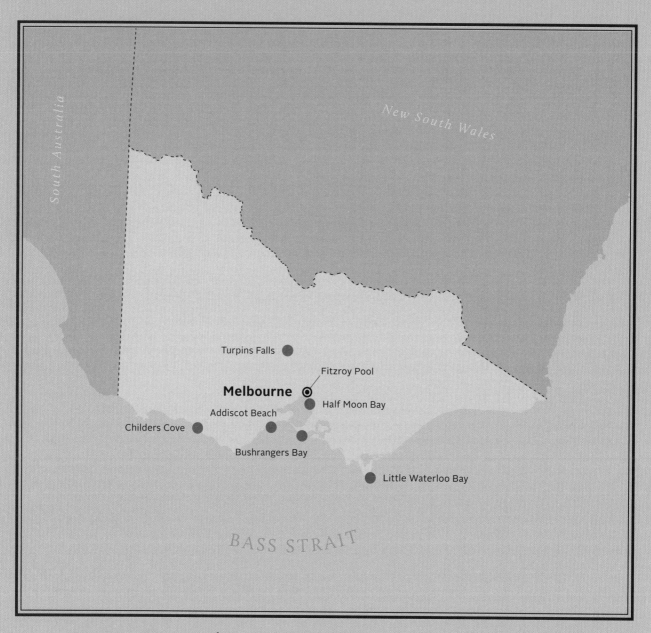

South Australia

New South Wales

Turpins Falls

Fitzroy Pool

Melbourne ◉

Half Moon Bay

Addiscot Beach

Childers Cove

Bushrangers Bay

Little Waterloo Bay

BASS STRAIT

When to visit

We like to say that Victoria has six months of great weather and eight months of bad weather (good maths, right?). Reliably warm days begin in November and water temperatures tend to peak in February/March and stay warm through May.

Favourite swim

BUSHRANGERS BAY
(*see* p. 53)

Best meal

VIET ROSE
(*see* p. 49)

Road-trip advice

If there is one thing that Victoria does better than most states, it's food and drink. And you don't have to be in the major centres to find great produce. Make discovering local gems a big part of your road trip, from country wineries to beachside breweries, servo sausage rolls to homemade cakes.

Victoria

Victoria is our home state and, therefore, the best.
Obviously. Or maybe that makes it the worst?

Like assessing yourself, it is impossible to be completely objective about places with which you have a long and intimate history. As a visitor you can glide into a landscape free of bias, whereas locals like us are encumbered by various emotional attachments. Fortunately, we are professionals, which means we've extended our exploration of the state far beyond regular haunts.

We had a great time looking at Victoria through the lens of *Places We Swim*. It gave us a perfect excuse to explore swimming spots that we don't normally get to. It was also a way of looking at familiar coastlines without the complications of surf forecasting. What a relief. To be fully transparent, we were determined to uncover hidden inland locations. Turpins Falls (*see* p. 40) was a revelation, feeling like a little piece of the Northern Territory in our backyard (complete with mid-strength tinnies). And yet, for all our exploring in the mountains, it was the ocean that won us over again and again.

Taking a step back, we realised there is an incredible variety of coastal landscapes packed into our small state. The sea is not just something to gaze down upon from the Great Ocean Road, but a force to feel and experience. From the end-of-the-earth beauty of Childers Cove (*see* p. 42) to our local nudist beach at Point Addis (*see* p. 44), to the lost piece of Tasmania known as Wilsons Prom (*see* p. 57), we have handpicked swims that reveal the soul of our state. The distances between each spot are not too great here, but the land and sea are defined by many unique microclimates. Naturally, local residents are absolutely convinced that they each live in the best place in the world.

It will take a little bravery to take the plunge in Victoria, as cold water is a universal theme. That said, we also get some of the hottest days in the country and swimming is a big part of the culture here. To enjoy Victoria you will also have to embrace the unpredictable: the weather is likely to change in an instant, and we all get about our business with the expectation that it will do so. But while you're never far from a great swim, nor are you ever far from a great meal; here, more than anywhere else, they go hand in hand.

WATERFALL

Best time to visit
December to May

How to get there
From Kyneton, travel 11km north on Kyneton–Metcalfe Rd. Turn right onto East Metcalfe–Langley Rd for 2.5km. East Metcalfe–Langley Rd becomes Shillidays Rd; continue a further 1.5km to the Turpins Falls turn-off on the right.

Access
Short dirt road to the carpark (suitable for 2WD). It's a quick but steep walk down to the falls, with a couple of sections that can get slippery when wet.

Cost of entry Free

Kid friendly Yes

Dog friendly No

Water temperature Cold

Open 24 hours

Facilities
None

Must bring
Waterproof sandals to wear into the water, over rocks and the sludgy bottom.

LOCAL KNOWLEDGE

In summer, try to visit mid-week when the crowds die down; if visiting on a weekend, be prepared to brave the droves of other swimmers.

Turpins Falls

LANGLEY, CENTRAL HIGHLANDS

A DRAMATIC WATERHOLE SURROUNDED BY A LARGE ROCKY AMPHITHEATRE THAT ATTRACTS FESTIVAL-LIKE SUMMER CROWDS.

On a hot summer's day, country Victoria can feel particularly landlocked – no wind, no water, no coastline to be found in any direction. So it was with welcome relief that we planned a trip to Turpins Falls in Langley – one of only a few places to swim locally – on a particularly sun-kissed afternoon in January.

We were staying with some friends in Trentham, about 30 minutes from Turpins Falls. They told us about their discovery of a *secret* water hole earlier that week, describing it as an untapped swimming spot where they had been the only visitors. We imagined there might be a few groups there on a weekend but, happy to share the bounty, we piled into cars and headed to the falls, just outside the neighbouring town of Kyneton.

As we descended into the gorge, a viewing platform revealed a clear view of the pool below – an impressive natural amphitheatre of rock surrounding a deep billabong located along the Campaspe River.

It turned out there was nothing secret about this location other than its discreet way of blending in with the surrounding paddocks. There must have been a hundred people in the water, paddling around on colourful floaties, and plenty more lazing on the banks. A veritable melting pot of locals, families and daytrippers from Melbourne, it felt like we'd arrived at a music festival as we stepped over crushed beer cans and conked-out sunbakers resting in the shade. But crowds are always a sign of a good thing, and Turpins Falls has plenty of redeeming features.

The water is blissfully cool on a hot summer's day and a lively scene of swimmers splash around, chatting in the shallows or floating in the deeper water. Some attempt to climb the slippery overhanging rocks at the lower part of the cliff, while kids line up to jump off big boulders near the water's edge.

When the season's dry, the term 'waterfall' is used loosely, with only a small trickle pouring over the 20-metres of rock into the refreshing pool below. Cliff diving was once popular, but has now been prohibited (says a foreboding sign upon entry), so the best spot to hop in to swim is via the rocky river outlet of the lagoon. Entry there is shallow, gradual and a little sludgy underfoot. This is a rich, particularly Australian setting and one to relish in warmer months.

We made a return trip to Turpins Falls in June and can confirm this place is truly a summer swimming spot. In winter the water is icy, and probably only good for a quick, breathtaking plunge. But the waterfall flows like it never does in warmer months, and you *will* get the place to yourself.

NEARBY

SOURCE DINING
72 Piper St, Kyneton

Previously known as Annie Smithers, before the eponymous Annie moved her bistro to Trentham (adding another great restaurant to the area), Source Dining is all about celebrating local produce, from the wine to the bread, cheese, meat, butter, and veggies grown in the back garden. Chef Tim Foster changes the menu seasonally, while his wife Michelle works the floor in the Nordic-inspired space.

THE ROYAL GEORGE HOTEL
24 Piper St, Kyneton

A treasured pub in a two-storey heritage building, popular with locals and visitors, just down the road from Source Dining. The Royal George is home to a classic country bar with good pub food (steaks, burgers and parmas) and a strong selection of beers on tap.

THE TRENTHAM COLLECTIVE
37a High St, Trentham

It's hard to resist stopping in at the cute historical towns in the area. Inside an old bank, the Trentham Collective has become a favourite cafe for coffee and cake or a pie for lunch. Everything is made in-house or locally, and everything is delicious, whether you're in for breakfast, lunch or dinner on Friday-night.

BEACH

Best time to visit
Summer during low to mid-tide. At high tide the water washes right up over the beach, so there's nowhere to sit.

How to get there
Turn off the Great Ocean Road about 19km east of Warrnambool (heading towards Melbourne) onto Childers Cove Rd. Follow the narrow, sealed road towards the coast for 7km, past Sandy Cove and Murnanes Beach. Childers is the third and final bay where you can park. It's about a 5-minute walk to the beach.

Access
Easy. Just drive, park and walk for a few minutes.

Cost of entry Free

Kid friendly Yes

Dog friendly Yes

Water temperature Cold

Open 24 hours

Facilities
Toilets and picnic tables at nearby Murnanes Beach

Must bring
Grab some picnic supplies and excessive quantities of cheese from Allansford Cheeseworld (5332 Great Ocean Road), the official cellar door of the Warrnambool Cheese and Butter Factory.

LOCAL KNOWLEDGE

The beach is not patrolled, so be aware of tides and water movement when you swim. It's part of a wild coastline and rips can drag out through the cove. Be sure to stay in the shallows and don't swim out into the mouth of the bay.

Childers Cove

MEPUNGA, GREAT OCEAN ROAD

A SECRET LITTLE BEACH, NESTLED AMONG DAIRY FARMS ON ONE OF THE WILDEST STRETCHES OF VICTORIAN COASTLINE.

It all started with a fortuitous meeting. We were flagged down on the road just outside Warrnambool by a guy who had seen the 'for sale' sign on the back of our car. We got chatting about swimming spots and almost immediately he suggested we visit Childers Cove, before jumping back into his car to lead the way. This was a promising local tip, given we'd spent the morning driving halfway around country Victoria only to conclude that the best swimming in the state is among saltwater and sandy beaches. It also reconfirmed the idea that local knowledge is the best kind.

So we were back on the coast, heading out of Warrnambool along the Great Ocean Road. A few kilometres down Childers Cove Road we were slapped with arresting scenes of towering limestone stacks and secret bays. Farmland meets the ocean here on this notoriously wild coastline, where dairy country of rolling green pastures sits high upon steep cliffs that look out over the Southern Ocean – these are truly head-turning, car-swerving landscapes.

Childers Cove is the third bay along this road, after Murnanes and Sandy, and the most protected of the three. Park in the carpark at the top and take the wooden steps down to the picturesque 100-metre-long beach. Before you get to the stairs, an undefined trail leading up to a lookout point is worth walking for a view of the idyllic setting from above. Down below, your deserted beach awaits.

The rugged and remote nature of this coastline is like no other part of Victoria. Harsh and extreme weather conditions erode the soft limestone cliffs to form caves, which become arches and eventually crumble into the sea, creating high rock stacks up to 50-metres tall. This natural seascape architecture has been made famous by the formations known as the Twelve Apostles and the coastal pilgrimages they inspire daily along the Great Ocean Road.

Despite its location off a well-worn highway, Childers Cove is the kind of place you will only hear about from a local. And although it's bittersweet to blow the lid off such a truly secret spot, our source was of the opinion that this natural bounty should be respectfully shared. Our fleeting encounter may not have ended in a car sale, but it did procure a new favourite place to swim on the Victorian west coast.

NEARBY

GRAZE
52a Kepler St, Warrnambool

A cafe and delicatessen serving house-made food, pantry goods to take away and coffee made with beans by Sydney's Will & Co. It's hard to go past a warm croissant filled with prosciutto and aged cheddar, but there are plenty of other great deli snacks to grab on your way out to the beach.

KERMOND'S HAMBURGERS
151 Lava St, Warrnambool

The Kermond family has been serving traditional-style burgers from this retro shop for more than 60 years. Made from scratch with meat supplied by local Lucas' Butchers, a Kermond's cheeseburger is both a local favourite and one that people travel for. Order a box of golden fries and a vanilla thickshake for the ultimate experience.

STANDARD DAVE PIZZA
218 Timor St, Warrnambool

A casual, neighbourhood pizzeria with a simple menu that also includes pasta, craft beer, local wine and cocktails. At Dave's the dough is crispy, the tunes are good and the mood is right – it's everything you want from a local pizza joint. Try the 'Tropical Warrnambool', made with Napoli sauce, mozzarella, leg ham and pineapple.

BEACH

◔ **Best time to visit**
November to May

◬ **How to get there**
Turn off the Great Ocean Road at Point Addis Rd (just after Bells Beach if you're coming from Melbourne) and follow it to the end. There is a carpark just opposite the boardwalk down to the beach.

⊖ **Access**
Easy. Walk a few hundred metres down the boardwalk to the beach.

⑊ **Cost of entry** Free

☺ **Kid friendly** Yes

⊗ **Dog friendly** Yes

◠ **Water temperature** Cool

◷ **Open** 24 hours

⊕ **Facilities**
Toilets (at the carpark)

◉ **Must bring**
A longboard

LOCAL KNOWLEDGE

If you're meeting friends, make plans before you get here. There's patchy phone reception down on the Point. Plus, nudity is optional here, so you don't want to be that creepy naked person carrying nothing but a phone.

Addiscot Beach

POINT ADDIS, SURF COAST

A PROTECTED HORSESHOE BAY THAT'S POSSIBLY THE FRIENDLIEST PLACE TO SWIM ALONG THE GREAT OCEAN ROAD.

It's hard to imagine a lifetime of swimming that doesn't include a beach like Point Addis on a coast as familiar as this one. We've spent more time trawling the stretch between Torquay and Apollo Bay than any other, chasing waves and good times on broody winter days, on sun-soaked weekends and on summer holidays.

Addiscot Beach is a favourite among many; in fact, this world-class strip can pull a crowd at almost any time of the year. It swells during summer and also around Easter when pro surfers invade neighbouring Bells Beach. During these periods, holiday houses fill and carparks overflow, delivering eager beachgoers to their beloved sandy spots.

It's widely known that the Great Ocean Road is exposed to some serious wave activity from the Southern Ocean, but this section (from Anglesea to Bells) is home to a protected reefy marine park, which is why Addiscot is so consistently calm. The beach sits tucked into a sheltered bay with outer reefs protecting the cove from swell, making it one of the friendliest spots for swimming along the coast. It's also an ideal beginner surf spot. Longboarders haul their crafts out here religiously, riding slow waves into the shore as they manoeuvre through schools of surfers, swimmers and dolphins.

Entry to the beach is a few hundred metres before the lookout point at the end of the road, and stairs take you on a short walk to the sand below. A viewing platform looks down onto Point Addis and its dramatic backdrop of crumbling sandstone cliffs. At the southern end of the beach are some caves, known as Pixie Caves, where rocks form an arch that you can walk under at low tide.

Although this coastline totally spoils us for choice with a host of swimming spots and iconic beaches, only a few are ideal for all swimming abilities in variable conditions. It'd be remiss not to mention equally friendly neighbour Point Roadknight Beach at Anglesea, but it's Adddiscot that gets the guernsey for its slightly more secluded location, with extra points for offering clothing-optional swimming – the north end of the beach has been a sanctioned nudist favourite since 1986 (and we presume much longer).

With bronzed buttocks and the scent of sunscreen permeating the salty sea air, Addiscot Beach is the quintessential Australian beach experience on a summer's day. We love to spend time here with family and friends as often as we can get down this way from Melbourne.

NEARBY

McGAIN'S NURSERY, CAFE AND FOODSTORE
1 Simmons Crt, Anglesea

This cosy cafe tucked inside a nursery is a hidden oasis in Anglesea. We come for the coffee and cake (usually the carrot or hummingbird), often stay for hours playing chess and leave with something from the foodstore for dinner. Take a seat out among the greenery or get lost in the garden.

AIREYS PUB
45 Great Ocean Road, Aireys Inlet

A cosy pub on the hill as your roll into Aireys Inlet. This place has a rustic, homey feel, with big fireplaces, local beers on tap, giant bowls of hot chips and other pub grub. Sit out on the deck in the sun or curl up near the fire on colder days after a swim.

FRESHWATER CREEK GENERAL STORE
670 Anglesea Rd, Freshwater Creek

We're not telling you about this servo-cum-general store because the petrol is cheap, though it is quite reasonably priced. It's the sausage rolls we flock to, almost exclusively. They are house-made, packed full of veggies and mince, and wrapped in flaky pastry – the perfect post-swim snack. You can buy them frozen to take home too. Last time we checked they were $5.

Fitzroy Pool

MELBOURNE

AN ICONIC INNER-CITY
PUBLIC POOL WITH A ROCKY
PAST, GREAT SIGNAGE AND
SUMMER DJ SETS.

POOL

Best time to visit
Mid-morning, mid-week, year-round.
Weekends in summer for high-volume
swimming and socialising.

Address
160 Alexandra Pde, Fitzroy

Access
Easy. Wheelchair accessible. For parking,
try the back streets such as Cecil St, or
lock your bike up out the front.

Cost of entry Adults $6.70,
kids 5–15 $3.50

Kid friendly Yes

Dog friendly No, but there is a dog park
on the same block.

Water temperature Warm (heated) in
winter, cool in summer

Open Mon–Fri 6am–8pm, Sat–Sun
8am–6pm, various hours public holidays

Facilities
Toilets, showers, outdoor shower, gym,
toddler pool

Must bring
Reflective sunnies if you want to check
people out. Helen Garner's *Monkey Grip* if
you want read about Fitzroy in the '70s.

LOCAL KNOWLEDGE

The 'Aqua Profonda' sign at the end
of the pool is famously misspelled and
should be 'Acqua Profonda', meaning
'deep water' in Italian. It was targeted
towards Italian immigrants at the time.
These days there are signs in Chinese
that translate to 'Don't spit'.

It's just after 7am on a warm Wednesday morning – peak hour at Fitzroy Pool. Regulars set the pace with strokes up and down the 50-metre red-and-blue roped lanes. On the sidelines, lifeguards set up signage for fast, medium and slow swimmers. The first sunbakers prepare their towels. A group of older swimmers chat in the spa. There's a similar thing happening at hundreds of pools around the country at the exact same time today: at Bondi Icebergs in Sydney (*see* p. 20), at Nightcliff Pool in Darwin (*see* p. 138) and at Merewether Ocean Baths in Newcastle (*see* p. 12).

The places we swim are truly an ode to the Australian psyche, each with their own deep legacy. Fitzroy Pool has long been our local, so it is with many fond memories, and a pinch of bias, that we include this one-time contentious inner-city pool.

In October 1994, more than 1500 yellow ribbons were tied to the fence and trees along Melbourne's Alexandra Parade, surrounding Fitzroy Pool, as locals occupied the site, blocking bulldozers from demolishing their beloved swim spot due to high maintenance costs. The protest lasted eight weeks in what was the most famous publicly fought decision about a pool in Australian history. Fitzroy Pool was reopened and the campaign to 'Save Our Pool' became an example of community spirit nationwide, and we're glad it did.

We've kicked, stroked and held our breath underwater for thousands of metres in this pool. We've spent cold mornings looking out over the frosty surface from the sauna, daring to invigorate ourselves outside. Then months later we've emblazoned tan lines on our backs while chatting to friends on the tiered concrete steps in the heat of the summer sun. Amazingly, much of our time has been spent trawling the lanes with people whose names we do not know but whose stroke styles, goggles' colour and lane preferences we are intimately aware of.

On weekends in summer, DJs play afternoon sets to an assorted audience of trendy twenty-somethings, Speedo-clad civilians, and young families smothered in sunscreen. This would be a scene from a Rennie Ellis photograph, if only we could swim topless, with a tinnie in one hand. Groups gather around the water; some take to the cooler, grassy area under the shade of trees near the toddler pool. At the deep end, the iconic 'Aqua Profonda' is painted on the wall – a reference used by more than a few artists and musicians over the years. It's a real inner-city Melbourne vibe; people are here as much to see as to be seen.

We revel in the hours when crowds subside and we have a lane almost to ourselves, be it on an unexpectedly warm afternoon, an icy winter's morning, or about 10am on a weekday (the golden hour). But a busy early-morning swim with friends is, without doubt, one of the best and most pleasurable starts to the day you can get.

NEARBY

NAPIER QUARTER
359 Napier St, Fitzroy

Just a few blocks up from the pool in the heart of Fitzroy is a cute, Euro-style corner cafe and bistro. In the space that was once Ici, Napier Quarter is a classic and sophisticated day-into-night kind of place, serving coffee, pastries and baked eggs early in the day and moving on to eating pasta, wine and roast chook. Sit out the front for breakfast in the sun and watch the world go by.

MILE END BAGELS
14 Johnson St, Fitzroy

Arguably Melbourne's best bagels. Prior to opening, the owners travelled the world and apprenticed with top bagel makers in the US and Canada. It shows. We've spent many mornings here post-swim, sipping bottomless cups of filter coffee and hot bagels freshly baked and smeared with cream cheese, tomato and basil oil.

VIET ROSE
363 Brunswick St, Fitzroy

Nothing warms you up after a swim like a bowl of hot, creamy laksa. It's the best. We don't order anything else here; in fact, we don't even look at a menu. Our order is the pork wonton laksa with egg noodles, Don't be swayed by the other options, you will only suffer food envy. This is no-frills dining at its best.

BEACH

◔ **Best time to visit**
November to May (or any day
the sun is shining)

◍ **Address**
232 Beach Rd, Black Rock

⊖ **Access**
Easy. Metered parking along the cliff-
tops and at Black Rock Yacht Club. Free
parking on neighbouring side streets.
Nearest train station is Sandringham,
2km away.

⑤ **Cost of entry** Free

☺ **Kid friendly** Yes

⊗ **Dog friendly** No

⌒ **Water temperature** Cool

◷ **Open** 24 hours

⊕ **Facilities**
Toilets, outdoor showers

⊚ **Must bring**
Small speaker to play music on the beach.

LOCAL KNOWLEDGE

There is a nudie beach on the north side
of the bay, near Red Bluff.

Half Moon Bay

MELBOURNE'S BEST CITY BEACH, COMPLETE WITH
A SUNKEN SHIP, COLOURFUL BEACH BOXES AND THE
SCENT OF FISH AND CHIPS IN THE AIR.

In our late teens and early twenties, when we had seemingly endless summers at our disposal, Half Moon Bay was the place we spent our time soaking up rays with friends. On hot mornings, we hastily packed our beach bags with tanning oil, a towel, water bottle, and fresh fruit. All of the essentials. Then, we'd pile into a car, slide in a Craig David CD and race down the Nepean Highway to Black Rock. We could easily spend entire days lazing underneath the red sandstone bluffs, scorching our pale bodies and reassuring one another that 'any burn we got today would become tomorrow's base coat'. The many nooks at the base of the cliffs gave us a sense of privacy, so we dropped our shoulder straps and hiked up our wedgies with impunity. We bobbed around in the clear blue water when our skin got too hot, but never fully appreciated the beauty of this place until we came back years later.

What appealed to us then, and now, is that this small, crescent-shaped bay is very close to the city, yet it still retains a sort of wild quality. The landscape is unexpected and imposing. Red, yellow and purple rocks meet the still blueness of Port Phillip Bay. The *HMS Cerberus*, an ex-navy vessel sunk as a breakwater in 1924, lurks below the surface. The wreck became a popular site for snorkelling and scuba diving over the years, but after some structural collapse in 1993 it became an unstable site and now has regulation swimming distances enforced around it. There have since been several campaigns to preserve the deteriorating ship as one of the only surviving vessels of the Australian colonial navies.

Half Moon Bay remains a hotspot for city-dwelling beachgoers of all ages, particularly on weekends. Its friendly, shallow and protected waters make it popular with families with young children and those who don't care for waves. Ocean swimmers do laps across the bay and people fish from the jetty. Teenagers still bring speakers to play music from their towels; other beach dwellers eat fish and chips from The Cerberus Beach House near the pier.

Because of its proximity to the city, Half Moon Bay is the best beach around for Melbourne kids. On busy days, there's hardly a free spot left on the sand.

Walk down the path from the carpark and take a right turn towards the cliffs to find more-secluded spots tucked into the rocky red bluff. At the other end of the beach (towards the pier) a surf life saving club sits next to colourful beach boxes, an iconic feature of beaches along this strip of inner-city peninsula.

Sure, this isn't Sydney's Bondi Beach, but bay-beach vibes on crystalline Port Phillip don't get much better.

NEARBY

THE CERBERUS BEACH HOUSE
Boat Shed 212, Half Moon Bay

A friendly beachfront hangout with a kiosk serving fish and chips downstairs and a casual restaurant upstairs. Open for lunch and dinner seven days a week through summer, and Tuesday to Sunday the rest of the year.

THE COLONEL'S SON
299 Beach Rd, Black Rock

Located opposite Black Rock Beach, the Colonel's Son feels more like a holiday house than a cafe. Wholesome dishes are cut with mild flavours inspired by the chef's Indian background, such as coconut chicken salad and crispy sumac calamari. This daytime eatery also opens for dinner from Thursday to Saturday.

DAVEY MAC'S
602 Balcombe Rd, Black Rock

This tiny, retro gelateria is a throwback to Italy, at the beach. Gelato and sorbet is made on-site, and piled high in cabinets. There are usually 40 classic and some special-edition flavours on offer. We tend to judge a gelateria by its pistachio or Ferrero Rocher, but the licorice here is very good (and popular) too. No harm in trying a few.

Bushrangers Bay

MORNINGTON PENINSULA

PRIVATE TIDAL ROCK POOLS
HIDDEN AMID A SURREAL
VOLCANIC LANDSCAPE.

ROCK POOL

Best time to visit
Low tide on a hot summer's day when a
north-easterly wind is blowing

How to get there
From the Cape Schanck Lighthouse
carpark (420 Cape Schanck Rd, Cape
Schanck), follow signs to Bushrangers
Bay. Walk east along cliff-tops for about
3km before dropping down to the beach.

Access
Easy. It's a 40-minute walk along a
well-defined path to the beach. Rocks
are sharp, slippery and uneven once you
get to the tidal pools. Be careful of your
footing and take it slowly.

Cost of entry Free

Kid friendly Yes

Dog friendly No. Flinders foreshore is the
best nearest option.

Water temperature Cool

Open 24 hours

Facilities
Toilets and picnic tables at Cape
Schanck Lighthouse

Must bring
Lunch, and lots of water. It can get
stinking hot among the black rocks and
you will be amazed at how much water
you can drink.

LOCAL KNOWLEDGE

Low tide only. I know we emphasise this
a lot, but the last thing we want is for
you to make the effort to get out here
only to find the whole place under
water. Try to arrive while the tide is still
dropping so you can enjoy your swim for
as long as possible.

The eastern side of Port Phillip is probably most famous for its blue-chip towns, Portsea and Sorrento, yet they are hardly a complete representation of what the Mornington Peninsula has to offer. A closer look reveals the true identity of this hook-shaped piece of land to be slow-paced and down to earth. The landscape is dominated by rolling hills, organic farms and some of the state's best wineries. Quality is a unifying theme around here, so it should come as no surprise that Bushrangers Bay is a top-shelf swimming option.

This basalt coastline is quite unlike anywhere else in the area, or even the state. Volcanic black rocks emerge from clear blue water. Deep pools are filled at high tide and slowly warm throughout the day. It has a distinct look and feel, so you can imagine how our eyes popped out of our heads when we saw this secret spot featured in the 2009 film adaptation of *Where the Wild Things Are*. Indeed, it seems like a natural place for a wild rumpus, and you will see lots of kangaroos if you arrive early in the morning.

We start our trip from the Cape Schanck Lighthouse carpark, from where it is a 3-kilometre one-way walk to Bushrangers Bay. Good snacks being essential, we often stop for supplies at Hawkes vegetable and farm store on our way down. Follow the well-defined track along the top of cliffs and through tunnels of coastal banksia. The trail eventually emerges onto the beach to reveal a storybook landscape of hulking, dark headlands. Don't be surprised to see waves exploding onto the beach, as it is exposed to a constant barrage of swells from the south. We prefer the safety and beauty of the nearby tidal rock pools.

Follow the beach east towards the rocky headlands. The most prominent feature is Elephant Rock and the best pools are distributed around its base, on the left-hand side. Water is always clear here and often a few degrees warmer than the ocean – Victoria's version of a spa bath. Remember, this is a low-tide-only spot, so take a moment to make sure that rogue waves aren't crashing into the pools before jumping in. Otherwise you may suddenly find yourself inside a washing machine or heading out to sea.

It is easy to spend the day exploring these pools and climbing the headlands. We feel like we discover a new swim or rock arch every time we visit. Natural baths come in many shapes and sizes, some small enough just for one, but all with million-dollar views – after all, we're on the Mornington Peninsula. All wild things welcome.

NEARBY

ST ANDREWS BEACH BREWERY
160 Sandy Rd, Fingal

A brewery in a former stables (owned by famed horse trainer Lee Freedman), this huge 180-capacity, mostly outdoor space is always humming. Currently they're producing four brews in-house – lager, pilsner, golden ale and pale ale – with plans to diversify. Food options include burgers, pizza, salads and seafood.

PENINSULA HOT SPRINGS
140 Springs La, Fingal

A delightful outdoor spa with dozens of pools filled with thermal mineral water. The property steps up a terraced mountain and is landscaped with lush gardens. Sit, relax, rejuvenate or float from pool to pool, to wash off the saltwater from your day at the beach. Arrive for sunset, so you can soak while the sun goes down. #romantic

POLPERRO
150 Red Hill Rd, Red Hill

Owned by winemaker Sam Coverdale (of Even Keel in Canberra). Small, single-vineyard winery Polperro opened as a cellar door for his local wine label, Polperro by Even Keel, specialising in pinot noir, chardonnay and pinot gris. It is also an elegant country bistro with a slick interior and a laidback approach. The result is spot on.

Little Waterloo Bay

A LOST PIECE OF TASMANIA,
STUCK ONTO THE BOTTOM OF
THE MAINLAND.

VICTORIA

BEACH

Best time to visit
February to May

How to get there
This beach is a popular stop along a roughly 40km multi-day circuit to the eastern coastline and back to Telegraph Saddle. You will need a map from the Tidal River visitor centre before attempting this walk. Little Waterloo Bay is located in the SE corner of the national park.

Access
Difficult. Trails are very well maintained, but distances are long. It's a 15–20km one-way bushwalk to get here. Most visitors stay overnight at Little Waterloo Bay campground before moving on (note: two-night limit at all hikers camps).

Cost of entry Free, but camping fees apply. Book online or at Tidal River visitor centre.

Kid friendly Yes (but must be capable hikers)

Dog friendly No

Water temperature Cool to cold

Open 24 hours

Facilities
Composting toilets, untreated water, campground

Must bring
Tent, sleeping bag, stove and food. Unless you are super-motivated, the only way to get here is via a multi-day backpacking trip. You will need to carry in, and out, all of your own supplies (untreated water is available at all campgrounds).

LOCAL KNOWLEDGE

During periods of low global sea level (ice ages), Wilsons Promontory forms the mainland entrance to a 'land bridge' connecting with Tasmania. It is the probable path that Aboriginal ancestors would have taken to populate Tasmania.

Wilsons Promontory is the southernmost point of the Australian mainland, a little appendage of land that extends far into Bass Strait towards Tasmania. Like God and Adam in the Sistine Chapel, Victoria and Tassie are locked in an eternal near-touch. A transfer of divinity captured in a snapshot lasting millions of years. In point of fact, the area looks and feels more like Tasmania's east coast than the rolling dairy hills of Victoria's South Gippsland. Granite mountains dwarf the neighbouring landscape, and fern-filled valleys lead to squeaky white beaches. Wombats, emus and wallabies frolic fearlessly in this Garden of Eden. The Prom is a masterpiece that people travel across the world to experience. Unlike the Sistine Chapel, however, you will be required to stay overnight and strip to (near) nakedness to properly enjoy it.

While the casual daytripper can have a great time visiting the Prom's easily accessible western shores, such as Norman's Beach and Picnic Bay, the best and most sheltered swims are all on the east coast. Even during frequent winter squalls, Little Waterloo Bay tends to be an oasis of calm. It's hard to get to (even for the prevailing westerly winds), which is one thing that makes it so special. The only way to arrive is by foot. It's a multi-day backpacking trip that offers protected coves and camp sites as a daily reward. While Little Waterloo is our favourite place, it's as much about the journey as the destination.

We try to get here at least once a year, monitoring the forecast for a few consecutive days of warm weather. There are a couple of ways to get in, but we like to do a clockwise circuit from Telegraph Saddle. We start at the carpark and walk 10.2 kilometres east (mostly downhill) to Sealers Cove. It's a large yellow-sand beach with a wide creek at the south end. There is a good camp site here, but we just stop for a quick dip and lunch before continuing a further 6.4 kilometres to Refuge Cove. This tight, heart-shaped bay often has a few sailboats moored in its calm waters. In front of the campground, granite slabs form ramps down to the turquoise ocean.

From Refuge Cove it's about 3.5 kilometres to Kersops Peak, where we get the first views of Waterloo Bay's flawless white sand. The large sweep of beach is subdivided into smaller bays, separated by small headlands of temperate rainforest and granite boulders. Little Waterloo is among these private bays, only a few kilometres beyond the lookout.

There is something about this stretch of beach that brings out the best in people. We've noticed this same effect at a few special places: the natural beauty is so overwhelming that it shifts everyone into a cheerful, communal mood. Little Waterloo Bay anchors its visitors in the present. We laugh like children, jumping over knee-high waves, crumb ourselves in sand like over-sized chicken fillets and fall asleep in the shade. By day and night, we swap stories and play cards with a motley crew of all ages and origins.

From here you can continue further south to the very bottom of the mainlaind, but we only walk about a kilometre further before turning inland. An intermittent boardwalk leads 4.7 kilometres to Telegraph Junction and then a service road takes us 6.1 kilometres back to the carpark. Hot showers at Tidal River offer some consolation as we transition out of our Eden. It can be difficult to leave, but like any masterpiece we can look forward to discovering something new with every visit.

NEARBY

TIDAL RIVER

The de facto cultural capital and activity hub of Wilsons Prom. This former military barracks turned tourist resort is home to a visitor centre, general store, campgrounds and accommodation. Good for a few basic supplies, a hot shower and phone service. A seasonal outdoor cinema runs through summer (just be sure to check with the visitor centre before setting your heart on a movie date). Good surf at Norman Beach on a north-easterly wind.

THE PADDOCK COFFEE SHOP
17 Falls Rd, Fish Creek

Fish Creek is the closet town to the Prom, and the Paddock is our go-to stop both on our way in and our way out. it serves the best coffee in the area, does a mean croque monsieur and sells pre-loved books. It also has some local pantry goods like eggs, jams and oils. Feels like heaven after a few days camping.

MOO'S AT MEENIYAN
89 Whitelaw St, Meeniyan

Meeniyan has become a foodie hub, with Moo's at its centre. This cute, eclectic converted home is open for breakfast, lunch and weekend dinners, with a glorious patio garden shining in the summer and a cosy wood stove that burns through winter. The focus is on local produce, and chef Trev is constantly updating the blackboards with seasonal dishes. You can get everything from an egg on toast to a three-course dinner with wine pairings.

Chef

MATT GERMANCHIS OF CAPTAIN MOONLITE

The walls are lined with old photographs of club members and plaques inscribed with the names of club captains; retired kayaks rest overhead in the rafters. Out on the deck, views open out over the cliff to the beach below. It might sound like any old surf life saving club in Australia, but this one at Anglesea is a little different.

Chef Matt Germanchis (ex Pei Modern and Movida) and his partner, front-of-house pro Gemma Gange (Pei Modern, Stokehouse and Jacques Reymond), have transformed the clubhouse into an eatery serving the best fish and chips on the Great Ocean Road. Since opening Captain Moonlite (named after a notorious Australian bushranger) in the surf club during the summer of 2016, they have created a comfortable spot for locals and visitors to sit

by the ocean and enjoy simple things such as grilled octopus and a beer.

In the small open kitchen, Matt is serving a 'coastal European' menu, of which 80 per cent of the dishes are seafood – think salt-and-pepper fish wings, bowls of whitebait, pickled sardines, fillets of blue-eye and plates of calamari. He's using almost entirely local produce, and picking up ingredients off the beach – saltbush for garnishes and ocean water for brine. Though this is no ordinary fish dinner, it's the setting here that really enhances the experience, looking out over Anglesea Beach. Captain Moonlite is a place where you can watch the waves crash while you dine, or walk straight down to the beach for a swim between courses.

...THERE ARE SO MANY WAYS TO THINK ABOUT SEAFOOD BECAUSE IT INVOLVES A DELICATE WAY OF COOKING.

Q. What's your connection to Anglesea?
A. Gemma's parents live here and we'd drive down from Melbourne to spend weekends, looking for somewhere to chill out. Gemma suggested we go check out the surf club one afternoon. We walked in and thought, this is great, let's do something here. It's like a Greek taverna near the ocean, and it really benefits the community. We donate a percentage of our takings to the surf life saving club.

Q. How do you approach the menu and work with fish suppliers?
A. The menu is predominantly seafood and that is purely because of the demand from customers. They come in here, they see the ocean and they want to eat fish. It's that simple. I try to focus a lot on Victorian seafood, so stuff from Lakes Entrance and up in Lorne, and it might be little esprit prawns, or bugs (they don't always live in Balmain). I do a lot of rock flathead too. I get mussels from Port Arlington. I ring my supplier and ask for what I want. Then he says, 'Yeah, boat's coming in on this day and this is what we have for you'. It's a great relationship.

Q. Do you cook more seafood now?
A. One hundred per cent. That's the exciting thing about it, because I can approach seafood in so many different ways now. Sometimes I'll age fish downstairs for a week; I'll get big albacore tunas in and age them for seven to 10 days, like you would meat. I'll hang these giant 30-kilo fish and come down with a knife and cut a loin off. It means having more opportunities to experiment, for instance with bugs or prawns: we can salt-and-pepper fry them; we can braise them or pressure-cook them; we can cook them with saltbush and serve them on bread. We have the opportunity to go through different cooking processes with one type of seafood and sell it in different ways. When you have a city restaurant you are restricted because you need a certain amount of meat dishes and veg dishes; you need this and that. But here I can put on a whole fish, fillets of fish, fish and chips, mussels – I can have five or six different seafood main courses on at once, with giant prawn crackers and cod roe on the bar menu. That dominates what we do here. The ocean has such an abundance of crustaceans and molluscs and fish, and there are so many different ways to think about seafood because it involves a delicate way of cooking.

Q. What local fish are you cooking at the moment?
A. Rock flatheads are super popular. There are lots of crayfish out there too. Flounders,

mussels, lots of cuttlefish from the area – I love using cuttlefish. We'll just cook whole eggplants and make an XO sauce out of dried prawns and dried fish that we have; we smear this intense sauce on the eggplant and we'll serve grilled cuttlefish on top of that. We like using things that generate quite quickly. Lots and lots of sardines from the area as well; we love to use sardines because it's a school fish. If we get big sardines in you can fillet them, rip the bone out and crumb them, or you get the small ones and pickle them and have them whole.

Q. What do you pickle them in?
A. We pickle them in a white-wine vinegar and lots of aromatics, like dill and bay and allspice, star anise, sugar and water. We get them raw and put a hot liquid over them. And they cook a little bit in the hot liquid, and they last like that for two to three days. You just have a salad with pickled sardines, and you're not losing the integrity of the fish.

Q. How do you make the brine with seawater?
A. The brine for us is essentially used as a curing or a preserving method. Sometimes we'll have fish like blue cod that is quite bland, and I'll try to bring back some of the natural ocean flavours. I'll get some ocean water and bring it up to boil to kill off any nasties. Then I'll chill it down and get some seaweed and put in lots of those umami, rich, salty flavours, and soak the fish in it for maybe 2 hours and sort of use it as a curing, so some of the flavour permeates the fish. Then we'll cook the fish, sometimes in some olive oil or some stock with the lid on and poach it. You can also brine lettuces. If I've got cos I'll just soak it in the seawater for half an hour and put it on the chargrill, so the cos has the sea notes to it and natural saltiness. I think seawater has a 2 or 3 per cent saltiness to it, so it's a natural consistent brine. It's like a curing liquor and you don't have to play with it; it's a natural product that we can utilise.

Q. Are these ideas/principles that you've thought about throughout your career, or is this something you've taken on in this new coastal environment?
A. Partly both. I've been cooking for close to 25 years now, so for me when I am in a certain environment I tend to think about it a little bit more – how you can do things better and work smarter and more naturally, with less elements but more of an impact on food.

Captain Moonlite is open Thursday to Monday at the Anglesea Surf Life Saving Club (http://captainmoonlite.com.au; 100 Great Ocean Road, Anglesea).

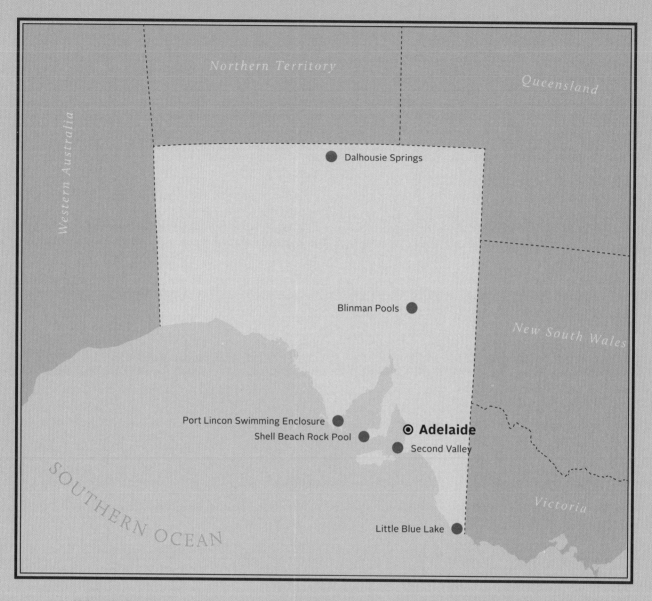

Northern Territory

Queensland

Western Australia

● Dalhousie Springs

Blinman Pools ●

New South Wales

Port Lincon Swimming Enclosure ●

Shell Beach Rock Pool ●

◉ **Adelaide**

● Second Valley

SOUTHERN OCEAN

Victoria

Little Blue Lake ●

When to visit

The outback is best from May to
October; all other places from
November to April.

Cliff-jumping best practices

For how to jump with safety in mind,
see p. x

Favourite swim

DALHOUSIE SPRINGS
(*see* p. 65)

Best meal

STAR OF GREECE
(*see* p. 75)

Road-trip advice

Stock up on food, water and fuel
whenever you have a chance. Good
supplies are few and far between
once you start travelling north and
west of Adelaide; there is nothing
worse than having to cut a trip short
because you're running out of water
(been there, done that). We carried
40 litres of water and always had a
sealed emergency log of salami and
some tinned herring for when salt
and morale were running low.

South Australia

South Australia is a huge state, yet so much of its population is concentrated in Adelaide that we never thought too far beyond its borders.

The City of Churches and the state's wineries steal the headlines, leaving very little room for other destinations. Locals know better, however, and our friends in Adelaide are quick to mobilise for a 6-hour drive with little notice. South Australians are always ready for a camping adventure; a weekend trip to a remote beach or desert swimming hole is part of life around here. The car is already packed, ready to go.

To the north and west, vegetation quickly shifts to sunburnt Australiana. In these humbling arid expanses it is easy to realise just how small we are. This is a land for people who don't like people. The thick fingers of the Yorke (see Shell Beach Rock Pool, p. 70) and Eyre peninsulas (see Port Lincoln, p. 72) dip into the Southern Ocean, catching crystal-clear water wherever it makes landfall. Wild isolation is multiplied as you travel north into the outback. The land becomes extraterrestrial, which makes swims all the more rewarding. Down the dusty, corrugated roads we found cold pools (see Blinman Pools, p. 68) and hot springs (see Dalhousie Springs, p. 65).

These places make Adelaide look like the Emerald City from *The Wizard of Oz*, an oasis on the frontier, to which we greedily returned to indulge in its generous hospitality before moving south. Heading along the coast, the land transforms once more, becoming soft and gentle. Where else can you mix wine tastings and cliff-jumping (see Second Valley, p. 74, and Little Blue Lake, p. 77)? Hint: best to do the jumping first.

Though it is seldom celebrated on the scale of other states, South Australia is a swimming giant and, just may be, the rock-jumping capital of the country. There are plenty of great swims around Adelaide, but anyone who ventures a little further will be immensely rewarded.

Dalhousie
Springs

A 38°C ARTESIAN HOT SPRING
IN THE TOP CORNER OF THE
SOUTH AUSTRALIAN DESERT.

SOUTH AUSTRALIA

THERMAL SPRING

Best time to visit
Year-round, but the cooler Dry season (April to October) is best.

How to get there
From SA, drive north from Oodnadatta to Hamilton Homestead (108km) and follow signs north-east to Pedirka and Dalhousie (71km). From NT, travel east from Kulgera to Finke (137km); continue south-east following signs to Federal and Dalhousie (174km).

Access
Roads are unsealed and generally rough. A 4WD is strongly recommended; however, a bit of patience goes a long way and we did see a couple of intrepid Subarus. Do not attempt this drive if there has been any rain, as roads will become an impassable boggy mess. For 4WD advice, *see* p. xi.

Cost of entry Free

Kid friendly Yes

Dog friendly No

Water temperature Hot

Open 24 hours

Facilities
Camping (free), toilets, showers, rainwater tank (emergency only)

Must bring
Food and water for a couple of days' travel, and a spare jerry can with fuel. There are no supplies available nearby.

LOCAL KNOWLEDGE

Take a dip early in the morning to see mist rising from the pool's surface.

With no working petrol gauge, speedometer or air-conditioning, we thought we were doing it pretty tough in our rusty 30-year old 4WD on the unsealed road of the Oodnadatta Track. That was until we saw a cloud of dust ahead and two bike riders pedalling the same path. After days of being overtaken by fellow drivers with superior suspension, we finally felt like we weren't the slowest travellers on the road. What we'd stumbled upon was a bike odyssey across the country by two ambitious architects (Owen and Bobbie, aka The Grand Section), who we joined for dinner and a float in the hot oasis that is Dalhousie Springs.

Located in Witjira National Park on the western fringe of the Simpson Desert, Dalhousie Springs is probably one of the most remote places that any of us will ever swim (or drive to). This group of 60 springs represents only a tiny fraction of the Great Artesian Basin, the world's largest and deepest artesian system. Water at this location has likely travelled thousands of kilometres over about a million years to reach the surface, which certainly puts any road trip into perspective. After hours and maybe days of driving through the hot, dry desert on corrugated, unsealed roads, the thermal pool makes for welcome respite.

Main Pool is a large thermal spring and the only designated swimming hole in the area. Though it is surrounded by dense, wetland vegetation, it can be easily accessed via stairs on the water's edge. The temperature sits at a reliable 38°C year-round, making it hospitable for all – most notably the six species of native fish, five of which are endemic to these springs. If you sit still long enough they will give you the full spa treatment, nibbling dead skin from any exposed part of your body.

Dalhousie Springs sits at a crossroads of the Oodnadatta Track, French Line, Rig Road and Simpson Desert Track, where weary travellers of all backgrounds drive in to soothe their bodies in the warm waters. On any given day there will be families in dusty caravans, grey nomads in custom 4WDs, and convoys of motorheads on the ultimate outback adventure with mates.

Most people only stay a night before getting back on the road – but not before taking a late-afternoon or early-morning dip. The water is deep in some parts, but sludgy footing can be found towards the centre. There is a permanent collection of pool noodles near the stairs, which swimmers can use to cut the perfect image of relaxation while they drift along to an evolving soundtrack of birdsong and travel stories. When the warm spring water is well noodled, the expression 'people soup' comes to mind, but it's also common to find that you have the pool all to yourself.

However long you stay and whatever path you're taking, you'll emerge from the water feeling rejuvenated and ready for the next leg of your journey.

NEARBY

DALHOUSIE HOMESTEAD
Witjira National Park

About 15 kilometres from the springs, this collection of limestone ruins fringed by 100-year-old date palms is a great example of pastoralism in an extreme environment. Poke around remnants of homes, a blacksmith's shop and cattle yards, which were abandoned in 1925.

MT DARE
Witjira National Park

Seventy very slow kilometres north of Dalhousie is a small remote town with an all-in-one outback roadhouse, including a pub, petrol station and campground, making it an ideal stop for a hike or an overnight stay.

KULGERA ROAD HOUSE
corner Kulgera Cres & South Stuart Hwy, Ghan, NT

This place is too quintessentially Australian to be contrived. Tough old dudes in cowboy hats gather around a fire; every wall is covered in vintage memorabilia, and autographed bras and stubby holders dangle from the ceiling. Visit for a cold beer and a burger, and sit up at the bar next to a couple of resident snakes.

ROCK POOL

◐ **Best time to visit**
February to May and September to November. It's too hot and there's not enough water over summer.

◬ **How to get there**
From the Outback Hwy at Parachilna, take the unsealed Parachilna Gorge Rd 17km east towards Blinman as far as Angorichina Village. The walking track begins from the village and becomes less defined as you travel upstream. Follow the riverbed and occasional markings for about 6km to the main pool. There are a couple of little swimming holes along the way and beyond, but you can't miss the Blinman; it's the biggest by a mile.

⊖ **Access**
Unsealed road for 17km – 4WD recommended. Walking trail (6km) is rocky and poorly defined. It's slow-going, so prepare to spend an entire day here.

⑤ **Cost of entry** Free

☺ **Kid friendly** Yes (but it's a long walk)

⊗ **Dog friendly** Yes

◠ **Water temperature** Cold

◷ **Open** 24 hours (but recommended during daylight only)

⊕ **Facilities**
None

⊛ **Must bring**
Good walking shoes – runners are fine. Extra drinking water.

LOCAL KNOWLEDGE

Driving at night in the outback is strongly discouraged because of roos and cattle. Roads around here are swamped with both – don't take the risk.

Blinman Pools

FLINDERS RANGES

A SERIES OF NATURAL ROCK POOLS AND WATERHOLES DOTTED ALONG A SEASONAL RIVERBED.

Like a cold swim after a long walk, the best kind of reward is one you have to work for. This is no more true than at Blinman Pools, a series of natural pools set along a dried-out rocky riverbed at the foothills of the Flinders Ranges, accessible only via a 6-kilometre walk.

Begin the walk at Angorichina Village, where there's a general store with petrol, basic food supplies and accommodation. The entrance is marked by a sign that reads: 'Real people only, no yuppies'. We didn't see either on the trail. Which was surprising. We'd been told by friends in Adelaide that Blinman was a popular spot on weekends, so were prepared for a small crowd. Signs advise to start the walk before midday in order to make it back before dark – pertinent advice.

There are two main pools along the mostly dry creek, the first 5 kilometres in. The walk is marked with signposts along a track that crosses back and forth over the dry riverbed several times. We're here in June: water flows, but it's bloody cold. We now realise why we might be the only people here, despite it being 'peak season' in the Flinders Ranges. You can imagine the relief it brings to those who visit in the heat of summer though. The first pool is bordered by a high cliff wall around one side with a small trickling waterfall. In warmer months, crowds pour in here to set up towels alongside their friends for the day, backpacks filled with cold drinks and music erupting from small portable speakers, echoing around the pool walls.

A kilometre upstream there is more swimming. The track rises slightly between the ranges, taking you to what can only be described as Modernist infinity pools, like something out of an architecture magazine, but cut naturally into the rock. They even have solar heating.

The dry, arid landscape here feels like a slap of Australiana: the land's hypnotic deep reds are set against rich blues of the sky, and not a puff of cloud to tarnish it. The warm kiss of the sunshine is enough to make you forget it's winter; it's easy to be misled when the sun is scorching and the sky is blue. But in the outback, what appears to be a hot day can soon become very cold as the sun goes down. Come summer, though, the heat here can be unbearable, and the harsh landscape provides little more shade than a few gumtrees dotted along the edges of the creek beds.

The 12-kilometre return walk to Blinman Pools will take you the good part of a day (approximately 5 hours, with time to swim and enjoy), and is a unique South Australian swimming experience.

NEARBY

FREE CAMPING
Parachilna Gorge Rd

Several free bush-camping sites lie along the Parachilna Gorge Road. With no visible signage, your best way to identify these spacious rest stops is if other campers have already set up there. You'll likely see them from the road, sheltered under a tree at the edge of the creek bed. Be mindful of flooding in these areas.

THE PRAIRIE HOTEL
High St & West Tce, Parachilna

A pub in the middle of nowhere, so it seems. This rustic lodging is also a frequent movie set with a top-notch bar and restaurant serving favourite pub specials and bush tucker (try the 'Feral Mix Grill', a platter of kangaroo fillets, emu mignon and camel sausage). Beer on tap is Fhager lager, made specially for the pub by Pikes Wines. There's also a local art gallery inside.

HEYSEN TRAIL

A long-distance, 1200-kilometre (two month) walking trail that runs from Parachilna Gorge in the Flinders Ranges, via the Adelaide Hills to Cape Jervis on the Fleurieu Peninsula. Day walkers can do small sections of this track. For more committed hikers, the full trail will take you through native bushland, pine forests, vineyards, farmland and historic towns.

ROCK POOL

◐ **Best time to visit**
Low tide, November to March

◈ **How to get there**
Shell Beach is a popular beach and campground on the north shore of Innes National Park (about 20km from the visitor centre) and the turn-off is well signed. Take the stairs down to beach and turn right to walk to the far end (east) until it becomes rocky and reefy. The pool is hidden among some tall rocks about 20m from the shore.

⊖ **Access**
Easy. Well-maintained unsealed road and beachside parking. The trickiest part is finding the rock pool.

⑤ **Cost of entry**
$10 per vehicle national-park entry fee

☺ **Kid friendly** Yes

⊗ **Dog friendly** No

◠ **Water temperature** Always refreshing. Guaranteed.

◷ **Open** 24 hours

⊕ **Facilities**
Toilet, camping (eight basic sites, $15 per vehicle)

◎ **Must bring**
Bug spray or a mesh face hood for flies. They will challenge even the most zen camper. Seriously, why do they always try to fly into your mouth?

Shell Beach
Rock Pool

INNES NATIONAL PARK, YORKE PENINSULA

A BEAUTIFUL HIDDEN ROCK POOL WITH THE RIGHT AMOUNT OF SECLUSION TO KEEP THE CROWDS AWAY.

After months driving around the country, we initially bypassed the Yorke Peninsula on our way east from Port Lincoln to Adelaide. But after a weekend spent in the capital, grilling friends on their favourite swimming spots in the state, Innes National Park kept coming up. We couldn't help feeling that we might have missed one of the best places to swim in South Australia.

FOMO got the better of us and we made a last-minute decision to backtrack and head to the tip of the coastline's middle peninsula. The drive took us about 4 hours west, to a coastal landscape where rugged cliffs and sandy beaches provided the backdrop. The following day was expected to be 35°C and sunny, so conditions were looking good for a hidden rock-pool adventure.

Our destination was Shell Beach, where a small campground is tucked into vegetation on the park's north shore, a couple of hundred metres' walk from the beach. The desired rock pool is discreetly located among rocky granite platforms on the east side of the beach (turn right at the bottom of the stairs). It's been made famous by Instagram, and many people have come looking for it via a location-tagged image, with no luck. So we followed another couple down the curving beach and over the rocks, determined to find the photogenic pool. You can't see it without scrambling around, but it's not too far around the headland, so keep looking until you find it. It's there and it's spectacular.

With water this enchanting, jumping from rocks at the pool's sides is the perfect entry. We plunge in with little hesitation, the chill of the water taking our breath away. It was a calm day when we visited, but this place can no doubt get pretty wild – it's tide and weather dependent, and can get swallowed up by the ocean. But on a still, 35°C morning late in November, it's a corker. The pool here is protected and impossibly clear, and you can dive down deep to explore an underwater world of small fish, coral, crabs and starfish.

We hear in the peak of summer this secluded spot can get quite busy, but we spend an hour alone before a wetsuited couple arrives with snorkels to dive for abalone. They tell us they are here instead of attending Schoolies, and we admire their choice to trade in beer bongs for barnacles.

For us, this place is a real discovery, and absolutely worth the two-day mission in the wrong direction.

NEARBY

BEACH BREAK
Shop 2, Yorke Hwy, Marion Bay

This a cute little coastal diner serves casual takeaway food such as fish and chips and chicken schnitzel burgers on sourdough. For most of the year it's open Friday to Sunday, but during summer, when the crowds arrive, they fire up the burners more regularly, serving hungry grommets after a surf.

PONDALOWIE BAY
Yorke Peninsula

A long stretch of beach on the south-west tip of the peninsula, 12 kilometres from Marion Bay. At the carpark, follow a winding kilometre of wooden boardwalk over sand dunes and down onto an incredible white-sand beach. There are a couple of nice surf breaks and a shipwreck that has washed up on the shore.

THE CORNISH KITCHEN
10/12 Ellen St, Moonta

A little further north on the west side of Yorke Peninsula in the town of Moonta is a damn fine bakery serving traditional Cornish-style pies and pasties. Popularity with the locals is a good sign and this place is always packed with farmers chatting about wheat prices, rainfall and state footy.

OCEAN POOL

◐ **Best time to visit**
Summer days from 6pm to sunset are absolute perfection.

◬ **Address**
Town jetty, Port Lincoln (across the road from 66 Tasman Tce)

⊖ **Access**
Easy. Walk down the jetty and jump in.

⑤ **Cost of entry** Free

☺ **Kid friendly** Yes

⊗ **Dog friendly** Yes. On-leash only from 8:30am to sunset.

◠ **Water temperature** Cold

◔ **Open** 24 hours

⊕ **Facilities**
Showers, toilets, picnic tables, BBQs

⊚ **Must bring**
Dinner. Despite a lifetime of being advised against it, there is something deeply satisfying about pairing swimming and eating. On a hot day, it can feel like half the town is sitting on the jetty, eating dinner and watching the sunset.

Port Lincoln Swimming Enclosure

EYRE PENINSULA

A LOCAL MEETING POINT AND PROTECTED SWIMMING AREA OFF THE SIDE OF THE TOWN JETTY.

The Eyre Peninsula is a legendary piece of arid land between Adelaide and the Nullarbor Desert. Its rugged, triangular horn extends about 400 kilometres into the Great Australian Bight, where its exposed western coastline collects enormous quantities of both fish and surf. It is impossible to talk to locals without receiving a fond commentary about its isolation. The same goes for ex-locals, though their fondness is for escaping that very same isolation. The peninsula's west coast is famous for its shimmering aquamarine water. However, conditions can change so quickly that many of our favourite places are unswimmable for most of the year. Port Lincoln's swimming enclosure, on the other hand, is a netted arena of tranquillity. For what it lacks in immediate wow factor, it more than compensates for as a highly functional public space.

Despite it being only 250 kilometres from Adelaide as a crow flies, getting to Port Lincoln requires a 7-hour drive around the Spencer Gulf. The small city is the hub for Australia's largest commercial fishing fleet and the lucrative abalone industry. This so-called 'seafood frontier' also happens to be one of the sharkiest coastlines in the country. Great whites are ever present, to the extent that one of the top tourist activities is cage diving. We surfed and swam all the way down the western side of the peninsula, but we definitely felt a heightened paranoia. Admittedly, a yawning gap exists between the perceived and real danger posed by sharks. In reality, we should all be much more concerned about melanoma. Yet, the peace of mind afforded by the swimming enclosure feels so much better than a smear of sunscreen.

The 50-metre floating ocean pool, which nestles against the town jetty, is essentially a raft of pontoons encircled by shark nets. A distant barrier of floating pipes smothers any would-be swell and ensures it doesn't get too wild in here. It's a natural adaptation to unpredictable waters. And, by virtue of being free, there is a distinctly communal culture among swimmers.

From the morning swim clubs to the afternoon school kids, people are enthusiastic and eager to share their prized pool. On a warm day, it can take on a festival atmosphere. Bikes are hurriedly abandoned along the jetty; people picnic and discreetly sip beers; kids are locked in endless cycles of flips and dives; anglers cast about; and lap swimmers glide through the water with the ease of knowing they aren't being stalked by a 5-metre predator. Everyone wins.

The swimming enclosure scratches our need for safety and ease. There's nothing more beautiful than golden hour here: as we finish our laps and roll up the paper from our fish and chips, we feel profoundly content.

NEARBY

PIZZERIA TRIESTE
33 Edinburgh St, Port Lincoln

Everyone we asked about food in Port Lincoln suggested this small Italian pizzeria. It might not look like anything special, but the handmade woodfired pizzas and paninis are traditional and wholesome. Open for breakfast, lunch and dinner, to dine in or take away.

THE FRESH FISH PLACE
20 Proper Bay Rd, Port Lincoln

On your way out of town, stop at this fancy fishmonger selling fish and chips, with dine-in cafe space available for lunch. It also sells fresh and frozen fish, house-pickled seafood (like mussels and pippies) and has a retail section selling wasabi, tartare, lemon juicers and fish knives. Probably the best place to get seafood anywhere along this coast. Closes at 6pm.

SLEAFORD BAY
Port Lincoln National Park

Park at Wreck Beach Road and walk up and over the huge sand dunes (part of an impressive dune system) to the exposed beaches looking out to the Southern Ocean. For a moment (before you see the water) you'll feel like you're in the Sahara. On a calm day the swimming is great here, but be on the lookout for rips.

CLIFF-JUMP

◗ **Best time to visit**
November to April
(very busy on hot weekends)

◭ **How to get there**
Follow Main South Rd south from
Adelaide for about 90km. Turn right
on Finniss Vale Dr and take it all the
way to the coast, where it dead-ends at
the Second Valley Caravan Park. Walk
downhill to the jetty and follow the
rough path on the left for about 800m,
traversing up until you see the cliff cut-
out and jumping pool below. Descend
and swim across to reach the jumps.

⊖ **Access**
Moderate. It's not a far walk, but you
do have to use your hands in places
and you can feel a little exposed
scrambling around.

⑂ **Cost of entry** Free

☺ **Kid friendly** Yes, but only very
capable swimmers

⊛ **Dog friendly** Yes

⌁ **Water temperature** Cold

◷ **Open** 24 hours

⊕ **Facilities**
Toilets (at carpark)

⊚ **Must bring**
Sunscreen. There isn't an inch of shade
out here, unless you swim into the cave.
Most people walk out absolutely roasted.

LOCAL KNOWLEDGE

Second Valley is the site of some of
the state's best diving and snorkelling.
Around the rocky shoreline of this
peninsula you may be lucky enough to
sight the mysterious leafy seadragon,
which looks more like a colourful piece
of seaweed or coral than marine life.

Second Valley

LEGENDARY CLIFF-JUMP DOWN INTO SURREAL
BLUE WATER.

Another day, another peninsula. South Australia's shoreline spreads its tendrilled fingers into the Southern Ocean, each swathe of coast offering an entirely different experience. The Fleurieu Peninsula is just south of Adelaide and stood out to us as the most hospitable of the lot, offering a welcome mix of indulgence and wilderness. Popular Maslin and Aldinga beaches mark the northern limits, and to the south the land gets exponentially more dramatic the further you travel. Rolling hills hide small farms and historic towns, not to mention the beloved McLaren Vale wineries. It was a tremendous surprise to us when golden fields abruptly ended at black cliffs. Below, the calm blue waters hardly stirred but for the splash of swimmers and divers at Second Valley.

This is the place that really cemented South Australia as the cliff-jumping capital of the country. To be clear, we are by no means adrenaline junkies and you don't have to do any jumps to appreciate Second Valley (for cliff-jumping best practices, *see* p. x). Kangaroo Island blocks most waves from reaching this coast, so on a windless day the ocean appears to be a glassy lagoon. Perfect for any type of swimmer.

To get here, walk downhill from the Second Valley Caravan Park carpark to the jetty (stop at the kiosk for all of your lunch needs). White-sand patches shift around this little bay and a lot of young families stop to play in the shallows. You can do a few low-key jumps from the jetty, and there is good snorkelling off the rocks. To continue to the main swimming hole, walk south beneath the cliffs to the next headland. There is a well-worn path and on a hot day you will be able to hear voices and/or music. It's a bit of a scramble, but a lot of people do it in thongs (we prefer something more covered to protect our feet when we climb and jump).

We've seen this place at different times of the year in all sorts of conditions, but the initial reveal is always priceless. Expansive views extend for kilometres down the coast and the exquisitely clear water beckons below. Sometimes you feel like you are discovering a secret spot, while other days it feel like a Schoolies party. You have to climb down to the water and swim across the narrow channel to get to any jumps.

Sit on the rocks and people-watch for a while, noting where to jump from and gauging reactions. There are always some who obviously don't want to jump and our hearts go out to them as they stand, frozen in terror, while their friends hoot and cheer encouragement. There are various ledges up to about 10 metres, and they all have reasonably safe landings. We don't stray beyond these, but you will see plenty of heroes flying from much higher up. This is a world-class place and a lot of fun. However, be very careful: we don't want to read about you in the newspaper.

NEARBY

LEONARD'S MILL
7869 Main South Rd, Second Valley

The beach is the main focus in Second Valley, but this beautiful old stone structure on the riverbank has had a flash new restoration, turning Leonard's Mill into a cosy silver-service restaurant, with boutique accommodation and a rustic yoga studio. The menu here features seasonal, local produce in dishes such as smoked snook, octopus sashimi and kangaroo tartare, plus McLaren Vale wines.

ALPHA BOX & DICE
8 Olivers Rd, McLaren Vale

Speaking of McLaren Vale wine, it'd be remiss for us not to mention one of the more innovative winemakers in the area. Alpha Box & Dice is a small-scale operation experimenting in European varietals, using grapes from farmers across South Australia. Visit the cellar door to sample their minimal-intervention approach to unpretentious wines.

STAR OF GREECE
1 Esplanade, Port Willunga

On your way back up the coast towards Adelaide, stop into the coastal town of Port Willunga for a swim and some lunch at this popular cliff-side shack. Fresh Australian produce meets Mediterranean influences, with seafood (oysters, kingfish, Moreton Bay bugs), zucchini flowers, brie tart, and summer pudding with house-made ice-cream. If you're coming through on a weekend, make sure to book. This place is a favourite among locals and visitors.

Little Blue Lake

MOUNT GAMBIER

A BOTTOMLESS BLUE LAGOON
IN THE MIDDLE OF A PADDOCK.

LAGOON   **CLIFF-JUMP**

◗ **Best time to visit**
November to May

◢ **How to get there**
From Mount Gambier, follow the Riddoch Hwy south-west, passing over the mountain and past the Blue Lake (Mount Gambier's water supply). Follow the road for about 10km out of town and turn right on Mount Salt Rd. Little Blue Lake is 3.5km further, on the right side of the road.

⊖ **Access**
Easy. You could drive right into it if you wanted to.

$ **Cost of entry** Free

☺ **Kid friendly** Yes

⊗ **Dog friendly** No

◠ **Water temperature** Cool

◷ **Open** 24 hours

⊕ **Facilities**
None

◉ **Must bring**
Dive equipment. Good visibility below 20m, and we are told there is a car at the bottom.

LOCAL KNOWLEDGE

For the last 20 years, the best-selling souvenir in Mount Gambier has been a little bottle of 'Blue Lake Water', selling for $5 a pop – a special memento to take home. We'd love to shake the hand of the genius who came up with that idea.

NEARBY

BADENOCH'S DELI
155c Bay Rd, Moorak

It doesn't do homemade or artisanal, but for generations this deli has been the place to go for the best ice-cream in town, and is just a short drive from Baby Blue.

OK PIE SHOP
66 Commercial St West, Mount Gambier

Back in town, this is Mt Gambier's famous 75-year-old bakery, and a place straight out of your childhood memories. We love the Greek lamb pie and the cream-filled brandy snaps, but it's the secret cheese tart recipe that has been a mainstay on the menu since it opened.

MT SCHANK

This is an inactive 100-metre-high volcano cone that you can hike up, then around the rim and down into the centre. The rim walk is nearly 2 kilometres around the edge, with views down into the densely vegetated green crater and out over surrounding farmland towards Mount Gambier.

We first arrived at Little Blue Lake, also known as Baby Blue, as a powerful storm was moving across the region. It hadn't rained all summer and the cold front suddenly blew in from the west, knocking us around the road, our frenzied windscreen wipers straining against their duty. We were determined to have a look, but could hardly even see the road to get us there. Yet, as we pulled into the carpark, the rain started to ease. After a few minutes, it stopped altogether and sun poured onto the shimmering blue water. Was it a sign? We think so.

The pool sits in an unassuming paddock about 15 kilometres south of Mount Gambier, looking a little lonely and out of place. It makes more sense when you learn that Baby Blue is a sinkhole, formed by the gradual collapse of an underground cave. The pool has an average depth of about 35 metres and it isn't unusual (but it is a little creepy) to see the odd diver suddenly emerge from below. In fact, this area is one of the best inland diving destinations in the world, with a Swiss-cheese network of 500 underground caves and 50 sinkholes to explore. For our purposes, however, surface swimming is just about the right speed.

Sheer 10-metre limestone walls make this an iconic South Australian jump and a rite of passage among locals. As a car full of tweens arrive from school, we think of a 10-year-old version of our friend Alice being pressured by her three older brothers to take the plunge. We watch kids peer over the edge as if they were looking into the Great Australian Bight. Instincts intact, they back away slowly, only to have their dad soar over the top of them and down into the pool. They look at each other and you can see the thoughts broadcast across their faces. Who's next? Do we really have to do this?

Like many places, signs forbid jumping here and there are murmurs of council-enforced fines, though nobody seems too concerned. Jump at your own discretion. Alternatively, take the steps down from the carpark side of the pool to a shiny new pontoon. This makes for a more gentle entry and is an easy introduction to the cool water. A few natural terraces extend back towards the road, providing a great vantage to sit and watch, like a swimming amphitheatre. As the clouds continue to lift and burn away, the water becomes more and more blue. We look off to the east and see Mt Schank, an extinct volcano, looming in the near distance. This is not a landscape we ever expected to see in Australia, but we are so happy to have found it.

Who's next?
Do we really have to do this?

Photographer and Travel Writer

JACKSON GROVES

Jackson Groves is a photographer and an adventure-travel blogger from Adelaide. He's been living out of a backpack since 2015, and making a racket out of it, taking photos and writing guides for brands and tourism boards from Sony to Tourism Australia. With hundreds of thousands of followers, he's Instagram famous, and is trading this huge online reach with his followers for experiences.

One day he'll be skydiving over Uluṟu, the next he's cruising out to the Great Barrier Reef to spend a night on a pontoon before taking a helicopter back to Cairns. Next week he'll be in the Philippines, then on to Israel before he returns to the outback for work (and some adventure). This is the life of a digital nomad in a time where pictures of bronzed adventurers, cliff-jumping, surfing and generally having a hell of a time swimming in impossibly blue waters are currency.

Jackson is a solo traveller. He spends his days doing the things that many of us don't have access to, or at least wouldn't have before the days of social media. He spends his nights editing photos and videos to share with the world – a constant stream of travel and holiday inspiration, and what seems like an endless summer.

I HAVE A 60-LITRE BACKPACK WITH ALL MY STUFF IN IT; THAT'S ALL I OWN – JUST CLOTHES AND TOILETRIES.

Q. How did you start on this path?

A. I was in Oahu (Hawaii) for the summer and my friend was shooting in the waves, which is quite a popular hobby for a lot of people, to shoot the barrels in the shore break there. It was too big for me, so I started shooting bodyboarders from the shore, then turned to shooting surfers, and bought some nice lenses. Then as we travelled Oahu, I began documenting our adventures.

Q. A lot of your photos are of you jumping off huge cliffs. Have you been doing this a while?

A. No, but I enjoy it. I started doing backflips off a boat in Indonesia from a couple of metres, then the heights got higher and now I manage to land on my feet from 15-metre jumps. But I don't have any other tricks other than a backflip. I think I just like the challenge of being scared and still doing it – the idea of being able to push through the fear despite my mind suggesting my body should not go ahead with it.

Q. We reckon South Australia is the cliff-jumping capital of Australia. Any favourite places?

A. My favourite spot in the world to jump is in Second Valley (see p. 74). That's a really nice spot, but it has to be the right kind of day – really hot with no wind.

Q. What are some of your other favourite places to swim in Australia?

A. Near Ormiston (see p. 121) in the NT, at Glen Helen Gorge (see p. 120). I rock climbed the back of one of those cliffs and then jumped about 20 or 25 metres. It doesn't look deep but it is. I always check the water before I jump. It's beautiful and there's nobody there, just two huge red cliffs and this big reflection. I also recently went to Babinda Boulders (see p. xiv) near Cairns – that was cool.

Q. You spend a lot of time overseas in South-East Asia, Indonesia and the Philippines. How do those beaches compare to Australian swimming spots?

A. In Australia we often have really uncrowded stretches of sand and some awesome spots, but you get different kinds of swimming in places like the Philippines where you have these epic limestone cliffs right on crystal-clear water. It's just something totally different from what you get in Australia. But we have a real mixture of stuff too, like Cape Tribulation where the rainforest meets the beach – that is unique.

I think Australians are a little bit spoilt, but there are great swimming places all around the world. There are many versions of a 10-out-of-10 beach. When you go to the Whitsunday Islands you call it a '10 out of 10', but then go you to a spot in the Philippines, which is so different – you can't give it an 11, and it's definitely not a nine …

Q. What are some other 10s?

A. If you start looking at surf, Waimea on Oahu is the overall best beach in the world – 12-metre-plus surf in the winter; it's where they have 'The Eddie' big wave comp. Then in summer it's completely flat. It's got a big rock to jump off into the water, turtles and tropical fish swimming around, boulders underwater; it even has a canal that connects to a river. For me, this beach has everything.

Q. When you go to a new place to swim or film or do a cliff-jump, what do you do to check out an area you don't know? What is your advice for swimming in a new place?

A. Firstly, if there is no one else swimming you have got to ask someone why – like around Cairns. Then, watch the water for a bit because the currents, particularly in the ocean, can be completely unforgiving. But generally, speak to the local people about places you haven't been before; ask around.

Q. From the outside, your lifestyle looks completely enviable. What do you love about it, and what are some of the realities or uncomfortable truths?

A. Pros would be that pretty much every day is on my terms. I don't have a boss and I also don't have anything tying me down to a certain plan. Whatever I want to do tomorrow is entirely up to me, which is probably the most freeing thing. The cons are that I have left my family and friends and whole life behind in Australia. Sometimes I just want a shelf to put my things on. And I'm completely reliant on good wi-fi connection.

Q. How much gear do you travel with?

A. I have a 60-litre backpack with all my stuff in it; that's all I own – just clothes and toiletries. Then I have a camera backpack with a laptop and camera gear, so I have two bags and I sling a drone (a Mavic Pro) on the outside. You need to be light when you're on the move like this.

Check out more of Jackson's nomadic life on Instagram @jackson.groves.

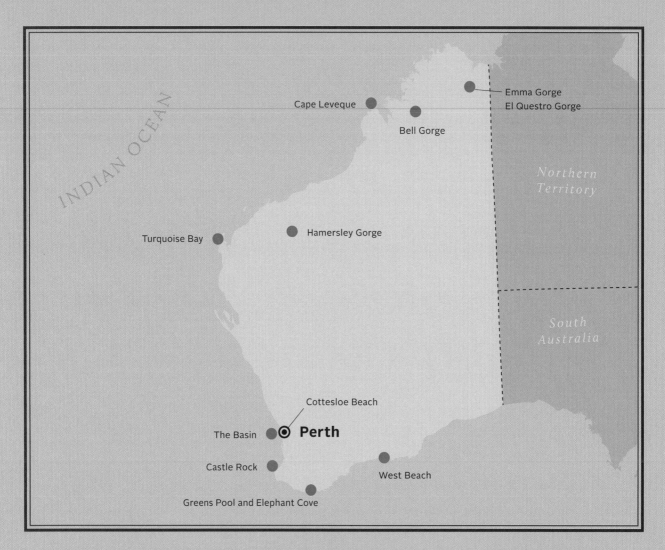

INDIAN OCEAN

Emma Gorge
El Questro Gorge

Cape Leveque

Bell Gorge

Northern Territory

Turquoise Bay

Hamersley Gorge

South Australia

Cottesloe Beach

The Basin ⦿ **Perth**

Castle Rock

West Beach

Greens Pool and Elephant Cove

When to visit

Kimberley, Pilbara & Coral Coast – April to September

Perth area – year-round

South-West – November to May

Favourite swim

GREENS POOL
(*see* p. 109)

Crocodiles

Croc populations are confined to the Kimberley region and are not as abundant as in the Northern Territory. The major tourist spots are surveyed, but not always signed. Before swimming, ask a local if it is safe. In the western Kimberley, around the Dampier Peninsula and Broome, many people happily swim at the beach, despite the slight risk of crocs. If there's a sighting in Broome, the beach will close, but it tends to be word of mouth further north. Stay away from estuaries, mangroves, and murky water. For more on crocodile safety, *see* p. 143.

Road-trip advice

Many of WA's wilderness areas are within national parks, and all have a $13 day-use fee. Rather than paying this at each place you stop, buy a pass before you get there and breeze in and out as frequently as you like. Annual passes cost $92 (concession $58) and $23 for WA residents, and one-month holiday passes are $46.

Best meal

OLD SHANGHAI AT FREMANTLE MARKETS
(*see* p. 105)

Western Australia

Western Australia makes up a third of our country's landmass, so it should come as no surprise that it possesses a supreme diversity of landscapes and swims.

We originally thought we'd include only a couple of places from this region, ticking just enough off the list while saving space for the east coast. But then we went there. The hardest part about writing this book turned out to be what *not* to include. We quickly discovered that WA is like Australia's answer to Iceland. From the freshwater gorges in El Questro (*see* p. 88) and Karijini (*see* p. 95), to near-shore coral gardens in Turquoise Bay (*see* p. 99), to sugar-white sand and vibrant blue water (*see* Rottnest Island, p. 104, and Esperance, p. 112) – WA is full of eye-popping destinations that clog everyone's social-media feeds. The land is raw and expansive, with moments of such profound isolation that you feel like you are on another planet. This, of course, begs the obvious question: If you take a picture without an internet connection, were you even there?

Given the state's immensity and diversity, you'll spend days on the road here. You need to have time to get to your swim, and also allocate enough time to enjoy it while you're there. It can be overwhelming once you actually start looking at the kilometres (and paying for the petrol). This is the state where we most envied the grey nomads we met. If they liked a place, they would set up shop for weeks. More than a few of them told us they were on SKI holidays: S-K-I. Spending the Kids' Inheritance. Their caravans had inspirational quotes scrawled on the back, like, 'Goodbye tension, hello pension!' We think Buddha said that. The nomads were good company and we ended up with more than a few surrogate parents along the way.

Visitors who make the effort will be rewarded mightily with pristine freshwater canyons, remote waterfalls, endless white-sand beaches, temperate rainforests and outlying islands. With just one person per square kilometre, WA has one of the lowest population densities on Earth. By comparison, Mongolia has 1.9 persons per square kilometre and Victoria has 26. But WA is a pleasure to travel, and you do so with a great sense of freedom. Though certain parts of the state can only be reached by 4WD, helicopter or boat, we have tried to create a list that doesn't require complicated access. These are the best swims in the state and we know that you will love them as much as we do.

Emma Gorge

THE KIMBERLEY

THIS CATHEDRAL FOR
SWIMMING IS ONE OF
THE HIGHEST AND MOST
DRAMATIC WATERFALLS
IN THE KIMBERLEY.

GORGE   WATERFALL

◔ **Best time to visit**
June and July

◬ **How to get there**
Emma Gorge is 80km west of Kununurra.
Take the Great Northern Hwy to the Gibb
River Rd, then head west for 25km until
you reach the turn-off. Very well signed
from all directions.

⊖ **Access**
Easy. Sealed roads to Emma Gorge
turn-off. 2WD access from Gibb River Rd
via well-maintained unsealed road to
Emma Gorge Resort. From there it's a
1.6km walk into the gorge via a rocky
riverbed path.

$ **Cost of entry** Free

☺ **Kid friendly** Yes, but it's a bit of a rocky
walk in.

⊗ **Dog friendly** No

◠ **Water temperature** Cool and refreshing

◷ **Open** 5.30am–4pm early May to late Oct
(Dry season). Access dates and times
may vary depending on the Wet. Late
in the Dry season (Oct), once the resort
has closed, trail access is only open from
6am–12pm.

⊕ **Facilities**
Toilets

◉ **Must bring**
Some sturdy footwear to scramble over
the rocky riverbed.

LOCAL KNOWLEDGE

On the right-hand side as you enter the
plunge pool below the falls, there is a
little hot spring pouring over some rocks.
If you can find it, it's lovely for a warm
shower after a refreshing swim.

It's hard to believe that Western Australia's Kimberley region is twice the size of our home state of Victoria. For us, and many of our fellow Victorians, it's probably the biggest place that we know nothing about. A distant world, tucked into a faraway state. A collision of the outback and the tropics. It's pristine land with one of the lowest population densities on the planet, we're told by local guide Scotty Connell, who we meet on the banks of Emma Gorge. It's the first stop on our swimming pilgrimage from Kununurra to Broome. People don't realise until they get here that WA is the swimming capital of the country, Scotty also tells us, before plunging into the crisp, turquoise water. He's a true local advocate and it's not the last time we'll see him on this trip.

Given a superficial look across the dusty, dry savannah landscape, it seems unlikely that this region could be the capital of anything but sunburn, yet here we stand among palm trees and delicate maidenhair ferns. Year-round springs feed deep gorges and wide rivers, and red cliffs fall into white sandy beaches.

The dramatic Emma Gorge falls pour over a 65-metre-high cliff into a large plunge pool, punctuating the end of the 1.6 kilometre hike in. The track begins at Emma Gorge Resort, and winds past the deep Turquoise Pool (also a great spot to swim, which we take note of for later) before arriving at the falls. The water is refreshingly cool, shaded by the looming cliffs for most of the day. Tourists dribble in and out, dropping piles of clothes on rocks as they stare up at the falls in awe before shocking their hot, sweaty bodies with the water's cool, pristine touch.

The plunge pool is deep and wide with a rocky bottom, but the water is so clear and fresh, you could drink it. We bliss out for a few hours before making out way back along the track past Turquoise Pool, where we take another plunge. The surface water here is lit up by the sun, giving it the turquoise colours it's named for, while people gather at the fringes to cool off. A rock jump begs us to plunge from a height rather than scramble over a slippery entry.

Emma Gorge is one of the most incredible places we've been, even late in the season when the water isn't flowing at its best. There's still enough for a great swim, and the crowds have all but dried up. Our mate Scotty assures us that we are only scratching the surface of the Kimberley swimming cult, and if this is a taste of what's to come – and it is – then we are the newly converted.

NEARBY

LAKE ARGYLE RESORT
Lot 512 Packsaddle Rd

Lake Argyle Resort caravan park has become an important stop on any trip in the Kimberley. At least, getting a photo of its spectacular infinity pool has. If you're not a guest, there's a $10 entry fee, but you can stay the day and will also have access to the swimming pontoon down on the lake.

ZEBEDEE SPRINGS
Durack Rd, El Questro Wilderness Park

This little oasis is a series of small thermal rock pools, tucked under spiral pandanus and towering palms. The water sits at a balmy 28°C year-round, which is surprisingly refreshing. Climb and slide between shallow pools; relax under small rapids; and kick-back like you're in a day spa. Try not to wear sunscreen in the water, to keep the natural springs clean.

THE GROTTO
Wyndham

Located just off the Great Northern Highway between the Gibb River Road and Wyndham, the Grotto is a spectacular cave system that drops down deep into a natural chasm. Entry is via a tiered rocky staircase. The Grotto fills during the Wet season, and Tarzan-style ropes hang from trees, ready for those daring enough to swing into the cool water.

ROCK POOL   WATERFALL

◐ **Best time to visit**
May to September

◭ **How to get there**
From the eastern end of the Gibb River Rd, head 33km along El Questro Rd to the turn-off to El Questro Station. Follow very well signed unsealed road towards the homestead. You will see a turn-off to El Questro Gorge after about 12km. It's a further couple of kilometres with one major water crossing. There is a map of the gorge at the trailhead. It's about a 7.5km return walk, but you should allow half a day.

⊖ **Access**
Moderate. 4WD only, as there is a fairly deep water crossing. Rock scrambling in the gorge, particularly after Halfway Pool, might not be suitable for everyone; however, we met plenty of kids and oldies who loved it.

$ **Cost of entry** Free

☺ **Kid friendly** Yes, but able-bodied kids only beyond Halfway Pool

⊗ **Dog friendly** No

◠ **Water temperature** Cool (perfect)

◷ **Open** 24 hours (though we don't recommend it in the dark)

⊕ **Facilities**
Toilets (at carpark)

⊛ **Must bring**
A waterproof bag for your things. You will have to walk or swim through Halfway Pool to continue upstream.

LOCAL KNOWLEDGE

Sunscreen is harmful to this fragile ecosystem so we advise that you leave it at home. Because very little direct sun reaches the bottom of the gorge, you really don't need it anyway.

El Questro Gorge

A LUSH RAINFOREST GORGE WITH PLUNGE POOLS AND A WATERFALL.

We'd long anticipated our arrival at El Questro. This working cattle station-cum-wilderness resort was at the top of most people's travel recommendations. Friends spoke of 'the Kimberley' in a reverent tone, often gazing thoughtfully to the horizon. Like Spanish sailors describing the lost city of El Dorado, they told us of a rainforest hidden in the craggy bush, of spring-filled canyons with water so clear you couldn't guess its depth. While these seemed like the exaggerated fantasies of heat-stricken travellers, we were determined to see what the fuss was all about.

El Questro does not disappoint. This is the first/last stop on the famed Gibb River Road and it presents a generous sample of the Kimberley in one compact package. In fact, it is so great that we broke one of our golden rules for this book and have written about it twice (*see* Emma Gorge, p. 85). Where Emma culminates with an awe-inspiring destination and borderline religious experience, El Questro Gorge is more of a swimming adventure that unfolds over many hours of discovery. Queue the *Jurassic Park* theme song.

To get to the trailhead you have to drive through a wide, sometimes deep, river. We were shitting ourselves, uncertain of both the roadworthiness of our car and our skills as amphibious drivers. Slow and steady won the race, and we avoided the public shame of getting bogged. We realised later that you could easily hitchhike from this point and would be enthusiastically transported by other drivers. From the crossing it is only about 1 kilometre to the trailhead.

Once on foot, sheer canyon walls immediately surround you, softened by sheets of iridescent green ferns. A canopy of spindly livistona palms reach gravity-defying heights, often contorting themselves along the canyon's contours. Even on the hottest days the gorge is an oasis of cool shadows and clear water. A 40-minute walk (about 1.2 kilometres) takes you to Halfway Pool, a deep swimming hole formed at the base of a few large boulders. Many people stop here, unable or unwilling to pull themselves over the rocks to reach the upper sections of the gorge.

From Halfway Pool it's just informal scrambling and rock-hopping. Follow the canyon up a further 2 kilometres until you reach MacMicking Pool, probably the best shower in the state. A delicate waterfall drops into a cave-like swimming hole, briefly illuminated by a beam of angelic light roughly between 10.30am and 1pm. Outside of that time it sits in still shadows, giving Mac some of the coolest water in the area.

If you're not in a rush, you can have El Questro Gorge all to yourself. We spent our days climbing and exploring, and drinking water from the stream when our supplies ran out. It may not be El Dorado, but it is the next best thing – a hidden rainforest in the desert.

NEARBY

EL QUESTRO STATION
El Questro Rd, El Questro Wilderness Park

For easy access to swims and bushwalks (including El Questro and Emma gorges), this is where you stay. Camping is $20 a night for an unpowered site with access to bathroom blocks, a camp kitchen and laundry facilities. Find a shady spot near the river. Bookings essential from June to August.

CHAMPAGNE POOLS
El Questro Rd, El Questro Wilderness Park

From a trailhead just after the river crossing at the entry to El Questro Station, a track follows the Pentecost River to a thousand-year-old boab tree, and then veers up and over rocky terrain. It's an exposed hike, so try to do this early morning. At the end a series of large, refreshing pools look out onto the red-walled canyon below.

AMALIA GORGE
El Questro Wilderness Park

Another scenic gorge walk through burnt Kimberley landscapes to clear green water. This is a 3.4-kilometre-return track (2 to 3 hours), and is best visited just after the Wet (from May) when water flows between pools. It is often one of the first places to dry up, so visit early in the season for the best experience.

BEACH

◗ **Best time to visit**
Cooler months of the Dry (April to October)

◬ **How to get there**
Drive north from Broome along the Broome–Cape Leveque Road for almost 200km to the tip of the peninsula.

⊖ **Access**
4WD only. This road is corrugated and unsealed for most of the way. There are some paved sections but it's mostly dry and dusty. It will take you upwards of 3 hours to get to the end of the peninsula.

⑨ **Cost of entry** Day pass $10

☺ **Kid friendly** Yes

⊗ **Dog friendly** No

◠ **Water temperature** Balmy

◷ **Open** 24 hours

⊕ **Facilities**
Toilets, showers, communal kitchen, glamping/camping (starting at $50 per car per night)

◉ **Must bring**
A beach umbrella or some shade for the beach; it's very exposed out here.

LOCAL KNOWLEDGE

The tides here are some of the biggest in the world and can change by up to 12 metres.

There are abundant mango farms dotted along the peninsula. Ask the locals if you can take a couple. Let the green ones ripen in the shade until they soften. The mangoes we had here were the best of our lives.

Cape Leveque

REMOTE WHITE-SAND BEACHES BOUND BY RED CLIFFS AND BLUE WATER.

Nothing can quite prepare you for a stretch of beaches like the ones you'll find on the Dampier Peninsula. After weeks of travelling unsealed, inland roads, we were relieved to get to coastal Broome before heading north along the peninsula. The sea breeze rushed in, cooling our hot bodies in the 35°C-plus heat of the Wet season build-up. A swim at Cable Beach was essential as we passed through the coastal port, but it was further north that the beaches really blew our minds.

Just when you think you've put dirt tracks behind you, the Broome–Cape Leveque Road offers up a 2 to 3 hour drive on unsealed corrugation. We try to drive these kinds of roads in the cooler times of the day, early in the morning or later in the afternoon. We tell ourselves that the worse condition the road is in, the better the reward is at the end, and Cape Leveque is a fine case in point. We're sure this road is deliberately left unsealed to distinguish those travellers content with the picturesque scenes of Broome from those willing to take on a little more adventure (and trips to the mechanics). We assure you, the drive is well worth it.

The Dampier Peninsula is a vast coastal landscape and the traditional home of the Bardi Jawi people. At Cape Leveque (the northernmost tip of the peninsula) is the incredible Kooljaman, an off-the-grid wilderness camp on Native Title land. The property is 100 per cent Indigenous owned and is operated by nearby Djarindjin and Ardyaloon communities. You can visit for the day or, like most people, get stuck here for weeks at a time. There are all levels of accommodation, from simple unpowered sites to beach huts and eco lodges. No matter your level of personal luxury, the democratic communal areas offer the perfect place to meet fellow travellers and swap stories of life on the road (i.e. car troubles and free camp sites).

On the western side of the peninsula, the Indian Ocean roars onto the beach. The currents are strong here and it's advised not to swim, though some people do try to fish. But watching a sunset drop into the water is picture-perfect – BYO drinks.

The east side, on the other hand, has a sheltered white-sand beach with crystal-clear water as far as the eye can see. This is not a mirage. The ocean is warm, still, and very salty – evoking the feeling of an enormous flotation tank. Perhaps the most relaxing way to ever get a sunburn. Take your own shelter to the beach if you plan to spend some time, or find shade under big boulders or inside 'humpies', where you can also stay overnight.

Cape Leveque is by no means a secret spot, but it is far enough out of the way to be unwittingly bypassed by many travellers on their way through Broome. The peninsula has some of the most pristine beaches in the country and Aboriginal custodianship means that they will likely remain low-key and respectfully developed for generations to come.

NEARBY

JAMES PRICE POINT

A great taste of the peninsula, only a short trip north of Broome. You can drive right along this wild, red coastline, even on the beach itself if you are feeling confident. Currently under threat from natural gas drilling.

LOMBADINA

One of many Aboriginal communities on the Dampier Peninsula, Lombadina is open for public visitors to spend the day or camp overnight. Eat tamarinds and mangoes from the trees; pick up a loaf of bread from the bakery; and drive on the beach. You'll probably have a virgin strip of sand all to yourself, all day long. Register your arrival into the community upon entry. Cost is $10 per vehicle and visits are allowed on weekdays only.

BROOME

It would be remiss for us to omit Broome and iconic Cable Beach from the book. If you're visiting the Cape, you will inevitably spend some time in this coastal city. Watch camels cross the beach at sunset while locals drive onto the sand to catch up with friends (a WA tradition). Have a mango smoothie at the Mango Tree Cafe; visit the local brewery Matzos for a ginger beer; and watch a movie in the world's longest-running outdoor cinema, Sun Pictures.

GORGE WATERFALL

Best time to visit
Mid-April to mid-October

How to get there
At the west end of the Gibb River Rd, turn off at a well-marked junction and drive 29km down an unsealed road into the King Leopold Ranges. It's a 2km hike into the gorge from the carpark.

Access
Difficult. 4WD only. The access road is unsealed and there are a few river crossings that can get quite deep (depending on road conditions and time of year). The road is boggy when wet. For 4WD advice, *see* p. xi.

Cost of entry WA national-parks pass is required or $13 day-use fee.

Kid friendly Yes

Dog friendly No

Water temperature Cool

Open 24 hours (but visit during daylight)

Facilities
Toilets (Bell Gorge carpark); camping ($13 per night), toilets, showers, drinking water, picnic tables (Silent Grove)

Must bring
Cash for camping fees at Silent Grove. As at many national-park camp sites, you pay by an honesty box.

LOCAL KNOWLEDGE

This is one of the few gorges and waterfalls along the Gibb River Road that flows year-round.

Bell Gorge

A TIERED WATERFALL INTO AN AMPHITHEATRE-LIKE GORGE ALONG THE LEGENDARY GIBB RIVER ROAD.

We were really pushing it for time on our trip to Bell Gorge – one of the Kimberley's most celebrated (and dramatic) swimming holes. It's the tail-end of the season by mid-October and we'd been passing the last bus loads of tour groups exiting the west end of the Gibb River Road, eager to make it to Broome. Moody storm clouds brewed overhead, threatening to unload onto the hot mess of dry landscape below. When we arrived at Bell Gorge, the carpark held just one other car. In such isolated and remote places, the presence of other people is always comforting; when truly alone, the feeling of tranquillity can be lost to that of being very far from anywhere and anyone else.

We pack a bag of snacks for the walk: homemade scroggin (trail mix), a tin of smoked mussels and some shortbread – and plenty of water, which by this point in the trip is never cold enough. In the heat we must be drinking five litres a day, each. Definitely overkill for this short hike, but we love our snacks and never know how long we will stay at a swim.

We wind through scrubby bushland, past sun-bleached rocks for about 2 kilometres to the first pool at the top of the falls. The incredible gorge opens up below us as we stand on the overhanging rock shelf with a slight sense of vertigo. The water is glassy, and the amber-hued rocks of the King Leopold Ranges rise up into the blue sky. It's a truly magical place and one of great significanceto the Imintji people.

The waterfall cascades quietly over the rocky ledge into a larger pool below. It's particularly mild at this time of year, and you can sit in the rapids as they swallow you in their cool embrace. We wonder what it's like here in the Wet season when the water thunders through the gorge.

Trail markers lead you over the upper pool to a path that runs around the top rim and down to the lower pool. Lizards and turtles splash around in the deep, cool water as it winds downstream through the high rock walls. Continuing on further will take you to other pools where you can swim and laze in the shadow of the rocks. In peak season, this place can get busy, and the pools deeper into the gorge will offer you some respite from the crowds.

We leave Bell Gorge with a true sense of calm. It feels restorative being in such a dramatic landscape. Just as we get back to the camp site the heavens open up – the first of the Wet season has reached us – relieving the parched, dry land. The rain doesn't stop for hours and we consider a midnight drive out, fearful that the river crossings might rise overnight, trapping us on the Gibb. But we stay put and make the mission out with some other travellers (with a winch) early next morning – our special memories of the place intact.

NEARBY

TUNNEL CREEK
King Leopold Ranges

Wading through Tunnel Creek in a dark cave that passes below the Napier Range is a real adventure – bring waterproof shoes and a torch. The creek is part of Western Australia's oldest cave system, and is also the site of the last stand of Aboriginal leader Jandamarra, who led a revolt against colonists from 1894–1897.

MANNING GORGE
Derby–Gibb River Rd, Derby

Located about halfway along the Gibb River Road is Mt Barnett Station, where you'll check in for camping, a further 7 kilometres away. The hike from the campground then takes you to yet another glorious waterfall where you can jump from rocks and swim through the gorge. It's a 5.6-kilometre return hike.

PUNAMII-UNPUU (MITCHELL FALLS)
Mitchell Plateau

It's a teeth-chattering experience coming into Punamii-unpuu (Mitchell Falls) in the Kimberley. The road into the national park is in bad condition, especially if you're coming from Kalumburu (the very north of the Kimberley region). But after seeing the falls and swimming at the top of them, the mind-numbing corrugation and the 3-hour trek in is well worth it.

Hamersley Gorge

KARIJINI NATIONAL PARK

AN EXPANSIVE AND VISUALLY
SURREAL LANDSCAPE WITH
TIERED ROCK POOLS AND A
DEEP GORGE.

GORGE   **ROCK POOL**

Best time to visit
May to October

How to get there
From Nanutarra Rd, take the turn-off to Hamersley Gorge, from where it's 3km to the carpark.

Access
Easy. Well-maintained dirt roads lead to a steep sealed descent. Suitable for 2WD but be careful of road conditions after heavy rain.

Cost of entry WA national-parks pass is required or $13 day-use fee.

Kid friendly Yes

Dog friendly No

Water temperature Cool-ish

Open 24 hours

Facilities
Composting toilets (at carpark)

Must bring
Water shoes with good grip and lots of drinking water. You'll want to stay all day.

K arijini is the heart of WA's Pilbara region and a welcome respite from long, dusty drives in all directions. It is a very sacred land for its Traditional Owners, the Banyjima, Kurrama and Innawonga peoples. To the keen eye, this ancient landscape is a bit like speeding across the pages of a geology textbook: 2.5-billion-year-old banded iron formations stretch into the distance and nearby discoveries of 3.5-billion-year-old fossils give evidence of the earliest land-based life on Earth. It's a truly ancient land of profound contrast. And the very same geological processes that make Karijini so unique and beautiful are responsible for its deposits of iron ore, lithium, nickel, gold and petroleum. This means that treasured wilderness often sits directly adjacent to some of Australia's biggest mining operations. Miraculously, the gorges of Karijini remain largely unspoilt as they carve cool paths through this arid land.

Freshwater creeks and pools sit beneath steep red walls here, making it a swimmers' playground. Sometimes you are confined to narrow slot canyons, and spider-walking along the walls, while other times you find pools blooming outwards in wide ravines, sharing space with trees and ferns. For days we struggled to distinguish between the excellence of one location and the next. That is, until we made it to Hamersley Gorge.

The gorge sits in the far north-west corner of Karijini, removed from popular locations and therefore seeing significantly less traffic or fanfare. A short, steep descent brings visitors to the edge of the water. To the left is a deep, expansive pool that extends for about 300 metres. After being assured multiple times that there are no crocodiles in the Pilbara, we swam a few greedy laps from end to end. Surrounding cliffs make for obvious rock jumps – just be sure to inspect the landing before taking any plunge.

Upstream of the main pool is a series of short cascades with small baths on each level. These give way to a larger swimming place set among thin, fissile layers of shale. Colourful rocks seemingly flow in place as they twist and curl into themselves. Water and land merge together to confuse the eye in a distortion of scale and perspective. It's an unlikely mash-up of colours and textures that evoke the surreal landscapes of M. C. Escher. We sat for hours in this strange and beautiful place, eating car-ripened mangoes and reading our books. We took turns swirling around the smooth walled Spa Pool and hiding from the sun under large rocks. This place may have taken billions of years to form, but it was worth the wait.

NEARBY

FERN POOL
Dales Gorge, Karijini National Park

From Dales Gorge carpark, walk along the ridge of the gorge before dropping down into Fern Pool – a large pool surrounded by soft green ferns and shaded by large rocks. Swim over to the small falls on the far side, or dangle your legs from the platform at the water's edge while small fish chew at the skin on your feet. Some people pay top dollar for a spa treatment like this, but here the resident fish offer pedicures for free. There's a peaceful feeling at this pool, which is a sacred Aboriginal birthing site; be mindful and respectful while visiting.

KERMITS POOL
Hancock Gorge, Karijini National Park

After a steep descent into the gorge, hike 800 metres through a narrow, high section of what feels like an adventure track along a stream. You might have to spider-crawl your way in, but it will lead you to a small, deep pool of dark-green water (hence the name). A magical place for spending some time soaking up rays of sunlight that make it through the cracks of the gorge before plunging back into the water.

KARIJINI ECO RETREAT
off Weano Rd, Karijini National Park

There aren't many places to sit and have a cocktail while the sun goes down in Karijini, unless you've got a bar in your van. The Karijini Eco Retreat is both a camp site with some luxe permanent tent suites and a restaurant with a bar. It's a nice spot to mingle with other travellers at the end of the day.

Colourful rocks seemingly flow
in place as they twist and curl
into themselves ...

Turquoise Bay

CAPE RANGE NATIONAL PARK,
NINGALOO REEF

ONE OF THE WORLD'S
LARGEST AND MOST
ACCESSIBLE FRINGING REEF
SYSTEMS, AND THE BEST
PLACE TO SNORKEL IN
THE COUNTRY.

WESTERN AUSTRALIA

BEACH

◐ **Best time to visit**
April to August. It tends to get really windy over summer and everyone but the kiteboarders leave town.

◇ **How to get there**
From Exmouth, follow Murat Rd north and turn left on Yardie Creek Rd, following signs to Cape Range NP. Continue around the peninsula, past the lighthouse and down the coast. The turn-off to Turquoise Bay is well signed.

⊖ **Access**
Easy. Jump in the water at the south end of the bay and let the current sweep you back to the carpark. Repeat.

$ **Cost of entry** WA national-parks pass is required or $13 day-use fee.

☺ **Kid friendly** Yes

⊗ **Dog friendly** No

◠ **Water temperature** Cool and very saline

◷ **Open** 24 hours

⊕ **Facilities**
Toilets

◉ **Must bring**
A snorkel, flippers and drinking water – there is no potable water available in the national park.

Marine Calendar

Months	J	F	M	A	M	J	J	A	S	O	N	D
Whale sharks				———————								
Coral spawn			———									
Turtles			————————————									
Humpback whales							—————————					
Manta rays	———————								———————			
Dolphins & dugongs	————————————————————————————————											

LOCAL KNOWLEDGE

Sun block is proven to be toxic to reef systems, so try to cover up with a rashie and wetsuit instead.

All right, we're going to say it: the Ningaloo Reef is the best reef in Australia. Wait, the world. Yep, this is guaranteed to rival anywhere else you've ever snorkelled. And the Great Barrier Reef deserves a break: all our attention has been hard on it over the years. So we've turned our sights to the west coast. Hopefully this one fares better.

For those who haven't heard of Ningaloo Reef, we're excited to break this news to you. This is something life changing and totally magnificent. Pack your zinc, your rash vest, your snorkel and your flippers and get yourself over to WA's north-west coast, *stat*. This World Heritage coral coast runs 260 kilometres down the west side of the Pilbara from Exmouth to Coral Bay, covering 705 hectares along the eastern Indian Ocean. It is Australia's largest fringing coral reef, and the only one positioned close to land, making it easily accessible – that is, you don't even need a boat to get there.

Driving into Exmouth, we were surprised to find the dry, harsh landscape of the Kimberley and Pilbara regions. Our tropical paradise must be elsewhere we thought. But what we found was a town with a keen interest in conservation, and of course a strong water culture: surfers, kitesurfers, divers, sailors and whale-boat skippers all have their seasons here.

At various times of the year, the water around the reef swarms with turtles, tropical fish, manta rays, humpback whales and the elusive whale shark. All of these animals, coral gardens and many hundreds of other species exist in such great abundance because of some very unique geography. A system of warm, shallow lagoons sits between the beach and the outer reef. Less than a kilometre from shore, the continental shelf abruptly ends, plunging down 500 metres. The deep water provides nutrients and allows large animals to move near the shore. The lagoons act as a sanctuary, nursery, and snorkelling mecca.

Turquoise Bay has a gentle tidal drag that pulls you down the beach. Walk to its south end to jump in, and float your way back across the bay over shallow lagoons formed by the reef, a diverse range of colourful coral and more than 500 species of fish. Because of the current, you'll hardly need to use your flippers. Dive down and swim around the sea cabbages and big bommies that create impressive underwater forests. Look all you want, but please don't touch anything – this is a delicate ecosystem.

Camping is the best way to access the area, putting you an arm's length from this pristine water. Around 15 camp sites are set along the coast in the park, all with beach frontage, and tucked into sand dunes to protect you from harsh winds that come up in the afternoons. Osprey is popular but we enjoyed the quieter set-up of North Kurrajong. Booking online before you get there is essential (there's no phone reception as soon as you leave Exmouth). Regardless of where you stay, you'll be sharing it with the locals – kangaroos like the beach too.

This whole coastline is so special and full of life, both in and out of the water. And one reason for this is the fact it hasn't anywhere near as much tourism as the Great Barrier Reef. Local businesses and tour companies are pushing a more sustainable model for Ningaloo, so this region can keep thriving. Its remote location has its advantages, but 'the best in the world' comes with some pretty high stakes. Tread lightly.

NEARBY

THE SHORT ORDER LOCAL
Town Beach, Exmouth

A brightly painted van run by two sisters serving coffee, juices, bacon and egg rolls, Reubens, grilled cheese sandwiches and freshly baked muffins (made by their mum). They're parked up at the side of the beach most days, and you can't miss their colourful set-up. They also do curry night on Wednesdays, burrito bowls on Fridays and Spanish night on Saturdays.

FROTH CRAFT RESTAURANT / MICROBREWERY
5 Kennedy St, Exmouth

After a day out on the reef, when the ice block in your esky has melted, a cold beer might be calling. Pull up a stool at Froth, Exmouth's local watering hole. They make their own brew, put beer in their cocktails and batter their chips in it. Things can get pretty wild here on weekends, when skippers, divers and tourists are locked in the delicate dance of courtship.

WHALE TOUR WITH LIVE NINGALOO
81 Nimitz St, Exmouth

There are many whale tour companies in Exmouth, so it's important to do your research on their approach to marine preservation. The Live Ningaloo team (Sonia and Murray) understands the impact of tourism on this precious environment, and makes conscious efforts to minimise their impact across every aspect of the business. These guys offer bespoke boat tours out to the reef to swim with humpback whales and whale sharks, as well as snorkelling tours and private boat charters.

BEACH

Best time to visit
Anytime, but summer is pretty special here. Arrive early to beat The Doctor.

Address
99 Marine Pde, Cottesloe

Access
Easy. Abundant parking. Bus 102 runs along the beach and Cottesloe train station is 1.4km away.

Cost of entry Free

Kid friendly Yes

Dog friendly Yes

Water temperature Near perfect: cool and refreshing.

Open 24 hours

Facilities
Toilets, beach showers

Must bring
Your wallet. There are lots of good places to eat and drink around here; you may want to graze all day.

LOCAL KNOWLEDGE

The Fremantle Doctor, the Freo Doctor or just the Doctor, as it is fondly known by locals, is the cooling (sometimes violent) sea breeze that comes in the afternoon during the summer months. Try to get to the beach before the Doctor arrives.

Cottesloe Beach

PERTH

A HIVE OF WATER ACTIVITY ALONG A CALM STRETCH OF AQUAMARINE COAST, AND PERTH'S FAVOURITE CITY BEACH.

Every time we go to Perth we think, what a place to live, what a life. The day here starts at 6am and ends at 6pm, or at least it does for the lifeguards on the beach. This city truly lives by the light – it's as though they get a few extra hours more than the rest of us. Perth is blessed with sunshine and warm weather most of the year, which puts it in good stead for swimming spots – of which it has a bounty. Like Sydney, Perth is known for its pristine city beaches (but has fewer crowds).

Probably the most well known is Cottesloe Beach, or Cott. There's always a healthy scene here right from the early hours of the day. Beach volleyball players, bodysurfers, runners, walkers, kayakers, surf lifesavers, and swimmers cross the beach from the rock groyne to the iconic black-and-white striped buoy. You can smell the sunscreen a mile off. Visitors pack the beach out by 10am, laying out towels on the sand or pitching up along the tiered green grass steps. Large hoop pines surround the iconic surf life saving clubhouse that takes pride of place, looking over the scene like a queen bee. Though the real queen bee is Maureen, a beloved local who can be found sitting under her striped beach umbrella near the rocks. Her deeply bronzed flesh redefines the word 'tan' and she is quick to point out that 'you can find me here any day that the sun is out' – which, in Perth, translates to every day.

Lifeguards in red and yellow sit high up in white beach boxes, watching over the water, some using new aerial surveillance to monitor for sharks. It's true this beach is no stranger to marine-life visitors, but nothing worth foregoing the pleasure of swimming. Cott is among some of the best patrolled beaches in the country, and if there is something out there, swimmers are notified immediately.

In fact, the accompanying overhead image was taken by aerial photographer Remy Gerega, who during his own photo shoot noticed a shark offshore and reported it to the coastguard. If you look closely, you can see that people are exiting the water. It made for a great photo but was unfortunately the end of Remy's shoot (though he had to continue paying for his time in the helicopter).

In March the annual outdoor public exhibition, Sculpture by the Sea, arrives on the shores at Cottesloe Beach, shining a spotlight on the seaside suburb. International pieces are planted on the sand for three weeks, part of the largest free public sculpture exhibition in the world. It's no surprise Cott was chosen as the second Australian beach to host the event (it's also held in October along the coastal walk from Bondi to Tamarama in Sydney). This is truly one of Australia's most well loved city beaches, a place that celebrates swimming as much as we do.

NEARBY

RED SPOON
88 Marine Pde, Cottesloe

This Italian-style gelateria has been on the Cottesloe Beach strip for more than seven years now and is still a favourite. Everything is house-made, all with natural ingredients. Try the Peanut Butter, the Ferrero, or the Black Hawaiian made with coconut water and cacao. This is some of the best ice-cream in Western Australia.

IL LIDO CANTEEN
88 Marine Pde, Cottesloe

It's hard to miss this colourful eatery on the corner of Marine Parade, just back from the action. Il Lido, meaning 'the beach' in Italian, is a mainstay in Cottesloe, and offers many iterations on the classic all-day diner. It's slick, sophisticated and fun, serving up breakfast, coffee, house-made pastries, antipasti, handmade pasta, dolce, aperitivo, lunch, dinner, cheese and wine. The same crew has also opened a pizzeria, Canteen Pizza, two blocks up.

COTTESLOE BEACH HOTEL
104 Marine Pde, Cottesloe

The Cott is an icon, with a reputation for a solid Sunday session. A classic old pub that has evolved over time to become a cool beachside bar, with a sunny beer garden drawing huge crowds for long lunches and afternoon spritzes. There's local beer on tap, oysters by the dozen and striped umbrellas to sit under. Someone once described it as 'Miami meets the Hamptons', which we think is quite apt.

BEACH

Best time to visit
Any time the sun is out, which is most days. The Boxing Day Raft Up is either the best or worst day to visit. Half of Perth and Freo sail to the island, and everything from yachts to dinghies are tied together near Parakeet Bay to form Australia's largest boat party. It gets loose.

How to get there
Ferries leave from Fremantle B Shed and Perth City every day, all day. First departure is typically around 7am. Confirm with ferry companies for complete timetables and pricing.

Access
Via a ferry or a private boat, then a short walk to the Basin from Thomson Bay.

Cost of entry Free, but ferries cost $60-plus for a return ticket.

Kid friendly Yes

Dog friendly No

Water temperature Fresh

Open 24 hours

Facilities
Drinking water, toilets, picnic tables

Must bring
Appropriate footwear for bike riding and walking. Bring your own bike if you have one.

LOCAL KNOWLEDGE

If you are going to rent bikes, hire from the ferry company so you can keep them until the return voyage. Bike rentals on Rottnest have to be returned by 3.30pm, which is way too early for all the activities you will want to do.

The Basin

ROTTNEST ISLAND

GLASSY AZURE WATER AND SNORKELLING ONLY A 30-MINUTE FERRY TRIP FROM PERTH.

'Rotto' is Perth's beloved island playground and WA's number 1 tourist destination. Although it's only about 17 kilometres away across a shallow sea, it is worlds apart from life on the mainland. Where the city has boomed and urbanised over recent decades, Rottnest Island has remained frozen in the early 1900s. Historic limestone cottages preserve a heritage streetscape and make for popular accommodation. The island's chequered history has seen it home to military barracks, a boys reformatory, internment camps and a prison. Now, it's a place dedicated entirely to recreation. Abundant reefs, sandy beaches and rocky headlands make Rotto a mecca for swimming, snorkelling, surfing, boating and fishing – pretty much the only thing you can't do here is drive a car.

We are currently searching for friends with yachts, but until then we will have to get to Rottnest Island via ferry. Which is a good thing, because the ferry services allow you bring a bicycle and also offer rentals of their own. Bikes are the best way to get around Rottnest and will enable access to every nook and cranny of the island. If the wind is blowing onshore, you can quickly ride to the other side. If you are having FOMO about not seeing all of it, you can do a gruelling lap before sundown.

If you aren't greeted on arrival by one of the 300 permanent human residents, you will receive frequent attention from the roughly 11,000 quokkas. These curious and confident marsupials are straight out of *The Princess Bride* (R.O.U.S. – rodents of unusual size), goofy rat-like creatures that stand on two legs long enough to photobomb and steal your lunch. They make for good company, but shabby lifeguards.

Having spent months driving across the outback, we were pretty keen to spin our legs on a bike. It's a quick pedal from the jetty at Thomson Bay to the Basin, where we found ourselves completely enamoured. This iconic patch of azure bliss is defined by its clear water, sugar-white sand and shallow reef. Wind, waves and currents seldom disturb this spot, making it a reliable place to snorkel. Most people, however, seem to do their swimming in an upright position – a gentle bob that we have come to call 'teabagging' (which is performed by 'teabaggers').

All of the island's bays and beaches are stunning in their own right, clear water being a common thread that binds them together. Choosing the best felt like a game of pick your favourite child. Nearby Parakeet Bay is an open beach with coffee-table-book vistas; Parker Point snorkel trail can't be missed; and legendary surf at Strickland Bay is worth coming back for. However, with every lap of the island we completed, we were always drawn back to the Basin.

NEARBY

ROTTNEST ISLAND BAKERY
Maley St, Rottnest Island

The bakery at Thomson Bay pumps out hundreds of fresh loaves, pies, rolls and jam doughnuts each day. You will pay island prices, but it'll be worth it when you've pedalled to the other side of Rotto and realise you have a chicken sandwich in your bag for lunch.

HOTEL ROTTNEST
Rottnest Island

A cold drink on the lawn at this historic beachside hotel is an important part of a trip to Rotto. Previously known as the Quokka Arms Hotel, this venue hums on hot afternoons, and the beer tastes best after you've pedalled a few kilometres in the sun. There are also rooms upstairs for an overnight stay.

OLD SHANGHAI AT FREMANTLE MARKETS
4–6 Henderson St, Fremantle

We love this hawker-style food court with multiple outlets selling dishes from across Asia – think Indian curries, big bowls of soupy noodles and Chinese barbecue dishes. Bring cash for the bar and sit outside on a balmy night, basking in the glow of the neon signs.

BEACH

◔ **Best time to visit**
December to February

◭ **How to get there**
Walk 2km north along Meelup Reserve Trail from Dunsborough. Or drive north on Cape Naturaliste Rd from Dunsborough and turn right on Meelup Beach Rd. Follow signs to Castle Rock and turn right onto Castle Rock Rd (1.7km from Cape Naturaliste Rd turn-off).

⊖ **Access**
Easy. A 20-minute walk along the coast from Dunsborough or a quick drive. The beach is only a couple of metres from the trail and carpark.

⊛ **Cost of entry** Free

☺ **Kid friendly** Yes

⊗ **Dog friendly** No, but there are many off-lead beaches in Dunsborough along Geographe Bay Rd.

◠ **Water temperature** Remarkably warm (about 20°C) from December to July thanks to the Leeuwin Current.

◷ **Open** 24 hours

⊕ **Facilities**
BBQs, picnic area, toilets

◉ **Must bring**
Did someone say rissoles? This is a prime place for a BBQ, so plan ahead: we strongly recommend a stop at the Bunbury Farmers Market (2 Vittoria Rd, Glen Iris) to stock up on edible supplies.

LOCAL KNOWLEDGE

Margaret River Gourmet Escape holds its annual beach BBQ here mid-November. It's a four-day festival that sees thousands of foodies swamp the region to eat, drink and party. This is either the best or worst weekend to be here, depending on your preference.

Castle Rock

CAPE NATURALISTE

AN ORANGE GRANITE MONOLITH SURROUNDED BY IMPOSSIBLY CLEAR WATER AND CALM SEAS.

The south-west corner of WA is a foil for the rest of the state. All of its water, fertile land, shade, food and wine seem to be concentrated in this region. The landscape is gentle and hospitable. Even the sun seems a little softer. The ocean is unbelievably clear and the coastline from Dunsborough to Cape Naturaliste is reliably calm and warm. It may have been all of the months we spent up north, but we constantly found ourselves fantasising about what our new lives would look like if we moved to Dunsborough, a cosy surf town with no waves. It would definitely include frequent visits to Castle Bay.

All of our favourite places to swim have some unique feature that makes them stand out, some special element that immediately grabs our attention. In a country full of beautiful beaches, white sand and clear water are just starting points. Here, the towering burnt-orange granite rocks stand in vivid contrast to glassy blue water and sky. We were immediately drawn to Castle Rock at the southern end of the bay on our first visit, and have kept returning to explore every piece of it.

Despite being 2 kilometres from Dunsborough, this beach gets far less attention than nearby Meelup or Eagle Bay. We walked along the Meelup Reserve Trail from town and met only locals along the way. Castle Rock looms high above the scrubby bush and is one of the tallest features in the area. On a warm day (which is most of the year) you can spend hours swimming around the boulders, lounging in rock pools, climbing, and jumping into the sparkling blue water. It is secluded, peaceful and – dare we say – romantic.

We like to sit on top of the rock in spring and welcome the arrival of humpback whales. Geographe Bay is a routine stopover on their 13,000 kilometre round trip from Antarctica to the Kimberley. From about September to November pregnant females come into the bay to calve. The little families stay close to the shore, no doubt drawn to the warm, calm waters for all the same reasons as us. They rest and nurse their young for a couple of months, swimming lazy laps between Busselton and Cape Naturaliste before continuing their journey south. Just like the whales, we may never move to the area full-time, but we will always go out of our way for a stopover.

NEARBY

ALBERT + NIKOLA
Shop 14/34 Dunn Bay Rd, Dunsborough

Dunsborough is a cute little town with lots of great food and wine. But if you're serious about your coffee, Albert + Nikola might be the place for your morning cup of joe. They showcase various roasters from around the country, on espresso, filter and cold drip. For food, they make raw treats, bagels and smoothie bowls.

RUSTICO AT HAY SHED HILL
511 Harmans Mill Rd, Margaret River

In a region abundant with vineyards and cellar doors, this winery came highly recommended by friends. Rustico is Hay Shed Hill's tapas bar, serving casual Mediterranean share dishes of scallops, paella, and salads with local cheese and figs. To make things easy, get the six-course set menu for $65 and make sure to try their sparkling pinot chardonnay.

EAGLE BAY BREWING CO
236 Eagle Bay Rd, Eagle Bay

A huge family-run brewery and winery on a vineyard with ocean views. This is a place where we always find ourselves staying longer than we plan to. It's easy to relax over a long lunch of pizzas, drinks in the afternoon, or a schooner of pale ale and a bowl of hot chips in the sun after a day at the beach.

Greens Pool and Elephant Cove

WILLIAM BAY NATIONAL PARK

A 250-METRE-LONG NATURAL
ROCK POOL AND COMMUNITY
MEETING PLACE.

WESTERN AUSTRALIA

ROCK POOL   BEACH

◯ **Best time to visit**
Summer (December to April) when the weather is hot and winds are light.

◭ **How to get there**
Located in William Bay National Park, about 20km west of Denmark. Turn off the South Coast Hwy at William Bay Rd and follow the well-maintained unsealed road 4km to Greens Pool carpark. The track will take you down some stairs to the beach.

⊖ **Access**
Easy. Roads and tracks are well maintained and well signed. You only have to walk a couple of hundred metres to the beach.

$ **Cost of entry** Free

☺ **Kid friendly** Yes

⊗ **Dog friendly** No

⌢ **Water temperature**
Cold. It gets down to 12°C in winter, and up to around 19°C in summer.

◷ **Open** 24 hours

⊕ **Facilities**
Toilets

◉ **Must bring**
A wetsuit and goggles so you can join the local swimmers and punch out some laps.

LOCAL KNOWLEDGE

Local swimmers know a few tricks about keeping warm in cold water. Thermal caps – even wearing two – can protect your ears and head from an ice-cream headache while swimming.

When people ask us about our favourite place to swim, our minds start racing through soggy, sweaty, sun-soaked memories, which almost always land at Greens Pool. After travelling through northern WA, where endless kilometres of unabated sun took us to dusty mining towns with no trees, we were looking forward to hitting the lush, southern corner of the state – abundant in nutrient-rich land growing hops, grapes and nurturing fat cows, open to the wild waters of the Southern Ocean and with a climate we were more at home with.

Located on the edge of William Bay National Park and just outside the coastal town of Denmark, Greens is the community's public pool. School swimming classes, bronze medallion training and games of Marco Polo happen here – it's a beloved natural asset.

Giant granite stones act as a protective boundary around this sprawling, reefy pool, which is almost entirely closed off from the wild oceanic waters beyond. A tight-knit, motley crew of swimmers do a 500-metre lap around the perimeter, along the rocks each morning. Because of these long laps, it's no coincidence that some world-class endurance swimmers train here. We meet a roster of regulars, varying in age and ability, many of whom swim year-round. They speak with great familiarity about every nook and cranny in the pool, naming the sea life they encounter (reef sharks, sting rays and turtles) and talk proudly of the warm Leeuwin Current that moves down the west coast, allowing them to swim here in winter. But even in November, some are wearing wetsuits and thermals caps. There's no doubt that this spot is completely weather-dependent, and on some days only for the boldest.

Just over the hill from Greens Pool is Elephant Rocks, a sheltered cove with granite boulders 20-times bigger than their namesake. Another glorious white-sand beach, the water here is clear and icy, and often all you can hear is the shrieking of other swimmers as they jump off the backs of the smaller 'elephants'. On calm days, when the tide is high and the swell is mild, you can swim between Greens and the cove. Or you can make the short journey over the headland, peering down from the backs of the herd.

With time on our side, we easily could have stayed a while. We'd made new friends, started reading the local paper and found a morning coffee spot. There's no denying we were reluctant to leave. What this revealed to us is that it's not just the swimming that makes us so fond of a place, it's the whole experience surrounding it.

NEARBY

MRS JONES
12 Mount Shadforth Rd, Denmark

This became our regular coffee stop in town, but really we were there for the house-made cakes – try the carrot cake or the melting moments, which you can also buy in buckets to take away. Using seasonal produce, Mrs Jones serves breakfast and lunch daily, plus dinner Fridays and Saturdays, with a selection of some of the best local wines. A friendly local spot.

BOSTON BREWING CO.
678 South Coast Hwy, Hay

We like to try the local beer wherever we go. Luckily, around here it's really good. Boston Brewing Co. is a family-owned brewery located on Willoughby Park vineyard, just out of Denmark. They brew, can and bottle all beer on-site, producing about eight different styles, from red and rye pale ales to Hefeweizen, a lager and a ginger beer. The impressive brewery also includes a tasting bar, a restaurant and a shop for takeaways.

FOREST HILL WINERY
1564 South Coast Hwy, Denmark

Forest Hill is one of the oldest wineries in a region known for its cool-climate wines. Sample their stand-out chardonnay or shiraz at the cellar door; take a few bottles with you; or stay and linger over lunch at the cosy winery restaurant Salt & Pepper, which looks out over the property. Open Thursday to Sunday.

BEACH

◑ **Best time to visit**
February to April, for consistent warm
weather and fewer windy days.

◭ **How to get there**
From the town centre, follow the
Esplanade south over the headland about
2.7km (it becomes Twilight Beach Rd).
West Beach is the first beach that you
will come across (also known as Firsties).

⊖ **Access**
Easy. The beach is just off the road and
a few staircases scale the cliff down to
the sand.

$ **Cost of entry** Free

☺ **Kid friendly** Yes

⊗ **Dog friendly** Yes

◠ **Water temperature** Cold

🕐 **Open** 24 hours

⊕ **Facilities**
Toilets

🕉 **Must bring**
Sunglasses: the sand is so white here it's
almost blinding.

LOCAL KNOWLEDGE

Further down the tourist drive is 10 Mile
Lagoon, a clothing-optional beach, if you
prefer to go without.

West Beach

A QUIET TOWN BEACH WITH IMMACULATE SAPPHIRE
WATER AND SHALLOW SWIMMING LAGOONS FORMED
BY LONG REEFS.

We've seen a lot of beautiful water and white sand – Whitehaven Beach (*see* p. 156) and Bay of Fires (*see* p. 173) are a couple of places that come to mind. However, not even they can compare to the immaculate clarity of Esperance's West Beach. What makes it even more amazing is that it exists in a low-key suburban neighbourhood, not in a national park or on a remote island. This is a quiet, no-fuss, local public space where people walk their dogs and jump into the water for a quick dip before work.

We arrived in Esperance dead-set on getting to nearby Cape Le Grand National Park; a quick stop to resupply in town was the only thing that stood in the way of our destiny. As we conducted an informal survey of town residents, while doing our grocery shopping, we were told repeatedly that West Beach gets the popular vote. Like so many times before, we then found ourselves unexpectedly backtracking to chase down a promising lead. Fortunately, it wasn't hours away on corrugated roads, but rather a 5-minute drive to the next suburb.

West Beach, or 'Firsties', is the first stop on Twilight Beach Road as it heads west along the tourist loop. Aside from the tranquil, blue water, its most defining feature is a long, shallow reef that follows the shoreline. At low tide, still lagoons form between the reef and the beach, providing long lap lanes. Any day of the year you will find people frolicking in the water, dogs herding children around the shallows, and picnickers looking on from the cliffs. Even as winter swells bring steady surf and chilling wind, few waves will make it over the reef and there is always a sheltered swim to be found.

Not far from shore are hundreds of granite islands that make up the Recherche Archipelago, referred to around here as the Bay of Isles. These islands are, in fact, an underwater mountain range that harbours enormous populations of Australian sea lions and fish. The mountains loom large from town and mimic the peaks in Cape Le Grand. Which, by the way, we did eventually make it to and we highly recommend. Explore the squeaky sand and pristine waters of Hellfire and Lucky Bay, especially during September and October when the wildflowers are in full bloom.

There is so much to see around here, you could easily spend a lifetime exploring the coast, both offshore and on. Better yet, you can get the best of it all without ever leaving town. West Beach is that good.

NEARBY

DOWNTOWN ESPRESSO BAR
Shop 1/94c Dempster St, Esperance

A cool little coffee bar on the main drag
in town, serving speciality coffee by
Melbourne's Dukes Espresso, pastries baked
daily and light lunch items – bagels, pretzels
and croissants. Text in your order, or sit up
at the bar for a chat.

OCEAN BLUES
19 The Esplanade, Esperance

Walk straight off the beach and into this
cute little coastal cafe with diner vibes,
serving breakfast, lunch and dinner.
Nothing fancy, but a good place to perch
for a burger, a thickshake or a game of
cards as you look out over the foreshore.

TAYLORS ST QUARTER
1 Taylor St, Esperance

A family-owned restaurant and bar with a
sunny deck and a breezy holiday feel in a
converted hospital that was previously the
local tearooms. Sunday sessions are popular
here, with live music, happy hour and a
bar menu of snapper ceviche, chargrilled
octopus and mac 'n' cheese croquettes.

Remote Pools

ROYAL LIFE SAVING SOCIETY WA

We acknowledge that it is almost impossible for us to talk about Aboriginal communities as outsiders without unintentionally causing offence or sounding like naive do-gooders. We are not educated in public health; we do not speak for these communities; nor do we claim to have solutions to the complex array of historical and social injustices that have been perpetrated against Australia's Indigenous peoples. We are, however, experts in observing when people are having a good time swimming. A public pool is an asset for any town, and during our time in the country's remote areas we saw how much they are loved and utilised. The Remote Pools project is an interesting initiative and we thought that, like us, other people would want to learn more about it.

WHEN I RUN MY SWIMMING LESSONS I DO A LOT OF SURVIVAL WORK, BECAUSE ONCE THOSE RIVERS START FLOWING ... THE KIDS ARE BACK SWIMMING IN THE RIVERS.

Remote Aboriginal Swimming Pools Project (RASP) began in 2000 and operates in consultation with community leaders to build and maintain pools in remote communities across WA. The program is a combined effort between WA's Royal Life Saving Society, the Department of Communities and private-sector funding (BHP is the principle supporter). According to Royal Life Saving, Indigenous Australians are four times more likely to die from drowning than any other group in the country, so there is a clear need for safe places to swim and for formal instruction. Their first pool was installed in Burringurrah and has expanded to five more communities: Jigalong, Yandeyarra, Bidyadanga, Warmun and Fitzroy Crossing.

Like anywhere in regional Australia, these remote pools often become the focal point of the town, and their managers integral community members. They are places for catching up with friends and offer something to do after school or work. Water hazards like large flooding rivers, crocodiles and Irukandji jellyfish are common in this part of the country, making a safe place to swim and to receive lessons all the more important.

Pools are typically open from the beginning of September to the end of May, with a few months break in winter. We caught up with Trevor and Adele Caporn, the husband and wife pool managers in Fitzroy Crossing; and also swam with the gregarious Bernie Egan in Bidyadanga. Like proud, sunburnt parents, they spoke of the kids with great excitement. They have a broad role in the community, often extending pool hours to host birthday parties and lifesaving carnivals, or acting as informal mentors and counsellors. 'Teaching kids is a skill, and a life-saving skill at that. If I can do anything to prevent a drowning, I've done my job', Adele explains. 'When I run my swimming lessons I do a lot of survival work, because once those rivers start flowing the pool doesn't get used very much – the kids are back swimming in the rivers.'

One of the most important functions of these pools is maintaining a safe space. When we showed up at Bidyadanga there were about 30 kids queued up out the front. Bernie opened the gate and they swarmed around her, rapidly firing off stories and re-enacting things that happened at school. 'There are kids that don't have someone to take them to the beach. They don't have anything to do after school, so this is it for them', she says. 'Kids can always come here, from when it opens until it shuts, and know that they are safe to play.' Indeed, this fits with the broader objectives of the pools, to improve social and emotional wellbeing, health, and community cohesion. It's an awful lot of expectation to put on a simple pool, but there is evidence that it is working. Research by Telethon Kids Institute shows that the incidence of ear problems dropped from 90 per cent to 54 per cent and severe skin sores dropped from 28 per cent to 3 per cent among study participants.

Again and again, we heard the word 'engagement'. Local schools follow the 'Go School, Go Pool' policy – kids can enter for free but are required to get a stamp from school to be able to swim. In nearly 20 years of the program, there has been a well-documented rise in school attendance, particularly among primary school aged children. 'Swim for Fruit' is another initiative – awarding one piece of fruit in exchange for 10 laps. After months of dusty roads and 40 degree heat, spiralised apple and cut watermelon never looked so good.

Pool managers are constantly trialling programs to excite kids and the communities, with the ultimate goal of handing over these facilities to local leadership. Bidyadanga has the first long-term Aboriginal employee and the next generation of Indigenous lifeguards are in training. This is by no means a silver bullet, but it certainly demonstrates something that we have observed all around Australia: a good place to swim helps to shape people and their communities.

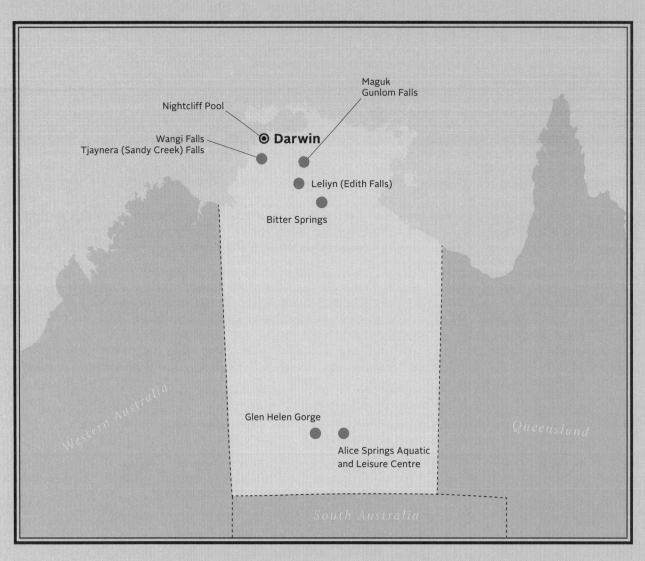

Nightcliff Pool

Maguk
Gunlom Falls

Wangi Falls
Tjaynera (Sandy Creek) Falls

◉ **Darwin**

● Leliyn (Edith Falls)

Bitter Springs

Western Australia

Glen Helen Gorge

Alice Springs Aquatic
and Leisure Centre

Queensland

South Australia

When to visit

Alice Springs region – During and after the rainy season (January to May) when the water is warm and swimming holes are full.

Top End – Access and swimming are best during the Dry season (April to September).

Crocodiles

For better or worse, the Top End is defined by our old friend, the saltwater crocodile. They are present in many waterways from Katherine to the Timor Sea. In this book, we only recommend places that are frequently surveyed by Croc Management. Even so, be vigilant, and make sure that swimming holes are marked as safe. To learn about crocodile safety, *see* p. 143.

Road-trip advice

The Alice Springs region and the Top End are so far from one another and so different that you could comfortably explore each area for weeks at a time.

Favourite swim

TJAYNERA (SANDY CREEK) FALLS
(*see* p. 136)

Best meal

RAPID CREEK MARKETS
(*see* p. 138)

Northern Territory

The Northern Territory is the Australia that the rest of the world imagines.

If we are honest, it may also make up a portion of how we imagine ourselves as a nation, despite our urban reality. Red dirt, snakes, crocodiles, road trains, tough old dudes in oil-stained hats, roadhouses with bras hanging from the ceiling. It's all there. Sometimes the Territory feels like a caricature, as it unfailingly delivers on every conceivable stereotype (or maybe that's just the Kulgera Pub; *see* p. 67). Most of the time, however, we found it to be far more forgiving and diverse than we ever anticipated. Water pours from the least expected places and life always finds a way to adapt and thrive. The land is filled with an ancient, wild, electric beauty.

For the sake of this book, the Territory can be thought of as two distinct regions – Alice Springs and the Top End. Alice is the outback that you see on postcards and in tourism campaigns. It is a proper desert, experiencing both extreme heat and extreme cold. In fact, we spent much of our first trip huddled under blankets; winter temperatures regularly drop below zero in the night-time. Not exactly what we prepared for when we left Melbourne. Once we allowed our preconceptions to fall away, a richer, more complex outback was revealed. We could never have imagined the imposing mountains and green valleys. Huge peaks and ridges that collect and distribute water through broad basins. Cool canyons that shelter year-round swimming holes, and seasonal rivers that open up infinitely more possibilities.

As far as we are concerned, the Top End begins around Mataranka. Geographers will disagree, saying it is too far south, but for us it is the dividing line past which things start to get troppo. The air is thick with humidity and the land pregnant with life. It's the point where the vegetation becomes interesting again after the 1000 kilometre drive to and from Alice (sorry, Tennant Creek). Monsoon season drenches the region from December to March, feeding enormous underground freshwater systems that comprise some of the cleanest, sweetest water on the planet. Distances between destinations are dramatically reduced, but crowds swell accordingly. The best areas are popular for a reason – places like Katherine, Litchfield and Kakadu cannot be matched in the abundance and scale of their swimming holes.

POOL

Best time to visit
Weekends in summer (November to February). Get here first thing in the morning to watch the natural light show on the mountains.

Address
14 Speed St, The Gap

Access
Easy. Abundant parking out the front.

Cost of entry Adults $5, kids 7–16 years $2.55, under 6 years free

Kid friendly Yes

Dog friendly No

Water temperature Cool

Open Mon–Fri 6am–7pm, Sat–Sun 9am–7pm

Facilities
Toilets, showers, indoor spa, water slide, toddler wading pool, kiosk, BBQs

Must bring
Speedos and sausages. 'Cos there is nothing better than a BBQ in your togs.

LOCAL KNOWLEDGE

Almost every single person who grew up in and around Alice Springs learned to swim in this pool.

Alice Springs Aquatic and Leisure Centre

ALICE SPRINGS

A LEGENDARY OUTDOOR PUBLIC POOL IN THE HEART OF ALICE SPRINGS, SET AGAINST A MACDONNELL RANGES BACKDROP.

It's a well-known fact around Alice Springs that there is no better way to stretch your limbs after a long car ride than by a kilometre of Australian crawl (freestyle). So after a few thirsty days spent out in the desert, we rolled into town ready for some laps, not yet realising that our best option was a swim in the city's legendary public pool.

On the doorstep of some of the most dramatic inland swimming holes and gorges in the country, the aquatic centre in Alice Springs is an unexpected gem. It might be the most geographically landlocked public pool in the country, but a dedication to providing the region with a high-quality swimming facility is clear. Having undergone some major upgrades over the years, the ASALC is seriously impressive. Features include a wellness centre, with a 25-metre indoor lap pool and a spa, two water slides, a toddler area and a lazy river.

The highlight for us is the heated outdoor 50-metre pool, set against the backdrop of the MacDonnell Ranges. It is also the only outdoor pool open during winter in the south of the Territory when temperatures can drop below zero. Early in the morning during the cooler months (June, July and August), steam rises off the water while the sun emerges from behind the mountains. It's worth braving a fresh start to experience sunrise in the pool.

During the week the pool enters an almost meditative state. Regulars drop in at various times of the day, pacing the lanes, drying off and leaving quietly. Lifeguards chat at the sidelines while friendly staff at the front desk hand out tips on other local waterholes, spruiking their favourite spots.

The ASALC is a true community hub, with resources dedicated to teaching kids of all backgrounds to swim, particularly those living in remote Aboriginal communities where they might not otherwise have access to lessons. Facilities include learn-to-swim programs for infants through to adults, and aqua fitness classes.

The pool here is surrounded by grass, and during summer it's a favourite spot for families to spend the day, picnicking and relaxing with friends while finding respite from the heat.

NEARBY

THE GOODS
11 Todd St, Alice Springs

Good coffee and good vibes are on offer at this appropriately named cafe in Todd Mall, the perfect spot to stop at after a swim. There's a small menu of smoothies, sandwiches and soups too.

JOHN HAYES ROCKHOLE
Trephina Gorge

A popular summer swimming spot with a chain of pools set between the red rocky cliffs of Trephina Gorge, an hour east of Alice. There are also some great bushwalks through this dramatic landscape, beyond the gorge and up along the ridge-top. 4WD accessible only. Swimming is only worthwhile after a big rain.

ELLERY CREEK BIG HOLE
Namatjira

A local favourite and the closest swimming spot to Alice Springs (just over an hour by car). Ellery Creek Big Hole is an important geological site with deep history, and deep water flowing year-round. The red gorge is an icon, and worth a visit even if you don't brave a swim.

The highlight for us is the heated outdoor 50-metre pool, set against the backdrop of the MacDonnell Ranges.

GORGE

◑ **Best time to visit**
December to April

⟀ **How to get there**
From Alice Springs, take Larapinta
Dr (State Rte 6) west for 46km. Turn
right onto Namatjira Dr (State Rte 2)
and continue 85km into Tjoritja/West
MacDonnell National Park. Turn left onto
Glen Helen Rd. The road dead-ends after
500m at Glen Helen Homestead.

⊖ **Access**
Enter through Glen Helen Homestead,
a mud-brick lodge with a restaurant and
sprawling campground. Follow the sandy
trail about 300m downstream to get to
the main swimming hole.

⑤ **Cost of entry** Free

☺ **Kid friendly** Yes

⊗ **Dog friendly** Yes

⌒ **Water temperature** Very cold

◷ **Open** 24 hours

⊕ **Facilities**
Toilets (at carpark)

⊚ **Must bring**
A great book. *Tracks* by Robyn Davidson
is a classic adventure memoir featuring
this very landscape.

LOCAL KNOWLEDGE

Water temperatures in the area are
always very cold, even in summer. Water
flows underground before reaching
the swimming holes, insulating it from
the hot air. Acclimatise yourself to the
temperature before jumping into deep
water. Sudden immersion in icy water
can cause loss of breath control and
complete disorientation.

Glen Helen Gorge

A QUINTESSENTIAL OUTBACK SWIMMING HOLE
AND REAL-LIFE CANVAS FOR FAMED ARTIST
ALBERT NAMATJIRA.

In a region defined by ephemeral rivers and waterholes, Glen Helen Gorge always has water, making it one of the most reliable places to take a dip. It also benefits greatly from not being the closest swimming hole to Alice Springs, so it never seems as rowdy or busy as other places in the West Macs. Think Bronte, rather than Bondi; Sunshine Coast, rather than Gold Coast.

Most swimmers congregate around the main pool, at the base of the gap, which feels like an open amphitheatre with a river running through it. Towering ghost gums and tall reeds line the banks, while endemic species of pink-flamingo, alligator and dolphin floaties can often be spotted mingling in deeper water. Hot days can get busy here, but most people don't stray beyond the most obvious entry points. You can easily escape the crowds by swimming downriver to hidden beaches on the south side of the ridge.

Many coastal dwellers will discover (too late) that Central Australia is literally freezing cold in the winter. Who knew? Those perfect blue skies and red rocks look so warm in photographs. We first visited in July and were limited to a series of daring plunges punctuated by whoops of giddy laughter and frantic, uncoordinated scrambling for the towel. Whether this type of swimming jump-starts the immune system or results in long-term nerve damage remains to be seen.

We didn't get it entirely wrong, though. Tourist high season is May to September, when consistently dry weather and cool daytime temperatures (rarely topping 23°C) foster perfect conditions for walking the nearby Larapinta Trail or taking sunset pictures of Uluru. Or camel safaris around Uluru. Or helicopter rides around Uluru. Whatever your Uluru fantasy, someone will sell you a ticket. However, when the temperatures rise and all the tourists go back home, the locals emerge to reclaim their swimming holes. December to April brings hot days and summer storms that pour fresh water into riverbeds, valleys and gorges.

Despite the heat, the West MacDonnell area is rejuvenated in summer when a seemingly inhospitable landscape is transformed into a swimming oasis. It's no wonder that nearly every single waterhole is a sacred site to the Indigenous Western Arrernte people, nor that many of these pools provided constant inspiration for Albert Namatjira's paintings. The places here are like nowhere else in Australia and Glen Helen Gorge is a monument to outback swimming.

NEARBY

RED BANK GORGE
West MacDonnell Ranges

A great place to visit on really hot days, because there are very few hours of direct sun in here. It's a deep, dramatic slot canyon polished by years of wind and water. Yes, canyon walls are swirls of red, but also contain purple, orange and yellow. Start at the main pool (1.3 kilometres from the carpark) and swim up the narrow gorge as far as your claustrophobia will allow. This is the start/end of the 223 kilometre Larapinta Trail, and a visit is well paired with a hike up Mt Sonder.

ORMISTON GORGE
West MacDonnell Ranges

Ormiston is a wide, high-walled canyon that opens up into the expansive Ormiston Pound. Close to the carpark is a deep, cool swimming hole, surrounded by native gum trees with permanent water, though it tends to go stagnant for a couple of months during winter. The main pool is popular with rock jumpers and usually attracts the largest crowds. Continue upstream for further swimming options and some privacy.

GLEN HELEN HOMESTEAD
1 Namatjira Dr, West MacDonnell Ranges

This homestead is a bit of an institution in the West MacDonnells, being the only place to get petrol, basic groceries and a warm meal. Slim Pickens has been performing the world's longest musical residency, going back to 2008, and doesn't seem to be slowing down. There are various tiers of accommodation on-site, but the campground is the best option for our money, with a fun, communal atmosphere and a good balance of returning campers and blow-ins.

THERMAL SPRING

○ **Best time to visit**
Dry season (May to September)

◇ **How to get there**
From the Stuart Hwy, head north out of Mataranka to Martin Rd. Follow Martin Rd to the end.

⊖ **Access**
Easy. Short stroll along a well-maintained palm-lined path to reach the springs.

⑤ **Cost of entry** Free

☺ **Kid friendly** Yes

⊗ **Dog friendly** No

⌒ **Water temperature** Warm

⊙ **Open** 24 hours during the Dry season

⊕ **Facilities**
Toilets (at the carpark), picnic tables

⊘ **Must bring**
A foam noodle or any other flotation device and cold mid-strength beer.

LOCAL KNOWLEDGE

These artesian waters are said to have therapeutic properties that aid the body's muscles, skin, lymphatic and nervous systems, and are particularly beneficial for those with arthritis.

Bitter Springs

MATARANKA, ELSEY NATIONAL PARK

A NATURAL, PALM-FRINGED ARTESIAN THERMAL SPRING WITH FOUNTAIN-OF-YOUTH POSSIBILITIES.

After days of never-ending horizons and flat, dry desert dotted with termite mounds, 'The Never Never' – a name for this vast remote area of outback Australia – never felt more apt. It also made arriving in Mataranka all the more sweet. Though the town itself is nothing more than a stopover, it is home to some oasis-like swimming spots. Our pick is Bitter Springs.

A natural palm-fringed artesian hot spring, Bitter Springs sits at a luxuriant 33°C year-round. It is part of a series of spring-fed natural thermal pools, supplied by the Wet season up north via the Roper River system. The Roper River begins east of Mataranka in Elsey National Park, and winds across the Top End over 1000 kilometres to meet the sea in the Gulf of Carpentaria.

Immersed in a natural setting of mossy green banks and river pandanus, the pool has a swamp-like feel (in a good way). Tall palms rise above the sun-flecked water creating shade, while lily pads float on the surface.

Throughout the day a constant flow of swimmers arrives at the springs for a balmy dip. Some wander in from a nearby campground in their swimsuits, with colourful foam noodles tucked under their arms. Others arrive in car loads or on bicycles. A couple are here for happy hour, floating downstream with tinnies of beer (no glass allowed). There is a convivial atmosphere as travellers strike up conversation with the person next to them, discussing car stories, highway routes and their favourite stops along the way. Family groups relish the opportunity for everyone to enjoy the comfortable water temperature, while older couples come to soothe their joints. The rejuvenating qualities give the spring a 'fountain of youth' appeal, conjuring up scenes from the movie *Cocoon* (1985).

Visitors enter the main pool at the stairs and drift around on floaties or dive with their goggles on. Submerged trees, branches and long grasses provide a waterlogged playground to explore below the surface. Other water life (fish, etc.) struggle to survive in the Dry season when the warm nutrient-rich water is low in oxygen.

Back above the water, visitors bob downstream on the current to explore other swimming areas along the 150-metre aqua trail. At the end of the gentle drift, a ladder gets you back onto the Bitter Springs walking path, to return to the main pool for another go round.

MATARANKA THERMAL POOL
Elsey National Park

The main springs in Mataranka, this pool is more a product of human hands than Bitter Springs, with a concrete bottom, easy access and a nearby canteen.

BITTER SPRINGS CABINS AND CAMPING
255 Martin Rd, Mataranka

Just a short walk from Bitter Springs, the local campground offers powered and unpowered sites, and cabins. You can hire a foam noodle here to float on for $1.

THE DALY WATERS PUB
16 Stuart St, Daly Waters

Two hours south of Mataranka, just off the Stuart Highway, is this historic Aussie pub dating back to the 1930s. Worth a stop for a cold beer and a classic pub meal. Although it seems too over the top to be real, this place is 100 per cent sincere in its kitsch.

Leliyn
(Edith Falls)

RED ROCK MEETS BLUE SKIES,
CASCADING WATERFALLS AND
COOL DEEP POOLS.

WATERFALL

Best time to visit
Dry season (May to September).
Closed in the Wet.

How to get there
The falls are 60km north of Katherine.
Turn off the Stuart Hwy at Edith Falls Rd
and drive east into Nitmiluk National
Park. The road dead-ends at the
campground and trailhead. Tracks are
all very well signed. It's 1.3km one way to
the upper pools.

Access
Easy. Short, albeit steep, hike to the
upper pools.

Cost of entry Free

Kid friendly Yes

Dog friendly No

Water temperature Cool

Open 24 hours

Facilities
Toilets, BBQs, picnic platform, kiosk,
camping (fees apply)

Must bring
A wide-brimmed hat for the walk

LOCAL KNOWLEDGE

You can drink the water in these
waterholes. Bring your bottle and fill up.

Despite bountiful numbers of waterfalls in the Northern Territory, a swim at one always feels extraordinary. This was our first falls swim in the NT as we drove up through the Centre, and it set some high expectations. It's not that the falls are incredibly dramatic here, but the whole setting has some very special energy, most importantly for the Jawoyn and Dagomen people who connect this place with creation, the Dreaming and ceremony.

Leliyn is a series of cascading waterfalls and deep pristine pools along the Edith River, just north of Katherine on the west side of Nitmiluk National Park. It is also the final destination of the Jatbula Trail, a 62-kilometre (five- to six-day) hike along ancient songline country, through an ever-changing landscape of sandy beaches, monsoon forests, rapid rivers and rocky canyons.

The main plunge pool at Leliyn is just a couple of hundred metres from the carpark, where there is a camp site and an open-air kiosk with ice-creams and cold drinks.

Just beyond this is a plunge pool at the base of the main falls, where a family in a blow-up boat is rowing merrily when we arrive. Eager to get to the top, however, we bypass this scene and take the trail to the top pools, a track that loops up around Leliyn. It's a steep 1.2-kilometre walk up the escarpment through long grass and we're relieved to find the water when we do. Piles of clothes and colourful bags lie dotted around the rocks at the top of the falls, telling us we're not the only ones who have discovered this paradise. It's a popular spot but feels like there is a quiet place for everyone.

We find shade, strip down and plunge into the cool, dark water. The pools couldn't be a more refreshing temperature in the heat of a Territory winter (still over 30°C most days).

People scramble over rocks and move between pools on the soft current. Kids play together, sliding and jumping into the deeper water, and some try climbing up under the slippery waterfall. The entire setting is blissful.

After a dip in the top pools, we recommend continuing along the trail towards Sweetwater Pools (another 3.4 kilometres). The path is guided by small triangular trail markers every few hundred meters and is popular with birdwatchers. Take plenty of water for the walk, and make sure you refill your bottle at Sweetwater. Spend the rest of your day lolling about in cool, croc-free waters. This is the Territory at its best.

KATHERINE GORGE
Nitmiluk National Park

This rest area of sandstone escarpments is actually home to 13 gorges. Explore by boat, on foot or on a high-rollers helicopter ride. Saltwater crocs inhabit the gorge system, so only swim in designated areas. Southern Rockhole is perfect after a bit of rain.

JATBULA TRAIL

A world-class hiking trail that spans 62 kilometres (a five- to six-day walk) across the western end of Arnhem Land escarpment from the centre of Nitmiluk National Park to Leliyn. Just 15 people are permitted onto the trail each day, and it can book out months in advance. This is definitely a 'bucket list' bushwalk.

SWEETWATER POOL
Nitmiluk National Park

A series of lush swimming pools a further 3.4-kilometre walk into the national park from the upper pools at Leliyn. Swimming holes here are separated by small rapids, and true to the name, the water here is actually sweet to drink. You'll likely see large water monitors sunbaking on the banks. This is also the last camp site along the Jatbula Trail. Highly recommended.

Gunlom Falls

KAKADU NATIONAL PARK

THE TERRITORY'S MOST
FAMOUS INFINITY POOL,
AND A MAJOR STOP ON ANY
KAKADU PILGRIMAGE.

NORTHERN TERRITORY

WATERFALL ROCK POOL

◑ **Best time to visit**
Dry season (May to October). The falls and plunge pool are closed during the Wet, so be sure to check before going.

◬ **How to get there**
Gunlom Falls is a major destination and the turn-off from Kakadu Hwy is well marked. Follow the unsealed road for 25km and turn left at the T-intersection. It's a further 10km drive to the main carpark, campground and plunge pool. A short, steep 2km (return) walk to the upper pools.

⊖ **Access**
Easy (but dusty). Well-maintained unsealed roads. Conditions can vary and while 4WD is handy for clearance, it is certainly not necessary.

⑤ **Cost of entry** International and interstate visitors over 16 years require a permit to enter Kakadu National Park ($40 per person).

☺ **Kid friendly** Yes

⊗ **Dog friendly** No

⌒ **Water temperature** Cool

◷ **Open** 24 hours

⊕ **Facilities**
BBQs, picnic area, toilet and showers, camping (fees apply)

⊚ **Must bring**
A camera. In the age of social media everyone wants a snap of the natural infinity-pool view, and for good reason – it's incredible.

LOCAL KNOWLEDGE

Crowds peak around lunchtimes and greatly subside from 3pm. This is a beautiful place to watch the sunset and you will probably have the whole place to yourself. Make sure to bring a torch for the return journey down.

You may be familiar with Gunlom Falls, even if you've never been to the NT. These days, it seems to find its way into every tourism campaign, or else it is clogging our newsfeeds, making city life feel incredibly unadventurous and grey. Many of us, however, will remember Gunlom, and indeed Kakadu National Park, from the *Crocodile Dundee* era. From a time when worn-out VHS tapes were passed from kid to kid. The golden age of leather vests and crocodile-skin hats. Kakadu has been firmly lodged in our minds ever since.

Needless to say, anticipation was great as we made our way to Gunlom Falls. Driving through parched savannah woodlands, it is almost impossible to believe that you will be rewarded with anything but broken aircon and dusty roads. It's like being stuck in a never-ending ad for mid-strength beer. The landscape works you into a swimming frenzy, and just before you crack, a towering escarpment looms and tall trees announce the presence of water. You are suddenly spoiled for choice. It's not a mirage. Gunlom Falls is a swimmers' paradise.

For all of our research, we had heard little about the enormous plunge pool at the base of the falls. Only 200m from the carpark, it sits like a hidden lake. The water is deep, clear and still, with a large sandy beach on one side. Anywhere else in the country, this would be a world-class swimming hole, yet we saw just a handful of families all day. The signs declared it was safe to swim, but where were the people? There is a certain eeriness to an empty pool in the Top End. Was there something we didn't know? Watching a lone child splash at the water's edge, one can't help but conjure a grim narrative involving large reptiles and school holidays gone wrong.

All of the people, it turns out, were racing up the escarpment to see the upper pools. It's an efficient trail, cutting a near vertical path 1 kilometre up the cliff. Your labour is quickly rewarded with sweeping views of the hills and broken ridges below. The sins of an overheating body are forgiven as it is lowered like a sizzling pan into cold water. Did someone say mid-strength tinnie?

It's impossible not to be dazzled by this spot, no matter how many other visitors there are nor how many photos you have seen. The front infinity pool offers the most famous view and the best people-watching, but we had our fun exploring the swimming holes further back, where there is a mini gorge with smooth walls and a number of shallow, spa-sized baths. Tall gum trees cast enough shade for anyone who needs it.

Despite the constant flow of people, Gunlom is never too busy to enjoy. By the late afternoon all of the tour buses depart, leaving only a handful of committed picnickers. If you are lucky, you will have sunset all to yourself. It's the perfect time to ponder life's greatest questions. Like, will I be able to wear this crocodile-skin vest when I'm back in Melbourne?

NEARBY

MOTOR CAR FALLS
Kakadu National Park

About 13 kilometres back from Gunlom Falls towards the main road turn-off at Yurmikmik carpark. Motor Car Falls is a lesser known and secluded spot with a deep pool and seasonal waterfall. It's a 7-kilometre return walk in from the carpark. Bring lots of water, as this can be a particularly dry walk.

JARRANGBARNMI (KOOLPIN GORGE)
Kakadu National Park

Only a small number of people are allowed to visit at one time and you need a permit to swim and camp here. A very special place with waterfalls, rock pool and a basic camp site. Most likely you'll have it all to yourself. Access via Gimbat Road, towards Gimbat day-use area. There is a locked gate at the start of the 4WD track (permits will include a set of keys). The track requires about 11 kilometres of high-clearance driving.

LAZY LIZARD TAVERN AND CARAVAN PARK
299 Miller Tce, Pine Creek

The town of Pine Creek is located on the Stuart Highway, near Kakadu's southern entrance. Stop in for a drink and a dip in the pool at this eclectic, outback pub, where they play '90s hits and serve pizza and pub food. There's a small general store next door for supplies, and a giant (fake) crocodile out the front.

GORGE

⟩ **Best time to visit**
Dry season (May to September)

⟨ **How to get there**
Follow signs to the turn-off along Kakadu
Hwy between Gunlom Falls road and
Cooinda. Head 14km east on an unsealed
road to Maguk carpark. Follow the track
about 600m and cross the stream on
your right. Continue for another 500m to
reach Maguk's bottom pool.

⊖ **Access**
4WD is highly recommended, as the
last couple of kilometres get very sandy.
Better maintained in the Dry season.
For 4WD advice, see p. xi.

$ **Cost of entry** International and
interstate visitors over 16 years require
a permit to enter Kakadu National Park
($40 per person).

☺ **Kid friendly** Yes

⊗ **Dog friendly** No

∿ **Water temperature** Cool

🕐 **Open** 24 hours

⊕ **Facilities** Toilets (at trailhead)

◎ **Must bring**
Lunch, so you can spend the whole
day exploring.

LOCAL KNOWLEDGE

If you can find the track to the top of the
falls, there are some great pools hiding
up there. One has a hole-in-the-wall
below the surface, so you can dive
down, swim through it, and pop up
in another pool.

Maguk

A SEEMINGLY BOTTOMLESS GORGE WITH A HUMBLE
WATERFALL AND HIDDEN ROCK POOLS.

The Top End holds its cards closely, seldom revealing anything until the very last moment. Unless places are highly celebrated, you are lucky to hear about them at all, especially in the crowded field of Kakadu swims. Maguk, with its huge, deep pool and sheer walls is just far enough off the beaten track that it slips under the radar of most visitors. Had it not been recommended by some local friends, it's likely we would have missed it ourselves.

Eager to beat fellow campers into the gorge, we rose early at the bush camp near the Maguk carpark (only $6 a night). From here it is only a couple of kilometres of sandy driving or walking to the trailhead.

The walk is a kilometre of damp (sometimes submerged) track that runs beside a creek and sports familiar crocodile warning signs along the way. Even when the water is a shallow puddle, you can't help but succumb to dark thoughts of what may be lurking below the surface. While the pool itself is surveyed before opening to the public, croc management doesn't guarantee anything about what is happening downstream. Don't be afraid, but be cautious, and stick to the trail.

The track eventually crosses the creek and dead-ends with a dramatic reveal of Maguk gorge. Like pulling back a veil, scrubby brush and spiral pandanus abruptly end at the water's edge. High canyon walls tower above to form a natural amphitheatre with a deep pool at its heart. It's easy to see why this place is considered extremely sacred to the Bininj Mungguy people. Keep that in mind as you enter the water, and remain both considerate and respectful of its significance.

The water's edge is shallow at first, but quickly drops into a dark abyss. You can't help feeling a little like Kevin Costner in the perennial classic *Waterworld* as you swim to the bottom looking for a bit of sand. We dove as deep as we could and always came up empty handed.

People perch on the rocky ledges that fringe the pool, eagerly soaking up the morning sunlight that bathes the western cliff-face. We sat here for ages, alternating between the hot rocks and cool water. We swam long laps from one end to the other, standing or floating beneath the small waterfall and allowing it to give us a shiatsu-like massage.

This place is popular for rock jumping, but signs explicitly advise against it. The best we can say is to avoid doing anything stupid and to assume responsibility for your actions. Every time someone gets injured, there is more pressure to police these beautiful, wild places.

On our way out, we noticed people taking a semi-hidden track to reach further pools above the gorge. The trail follows the top of the escarpment, with vertigo-inducing views of swimmers below. The top pools are narrow and deep, defined by smooth, weathered rock formations, with an underwater passage from one pool to another.

In our opinion, Maguk is the jewel in Kakadu's crown – it's dramatic, super-swimmable, and delights us with its variety of experiences.

NEARBY

JIM JIM FALLS & BARRK MALAM BUSHWALK
Kakadu National Park

Open during Dry season only (though popular for helicopter photography in the Wet), Jim Jim Falls is accessible via a rough, 4WD track. The walk in is a kilometre through monsoon forest and over large boulders to a deep plunge pool (and one of the NT's best beaches) flanked by breathtaking 250-metre-high cliffs. During the Dry season the water may only be a trickle. The Barrk Malam Bushwalk is a steep 3-kilometre hike (one way) on a rough track up through rugged stone country to the top of the falls. Here you will find more plunge pools, incredible views and, if you're lucky, some beautiful hidden rock art. Look, but don't touch.

TWIN FALLS
Kakadu National Park

Off the same road as Jim Jim, these spectacular falls are accessed by a boat shuttle service and a walking track over boulders and sand. The last section of the road involves a deep-water crossing. High clearance 4WD with a snorkel is recommended.

UBIRR ROCK ART SITE
Kakadu National Park

Kakadu's rock art represents some of the longest historical records of any group of people in the world. At Ubirr, several Aboriginal rock art galleries document Indigenous stories through naturalistic paintings of animals, changing landscapes and the first European contact. Climb to the top of the rocky lookout for views over the Nadab floodplain, a particularly beautiful spot at sunset (bring mozzie repellent).

WATERFALL

◐ **Best time to visit**
Dry season (May to November)

◬ **How to get there**
A 2-hour drive south of Darwin into Litchfield National Park. The falls are located on Wangi Falls Rd. It is very well signed.

⊖ **Access**
Easy. A two-minute walk from the carpark.

⑂ **Cost of entry** Free

☺ **Kid friendly** Yes

⊗ **Dog friendly** No

⌒ **Water temperature** Refreshing

◷ **Open** 24 hours, in the Dry season. Swimming is not possible during the Wet; check with the national park before visiting.

⊕ **Facilities**
Toilets, BBQs, picnic tables, kiosk, camping

⊚ **Must bring**
A GoPro or similar waterproof camera for filming in the waterfalls

---

LOCAL KNOWLEDGE

Arrive early in the day before the crowds and stay late to watch them all leave.

Wangi Falls

A SACRED WATERFALL AND HUGE PLUNGE POOL SURROUNDED BY LUSH, MONSOONAL RAINFOREST.

Wangi Falls (pronounced 'wong-guy') is Litchfield National Park's most popular and easily accessible swimming spot. Two waterfalls cascade down the rock face into a huge pool at the bottom, surrounded by greenery and birdlife.

Visitors come from far and wide by the bus load to plunge into the waters. They wear colourful swim suits, and grip inflatable floaties and waterproof cameras on selfie sticks as they wade at the water's edge. For many, Wangi Falls is the first stop on a swimming pilgrimage around the national park that has become a rite of passage in the Top End.

The water is crisp and clear and the falls flow year-round, but it is only safe for swimming in the Dry. More than a dozen types of fish live in the water at Wangi, including eel-tailed catfish, purple spotted trout and black-banded rainbow fish. Turtles can be seen here too, surviving on the large river Pandanus fruits that break apart and fall into the pool. Small fish and shrimp may nibble at your feet in the water, but they are harmless.

Families unload picnic rugs and eskys from their cars, full of snacks and drinks for the day ahead. Some lay out their towels to sunbake in the shade; others fire up barbecues while kids run around in wet swimsuits with ice-cream dripping down their chins. Various accents can be heard among the sounds of the landscape – the delicate hum of people, birds and the click of phone cameras. This is the Territory's equivalent of the beach.

We swim out to the falls on the right side for a heavy shower. On the left, a small spa-like plunge pool has formed where a handful of people can sit submerged, looking out over the main pool. Rock jumping is not encouraged, but we certainly see some fellow enthusiasts.

A boardwalk wraps around one side of the pool, and splits off towards a lookout and the ridge-top Wangi Falls Walk. The ridge-top trail begins at the plunge pool and is approximately 1.6 kilometres return. It takes you through the lush, monsoonal rainforest – filled with psychedelic butterflies and colourful spiders – and around the top of the falls for a full circuit loop back to the water's edge.

You'd be lucky to get this place all to yourself, but don't let the crowds deter you: no number of swimmers could make this spot feel full. It's popular for a reason.

NEARBY

BERRY SPRINGS
Just an hour south of central Darwin, Berry Springs is a popular stop for a dip on your way to Litchfield. Signs here advise not to put your head underwater. We advise to bring a pool toy to help keep you floating on the surface.

WALKER CREEK
Litchfield National Park

A series of eight secluded camp sites sit along Walker Creek, each with its own private swimming spot. Sites 2, 3, 7 and 8 are our picks. Leave your car in the carpark and walk in to the individual camp sites. There are drop toilets at the trailhead and near site 7.

LITCHFIELD HELICOPTER FLIGHTS
Helicopter flights can be booked at the Wangi Falls information centre. Fly over Wangi and north across the Litchfield escarpment for a birds-eye view over inaccessible cascading waterfalls and lush, green national park. Six minutes of highly indulgent visual pleasure and worth every penny.

◫

WATERFALL

◐ **Best time to visit**
Dry season (May to November). The pool receives sun from midday onwards.

◬ **How to get there**
Turn off Litchfield Park Rd onto a well-marked 4WD track about 8km south of Wangi Falls. After a short river crossing, it's a further 8km of easy driving along the track to the Sandy Creek campground, carpark and trailhead. Walk the well-maintained track 1.4km to reach the falls.

⊖ **Access**
A 4WD is required for a small river crossing and patches of soft sand.

⑤ **Cost of entry** Free

☺ **Kid friendly** Yes

⊗ **Dog friendly** No

⌒ **Water temperature** Cool

⊙ **Open** 24 hours

⊕ **Facilities**
Camping, toilets and picnic tables (at the campground)

⊚ **Must bring**
Camping gear to stay the night and cash to pay the fees

LOCAL KNOWLEDGE

Don't be afraid of the river crossing. If the water level is lower than the engine, you don't even need a snorkel. Look for the depth indicator marker at the deepest point for peace of mind before crossing. While conditions can vary, levels are generally very low in the Dry season, and the bottom is packed with rocks, so you're unlikely to get stuck. For 4WD advice, see p. xi.

Tjaynera (Sandy Creek) Falls

LITCHFIELD NATIONAL PARK

A MIRACULOUSLY PRIVATE WATERFALL HIDDEN IN THE TOP END'S BUSIEST NATIONAL PARK.

We heard about Tjaynera from some friends living in Darwin. They were finishing a two-year stint and had spent most weekends exploring waterholes in the Top End. Needless to say, we leaned on them heavily for information. We spent an entire evening going over their tattered and heavily annotated map, passing it around the table like a sacred text – our own personal Dead Sea Scrolls; better yet, the original Coca Cola recipe. Tjaynera was circled twice and highlighted. Not many places on the map got that kind of treatment. We'd had a few other people tell us about it too, often speaking in hushed tones.

Tjaynera isn't on the usual Litchfield circuit, despite being only a few minutes from popular swim spot Wangi Falls (see p. 134). The small river crossing (stream crossing may be a more accurate description) tends to intimidate people, including us, and especially those who aren't seasoned Territorians. We drove to the edge of the river and looked at it for a long time. We discussed the pros and cons. We watched other cars make the crossing. On one hand we may see the best swimming hole of our lives, we thought; on the other, we could stall in the river and get eaten by crocodiles. Both seemed highly probable. We turned around and drove back out to the sealed road, dispirited and marinating in the silence of our cowardice. We probably wouldn't have gone back if it wasn't for some grey nomads heckling us. They gave a us crash course in river crossings and agreed to rescue us, if necessary. Like most things, it wasn't as difficult or scary as we feared.

Once over the river, an easy dirt road leads to the Tjaynera camp site and carpark, from where it's a further 1.4 kilometre walk to the waterfall. The trail follows a small creek up an open valley, making you doubt there could be any significant body of water ahead. Which means expectations are wildly exceeded on arrival. The scale of both the waterfall and the pool below are as grand as anywhere in the Top End, yet the crowds are among the smallest. Even at the peak of school holidays, on a hot Sunday afternoon, we shared the water with about eight other people. Just enough to confirm that it is safe to swim, yet still feel like you are off the beaten track.

The falls take a 48-metre dive from the overhanging sandstone cliffs into a deep, wide pool. Layers of yellow and red rock are angular and sturdy, covered with ferns, trees and vines in a way that suggests the remnants of a lost city. Pandanus trees perfectly frame your vision from every angle. The setting has a weight of significance to it that goes beyond many other pools we have seen. You can't help but feel a wild sense of discovery that is hard to walk away from. We stayed all day, watching the sun track across the water before it finally climbed the cliffs and disappeared over the top.

NEARBY

FLORENCE FALLS
Litchfield National Park

An iconic double waterfall with high cliffs on three sides for shade and a lazy grotto-like vibe. Florence is one of the best places in the NT on a good day, but it does get busy and can't handle a crowd as well as other pools.

BULEY ROCKHOLE
Litchfield National Park

A series of small yet surprisingly deep rock pools fed by one of the cleanest, sweetest springs we have ever encountered. This is a low-energy waterhole for reptilian people who want to slide back and forth between hot rocks and fresh pools. Natural butt nooks and stubby holders abound.

CRAZY ACRES MANGO FARM AND CAFE
70 Reedbeds Rd, Berry Springs

A classic stop for anyone travelling from Darwin to Litchfield or Berry Springs. These guys manage to work mango into just about every dish. Mango smoothies or homemade mango ice-cream always hit the spot. Only open during the Dry season.

POOL

◑ **Best time to visit**
Anytime. It's always warm in Darwin and public pools are the best swimming option. Sunset is a particularly nice time to do laps along this cliff.

△ **Address**
259 Casuarina Dr, Nightcliff

⊖ **Access**
Easy. Parking and bike paths out the front.

⑤ **Cost of entry** Adults $4, seniors $3.40, kids/concession $2

☺ **Kid friendly** Yes

⊗ **Dog friendly** No

⌒ **Water temperature** Warm

◔ **Open** Mon–Fri 5.30am–7.30pm, Sat–Sun 8am–7.30pm (may vary slightly)

⊕ **Facilities**
Toilets, showers, picnic tables, BBQs, table tennis

◎ **Must bring**
Cash to spend at the food trucks that park out front.

LOCAL KNOWLEDGE

This place is located on top of a fairly high cliff, yet a rumour persists that a croc once washed up into the pool. We imagine you could say the same about every pool in the Top End.

Nightcliff Pool

DARWIN

A BALMY, CLIFF-SIDE PUBLIC POOL OVERLOOKING THE TIMOR SEA.

We have yet to determine whether residents of Darwin are masters of self-control or self-punishment. Every day they wake up to the inhumane combination of hot weather and beautiful, blue, crocodile-filled oceans. Every day a thousand perfect beaches and palm-fringed coves go completely unswum. It is ocean abstinence in its cruellest form. Surely this constant swimming repression is what makes people go troppo. As the heat rises, they flirt with the water's edge in every imaginable way, but always stop just short of submersion. Fortunately, for those looking for the next best thing, there is the 50-metre Nightcliff Pool.

Located on a rocky bluff along the Nightcliff/Rapid Creek foreshore, this unpretentious community pool is as close to ocean swimming as you can get without risking life and limb. Large lawns and tropical gardens foster an especially relaxed atmosphere that encourages swimmers to stay longer than intended. Regulars are quick to make you feel welcome and it isn't unusual to find a cup of tea in your hand after morning laps. Evenings tend to escalate and are known to produce spontaneous barbecues and enthusiastic conversation.

We would be remiss to deny that our love of this pool isn't also influenced by our love of the neighbourhood. We found it to be full of thinkers, dreamers, teachers and travellers. Some of Australia's finest interstate and international transplants land themselves in Darwin, at least for a period of time. During the Dry season, the entire foreshore becomes every resident's second living room. It takes on a festival atmosphere as large groups gather to have picnics and watch the sunset. Food trucks line Casuarina Drive, laying out chairs or bean bags beneath festoon lighting. As a cool breeze pushes ashore from the Timor Sea, you can't help but feel that Darwin has perfected outdoor living.

NEARBY

FOOD TRUCKS
Casuarina Dr

A selection of food trucks park in front of the pool and along Casurina Drive most nights of the week. We couldn't keep ourselves away from the Thai, though a Greek truck was carving slabs of marinated lamb like a virtuoso. Darwin's best pizza is served from the intersection of Chapman Street and Casuarina Drive, and there is a wide offering at the Nightcliff Jetty most nights.

PARAP AND RAPID CREEK MARKETS
3/3 Vickers St, Parap and
48 Trower Rd, Millner

Food markets are by far Darwin's culinary highlight. Parap Market is a local produce and exotic food market held every Saturday (8am–2pm), all year round. Bring cash and graze your way through Malaysian, Thai, Sri Lankan, Indian and Laotian cuisine. Many of the same vendors are found also at Rapid Creek Market on Sundays (6.30am–1.30pm).

LUCKY BAT CAFE
3/7 Pavonia Pl, Nightcliff

A casual neighbourhood cafe, and a favourite of the local swimmers. Wood-oven sourdough bread is baked daily on the premises and the seasonal menu is largely sourced locally. We've enjoyed more than a few iced coffees and mango smoothies from the sunny courtyard.

Senior Ranger

STUART WOERLE

As Australians, we take a lot of pride in our deadly animals – at least, that's the impression we like to project. Hoop snakes, drop bears ... the danger knows no limits according to many inner-city dwellers. Nevermind that our most harrowing encounter is likely to be with a curious possum in the botanic garden or the occasional swooping magpie.

For all our sharks, snakes, and spiders there is very little appreciable danger. Those animals do everything they can to avoid humans and you have to be extremely unlucky to get into any trouble with them. Crocodiles, however, should not be taken so lightly.

When swimming in Australia's Top End (whether in Western Australia, the Northern Territory or Queensland) you will inevitably enter crocodile country. There is no getting around the fact that the saltwater crocodile (Crocodylus porosus) is a survivor. It's a living fossil and the world's largest reptile. In short, it's a dinosaur. Salties are cold-blooded opportunists with ironclad patience. They will eat whatever they can get, but, although the danger is real, some basic knowledge is all you need to avoid any unwanted encounters.

We were lucky enough to sit down with one of Australia's crocodile experts, Stuart Woerle. He is a senior ranger in the NT's crocodile management program and a seasoned campaigner in the park system. Stuart is the son of a park ranger and has worked for the national-park services since 1983.

A BIG CROC CAN BE IN A FOOT OF WATER AND YOU'LL NEVER KNOW IT'S THERE.

Q. What should people know about swimming in the NT?
A. The first thing is don't swim unless there is a sign saying you can swim. If it's a safe area, it will be advertised. Otherwise, assume there is something in there. Most fatal crocodile attacks in the NT in the past 20 years have occurred when people have entered the water outside of designated swimming areas. Educate yourself before coming. Go on the CrocWise website.

Also, camp at least 50 metres from the water's edge. If you are camping in the bush, expect there to be a croc. If you are boiling a billy, put it on a stick, throw a rope; don't enter the water or go near it.

One thing Dad told me growing up, if you get your water at a waterhole, take it from a different place each day. He reckoned if you keep going back to the same spot the croc would watch you the first day, confirm it the second day, then he's there to get you the third day.

The main thing is safety around the waterways. Don't do anything that will put yourself in danger. Fishing off the bank of the river, put a tree between you and the river. We see all sorts of silly things: fishing in knee-deep or thigh-deep water. It amazes me there are not *more* attacks.

Q. What are the big misconceptions about croc safety?
A. A good one is, 'Oh, there are freshies here so there can't be any salties'. They think it's safe to swim. That is the worst one. Freshies and salties can live in the same body of water. If a place is safe, there will be a sign telling you it is okay to swim.

Another misconception is that if you are in knee-deep water it's safe – it's not safe. Especially murky water. A big croc can be in a foot of water and you'll never know it's there.

Q. How do crocodiles get into these swimming holes?
A. During the Wet season the crocs will generally travel upriver looking for food. Then often they'll go back down with the water too, depending on the source. You'll have a large croc with six to 10 females in the area that he services, and he'll guard that area from other males. So when you get younger crocs who become sexually mature, they'll be looking for an area too. Sometimes they'll take on the big crocs and get a flogging, then often you'll find those injured animals looking for a place to heal. So they'll go into quieter areas, upriver, which is often where people go.

Q. Can you describe the process of management coming out of the Wet season and preparing places for visitors.
A. Parks and Wildlife have a standard operating procedure. Any area that is deemed a safe place for people to swim, after the water recedes, they survey it. And they survey a minimum of three nights in a row. The rangers do it at night so they can see the crocs' eyes with a spotlight. Even if a croc is shy, you will see the eye flash. Some waterholes have freshies in there and that's fine, they're just freshies, they leave them. If they're large freshies or salties, they are removed. Put a boat in at night-time and harpoon them, or install a trap. Pools won't open until we are satisfied that there is nothing in there.

Q. What do you do with the crocs you catch?
A. With a large freshwater croc, they just relocate it to a different water cycle. Salties are like homing pigeons, they tend to come back. So you don't relocate them. They all go to croc farms.

Q. Can you tell us about the CrocWise program?
A. It's an educational program for school groups but useful for anyone really, to educate people about crocodiles – 'cos you can't educate crocs about people. There are a lot of calls for culling and removal of crocs, which is a government decision, but until then the only way to make things safe is to educate about the dangers of crocs and how to operate. At the end of the day, we have to understand that it's their home too, and they were here long before we were.

For more on croc safety, see CrocWise: https:// nt.gov.au/emergency/community-safety/ crocodile-safety-be-crocwise/how-to-stay-safe.

Jim Jim Falls, Kakadu National Park, Northern Territory

Crocodile habitats in Australia

● Saltwater crocodile
● Freshwater crocodile

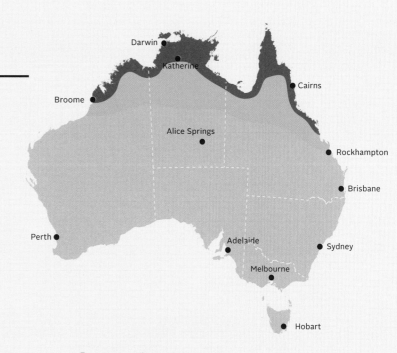

Darwin
Katherine
Broome
Cairns
Alice Springs
Rockhampton
Brisbane
Perth
Adelaide
Sydney
Melbourne
Hobart

Crocs by state

Northern Territory has the largest saltwater crocodile population, as a function of both geography and suitable habitat. Salties are present throughout the Top End, extending north from Mataranka. Management and surveying is very active, so you can swim with confidence in designated areas. If it is safe, there will be a sign. Otherwise, steer clear.

Western Australian populations are not as abundant or easy to access, being confined to the Kimberley region. The major tourist places are surveyed, but not always signed. Before swimming, ask a local if it is safe. In the western Kimberley, around the Dampier Peninsula and Broome, many people happily swim at the beach, despite the risk of crocs. If something is sighted they will close the beach in Broome, but it tends to be word of mouth further north. Again, if you are unsure, ask a local.

Queensland salties inhabit waterways from Cape Yorke to as far south as Maryborough. Popular beaches are regularly patrolled and will be signed if there have been any recent sightings. Beaches north of Port Douglas are very risky and swimming near shore should be avoided for the most part. Always chat to locals before jumping in the water north of Hervey Bay.

Best practices

○ Only swim in designated areas.
○ Avoid swimming in areas where crocodiles may live – rivers, streams or beaches near river mouths – even if there is no warning sign.
○ Ask locals where it is safe to swim.
○ Never provoke, harass, feed or otherwise interfere with a crocodile (even little ones).
○ Avoid places where animals and livestock drink.
○ Be extra careful around water at night.
○ Be extra careful during breeding season (September to April).

Salties vs freshies

Freshwater crocodiles are shy and elusive. If you have ever swum in the Top End, chances are you have been hanging out with these guys (even if you didn't know it). They generally keep to themselves and eat small critters such as fish, lizards, snakes and frogs. Like any wild animal, however, they will give you a warning bite if they feel threatened. If you see one, don't try to pat it on the head, take a photo, or give it a cuddle. Just leave it alone.

Saltwater crocodiles grow larger, live longer and will eat anything. Turtles, catfish, barramundi, you name it. They enjoy little critters as much as the next guy, but will also eat whatever comes to the water's edge for a drink – pigs, horses, cattle, Jonno, etc. Despite their name, they populate both freshwater and saltwater environments.

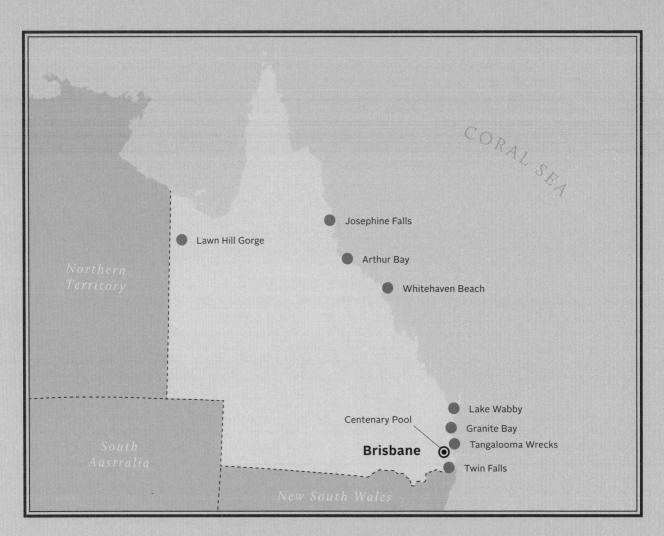

CORAL SEA

Josephine Falls

Lawn Hill Gorge

Northern Territory

Arthur Bay

Whitehaven Beach

Lake Wabby

Centenary Pool

Granite Bay

Tangalooma Wrecks

Brisbane

South Australia

Twin Falls

New South Wales

When to visit

Gold Coast to Bundaberg – Great year-round. Always busy during school holidays.

Bundaberg to Tropical North Queensland – Best from May to October. The weather is mild and you don't have to worry about stingers or floods.

Road-trip advice

This is one of the best places to free-camp; in fact, it is encouraged. There are numerous well-maintained rest stops north of Brisbane, all the way to Cape Tribulation.

Best meal

GAUGE
(*see* p. 165)

Favourite swim

JOSEPHINE FALLS
(*see* p. 149)

Stinger season

Marine jellyfish such as the Irukandji and box jellyfish are most active and copious from November to May. During this time, a stinger suit (see also unisex burkini, see also futuristic spacesuit) is recommended north of the Sunshine Coast.

Crocodiles

Very abundant north of Port Douglas, but present as far south as Maryborough. In this book we only recommend places that are known to be safe. While in north Queensland, always check for signs and ask locals if it is safe to swim (*see* p. 143 for more on crocodile safety).

Queensland

Let's get the long list of superlatives out of the way.

Queensland is the sand island capital of the world (*see* Fraser Island, p. 158, and Moreton Island, p. 162). It is home to the world's oldest continuously surviving tropical rainforest, the Wet Tropics (*see* Josephine Falls, p. 149). It houses much of the Great Artesian Basin, the world's largest and deepest freshwater basin (*see* Lightning Ridge, p. 10). It has the world's largest coral reef system, the Great Barrier Reef. Oh yes, and thanks to all the sunshine, it happens to be the skin-cancer capital of the world.

For a lot of us, Queensland exists as an idea as much as a place. It has always been a soft target for interstate sniping. Bogan. Banana bender. Troppo. Gold Coast. It's a place to vacation. As Melburnians, we are quick to rattle our sabre of sophistication whenever someone denigrates our home state's climate. Our personal biases skew towards the belief that the worse the weather, the better the culture. Therefore, a place with perfect weather would have to be one dimensional, right? Sunshine + winter = intellectual backwaters. It's a simple equation. Unfortunately, there is no such balance in the universe. Not only is Queensland home to many of Australia's most distinctive landscapes, it also houses our favourite gallery (GOMA, *see* p. 165) and restaurant (Gauge, *see* p. 165). Sorry, Melbourne.

Call it an affair, call it an epiphany, call it low expectations – we fell in love with this state. Though it is rightfully famous for beaches and islands, we were equally impressed by the waterfall-filled hinterland, crystal-clear rivers, rock pools, perched sand lakes and artesian baths. Queensland is an easy and welcoming place to travel, where people always have time for a chat (even the mechanics were in a good mood). Best of all, you can hardly drive an hour without passing a roadside fruit stand. We gorged on mango, lychee, papaya, dragon fruit and watermelon until our stomachs were swollen and aching. Then we ate some more.

GORGE

A GLORIOUS GREEN OASIS IN THE FAR REACHES OF THE
QUEENSLAND DESERT.

◐ **Best time to visit**
Dry season/winter (June to August),
when it's not too hot and you're
95 per cent guaranteed it won't rain.

◭ **How to get there**
You can approach from any cardinal
direction, but the least painful is via
Gregory. Follow signs from Gregory to
Adels Grove/Boodjamulla (Lawn Hill)
National Park (the road signs still hadn't
been updated with the new park name).
It's about 85km of unsealed road to Adels
and another 10km into the national park.

⊖ **Access**
Moderate. Conditions can vary and there
are a couple of stream crossings. 4WD
recommended for full confidence. Expect
corrugation and occasional potholes.
Take it slow and enjoy the serenity.

⑤ **Cost of entry** Free

☺ **Kid friendly** Yes

⊗ **Dog friendly** No

◠ **Water temperature** Cool (refreshing in
the desert heat)

◔ **Open** 24 hours

⊕ **Facilities**
Toilets, cold showers, camping (fees
apply; pre-book online), drinking water

◉ **Must bring**
A kayak, if you have your own. If you
don't, you can hire them from the
reception at both Adels Grove and
Lawn Hill Gorge.

LOCAL KNOWLEDGE

Aim to be there after 3pm when it is
much quieter – you might even have the
gorge all to yourself. A lot of people have
already left by then for afternoon drinks,
showers and to get dinner started.

Part and parcel of travelling on the open road for months on end is
doing our research along the way. That is, not just simply googling
in the car on the highway (though we do that too), but chatting to
people at every opportunity, especially those who might get as excited
as we do about driving days off course to find a far-flung oasis. Before
we arrived in Queensland, we'd asked other travellers around the
country about their most memorable swims. More often than not,
they mentioned Lawn Hill Gorge in Boodjamulla (Lawn Hill) National
Park, known by most as Lawn Hill.

Located in the remote north-west corner of Queensland, near
the NT boarder, Lawn Hill is a dusty trek from basically anywhere, so
you'll have to make a point of it by travelling through remote savannah
country. Before you get to the national park, you come to a small
town called Gregory River, home to a pub, a general store (nice coffee
and muffins too) and a famous stream in the gully with the clearest
water you will have seen in weeks. It's usually chock-a-block with grey
nomads who set up in fancy caravans at the free site.

There are two parts to Lawn Hill: the national park and a camp
site called Adels Grove. Adels is a 32-hectare privately owned property
with a fascinating history that involves an experimental botanical
garden early in the 20th century (look it up). It offers idyllic shaded
spots for campers, set on the banks of the river. Swimmers head for
the pontoon that floats in the middle, while others bob around in the
shallow communal swimming hole. This waterway winds down from
Boodjamulla National Park, like the eponymous Aboriginal serpent of
the Dreaming, who formed the gorge to keep his skin wet. From Adels
Grove it is then another rough 10-kilometre road into the park.

One of the joys of arriving at Lawn Hill Gorge is that you work so
hard to get here, ticking up kilometres in the outback. The other is that
you probably haven't seen a freshwater swimming hole for quite some
time. This is what blows us away. You travel through coastal places
where you can't swim because of crocs or jellyfish, and then through
this dry, barren land where not only do you find cool, shady places to
camp, but water that's incredibly beautiful, expansive, clear and green.
You can swim with no fear. It's literally an oasis.

Days can be spent in the national park, hiking up rocky red plateaus
through palm-fringed gorges to lookout points (Indarri and Duwadarri)
and gazing down to the spring-fed emerald-green water below, which
bubbles up from the Georgina Basin, then making your way back down
to the water to cool off. Calcium build-ups in the water form natural
dams, which divide pools with a few metres of overhanging greenery.
Water pours from the upper pools, creating beautiful waterfalls that
you can sit under. This is truly a picture of paradise, and we're certainly
not the only ones who think so. Just ask anyone you encounter on
the road.

NEARBY

UPPER GORGE WALK
Boodjamulla National Park

The 7-kilometre Upper Gorge Walk begins at the eastern end of the camping area, ascends a ridge and meanders along the edge of the gorge, offering spectacular scenery from two lookout points – Indarri and Duwadarri. These are real revelatory moments. The loop track returns along the creek edge where you can plunge into the water to cool off.

ADELS GROVE CAMPGROUND

Set in natural bushland in the shade of the Lawn Hill Creek, this serene camp site offers two areas to set up in: Top Campground, ideal for those with solar panels and pets, and the Grove, popular with family groups for its large shaded areas. All sites are unpowered and cost $18 per person per night. Adels Grove also offers permanent tents and cabins, a restaurant and hot showers.

GREGORY DOWNS HOTEL
150 Main St, Gregory

This pub has been an iconic stop in the old Savannah Way since the days of camelsconvoys and covered wagons. It's definitely worth a stop in to freshen up a dry mouth. Mid-strength lagers never seemed so appealing.

Josephine Falls

WOOROONOORAN
NATIONAL PARK, TROPICAL
NORTH QUEENSLAND

EMERALD WATER CREATES A
NATURAL WET'N'WILD PARK
AMONG GRANITE BOULDERS
AND TALL TREES.

WATERFALL ROCK POOL

Best time to visit
Anytime it isn't flooding. Most reliable from April to December, but can be great year-round.

How to get there
From Bruce Hwy take the well-signed turn onto Bartle Frere Rd (about 75km south of Cairns). Continue through sugarcane fields for 7km and turn right onto Price Rd, which dead-ends at the Josephine Falls carpark.

Access
Easy. Sealed roads into the carpark and paved, level paths to the water.

Cost of entry Free

Kid friendly Yes

Dog friendly No

Water temperature Cool

Open 24 hours

Facilities
Toilets

Must bring
Waterproof phone case – for taking photos of friends sliding down the boulders.

LOCAL KNOWLEDGE

An advertising company must have really run with the idea of 'refreshing': Paul Hogan and his offsider, Stropp, once filmed a Winfield menthol cigarette ad here, diving off near the falls. It may be the reason for Josephine Falls first coming into the spotlight. Look the ad up for a laugh.

One of the things that surprised us the most about Queensland was the state's inland swimming spots and waterfalls. We visited in the Wet season, which locals like to call 'waterfalls' season; it's a magical time, such a contrast to the island hopping you see in postcards, and gave us a different impression of Queensland than what we'd anticipated. We visited more waterfalls than we did beaches in the weeks we were here, spending days moving between mountainous, tropical hinterlands, down rainforest tracks and climbing over slippery rocks to see incredible plunging falls.

During this part of the trip, the weather was hot, and sunny (unusual during the Wet in a place that rains 250 days of the year). A friend from Sydney joined us in the van for our mobile mission – we'd promised him a weekend of swimming adventures. We were charged to find 'the one', and told him, despite the waterfall fatigue we were beginning to feel, that like love, when you know, you know. We'd spent the good part of a week zipping around the Atherton Tablelands, engaging in a bunch of casual encounters to entertain ourselves, but knew deep down that none of them was quite right. It wasn't until our friend's last day that we landed the real keeper: Josephine Falls.

It could only be described as lust when we laid eyes on this series of tiered granite rock pools and waterfalls just south of Cairns in Wooroonooran National Park. This lush mountainous land, right on the coast, covers 75,000 hectares of the Bellenden Ker Range and forms part of the Wet Tropics World Heritage area. The range includes Mt Bartle Frere, Queensland's highest mountain (1622 metres). Josephine Falls sits at the base, with a constant flow from streams that cascade down the mountain, creating some of the cleanest waterways in the world.

From the carpark, a paved path (about 700 metres) takes you through green vine forest of large leaves, buttressed tree roots, robust woody vines and basket ferns. Green spotted triangle butterflies flutter past iridescent blue Ulysses, while king parrots and rainbow lorikeets sit higher overhead, singing love songs to each other. It's a romantic place and we're totally seduced.

There are three spots to stop along this boardwalk. The first is where you get in to swim. We find people sitting and chatting in crystal-clear shallow pools, while others laze on big boulders in the dappled light. The biggest rock pool has a sandy bottom and is bordered by a giant piece of slippery granite that people are queueing up at to slide down, some wearing inflatable iced strawberry doughnuts. Scrambling further up takes you to more rocky slides into smaller pools, and families splashing about and fishing for yabbies.

The second stop is a deck that looks over the rock pools onto swimmers below. Continuing along the rainforest walk takes you to the third stop, a large viewing platform looking up to a flowing waterfall with a deep plunge pool. It's probably the most impressive of them all but, unfortunately, is not open to public swimming.

Our love affair turned tumultuous when we returned later that week, and some heavy Wet-season rains provided a very different setting. Water gushed ferociously downstream over the boulders we'd laid our towels on only days earlier. Swimming was closed and things looked rocky, but we were already smitten.

NEARBY

BABINDA BOULDERS

Babinda Boulders is a natural pool at the confluence of three streams among a group of boulders near the town of Babinda. When we visited, they'd just had the first rain of the Wet. The river was deep with cold rainwater rushing through lush, green rainforest and wrapping around giant granite boulders. It's the kind of landscape you don't get anywhere else in the country.

BABINDA INDEPENDENT BAKERY
35 Munro St, Babinda

On the way to the Boulders, a stop at the celebrated local bakery in the quaint town of Babinda is essential. Its slogan is 'Fresh and Fantastic'; certificates of appreciation cover the walls; and the staff all wear Hawaiian shirts. This may have been our favourite bakery experience in Queensland (and there were many). Try a sausage roll or the lamb and rosemary pie, and douse it in locally made jalapeño hot sauce, also sold by the bottle to take home.

MT BARTLE FRERE

Although the summit is lost in clouds eight days out of 10, it's a real feat to say you've climbed Queensland's highest mountain. Mt Bartle Frere reaches an elevation of 1622 metres, and the hike to the summit will take 10 to 12 hours. Camping overnight and doing it in two days is possible, and may make the climb more leisurely.

Arthur Bay

MAGNETIC ISLAND

A DRY TROPICAL ISLAND
WHERE YOU CAN'T HELP
BUT CHANNEL YOUR INNER
ROBINSON CRUSOE.

BEACH

Best time to visit
May to October

How to get there
From Townsville, a 25-minute passenger ferry regularly departs Breakwater Terminal, and a slower car ferry leaves from Ross St. Both arrive at Nelly Bay. Catch a bus towards Florence Bay and get off at the Forts stop. Walk down the hill via Radical Bay Rd to Arthur Bay (1km).

Access
Easy. Ferry and public transport to trailhead. A paved path will take you to the beach.

Cost of entry Free

Kid friendly Yes

Dog friendly No

Water temperature Like a warm bath

Open 24 hours during the Dry season

Facilities
None

Must bring
A plan. No camping on Magnetic Island, you'll need to arrange accommodation.

LOCAL KNOWLEDGE

Magnetic Island is surrounded by several shipwrecks, making it a popular place to dive. Sites at Florence Bay, Arthur Bay, Alma Bay, Geoffrey Bay and Nelly Bay, attract large schools of angelfish, sergeant majors, parrot fish, batfish and trevally.

We love finding places that are easy to access, yet still retain their wild beauty. Magnetic Island perfectly meets the brief. A 25-minute ferry from Townsville will land you on this relaxed, mountainous and secluded island. We arrived desperate for a dip, having spent the previous weeks around Cairns watching our favourite swimming holes become raging torrents and our towels transformed by mildew. What a relief to be in the 'dry tropics'. Sunshine and 30°C is what most people expect around here, and you are pretty much guaranteed to get it.

A single road winds its way along the perimeter of the island, with regular buses shuttling people between the four municipalities – Picnic Bay, Nelly Bay, Arcadia and Horseshoe Bay. It's easy to jump on and off as you please, getting close to your desired beach. There are 23 in total, but most can only be accessed by foot or boat. Despite the island being such a popular destination, there are so many spots to swim that you rarely share a beach with a more than a handful of people.

A short walk took us through open eucalyptus forests, past grunting koalas, down to Arthur Bay. To set the scene, the bay is bounded on both sides by granite headlands, where tall hoop pines find their footing among rounded boulders. A semi-permanent creek makes a natural wading pool at the back of the bay, shaded by pandanus trees. The main attraction, however, is the intense blue-green water of the beach. We were stinging for it by the time we reached the shore and our clothes have never come off so quickly. Underwater visibility is excellent here and we spent much of the day swimming around to the fringing reef on the north end of the bay.

Stepping back onto the sand, thoroughly contented, we saw an alternate life path unfold in front of us. In this world, we build a driftwood shack and live off the sea. Our long, sun-bleached hair tumbles in tight ringlets around our brown shoulders. Strong, sinewy, sun-spot-covered arms pull in the catch of the day. We live easily, nourished by abundant marine-turtle tails and koala jerky. It's a faultless, simple life until one of us succumbs to an entirely treatable infection. At this point, the reflection shimmers and we return to reality. Maybe we are better off just enjoying it as visitors.

NEARBY

BALDING BAY
The only bay on Magnetic Island's east coast that is not accessible by car (or the beach buggies everyone drives around here), Balding Bay is the calm, protected beach before the township in Horseshoe Bay. Follow a rocky track east to be rewarded by velvety soft sand and big granite boulders at either end of the pristine beach. There's a toilet here, but no drinking water.

MARLIN BAR
3 Pacific Dr, Horseshoe Bay

Horseshoe Bay's beachside strip is rowdy with locals and backpackers, and on weekends people spill from the doors at Marlin Bar, a popular place for a beer and a counter meal. The footy may be screening on one of the TVs in the main room, diverting some attention from the jovial atmosphere at the bar.

HORSESHOE BAY FISH AND CHIPS
1/6 Pacific Dr, Horseshoe Bay

A straight-up fish and chip shop serving seafood caught right out the front – barramundi, whiting or Spanish mackerel; battered, crumbed or grilled. Get yours to take away with a good serving of chips; pick up a longneck from the bottle shop and head to the beach to unwrap your hot newspaper package.

Stepping back onto the sand,
thoroughly contented, we saw
an alternate life path unfold ...

BEACH

Best time to visit
Winter (June to October). But November can bring 'glass out' days, where there is not a breath of wind and you can't see the horizon (a rare spectacle).

How to get there
Boat cruises leave from Airlie Beach to the island daily and there are tons of operators that cater to all levels of travel. Camping Whitsundays and Island Camping Connections offer drop-off/pick-up service to camping areas. Bookings essential for all. Check whitsundaycamping.com.au for more info.

Access
Difficult. Boat or helicopter. Most people come on an organised tour.

Cost of entry
Free to access the beach, but there are transport costs to get there.

Kid friendly
Yes

Dog friendly
No

Water temperature
Balmy

Open
24 hours

Facilities
Toilets (at the lookout between Tongue Beach and Betty Beach)

Must bring
Depending on the time of year, you may need to bring a stinger suit to swim. Stingers are more prevalent from November to May.

LOCAL KNOWLEDGE

The sand is so fine here you can polish your jewellery in it.

Whitehaven Beach

WHITSUNDAY ISLAND

THE WHITEST SAND IN THE WORLD, ELECTRIC-BLUE WATER AND BUSH CAMPING.

The third most photographed place in Australia, the second best beach in the world, the purest sand on Earth. Prestigious accolades roll off the tongue when you mention Queensland's sublime Whitehaven Beach. You've seen it on postcards, in magazines and Instagram feeds. But you haven't really seen it unless you've visited, taken a picture and captured it for your own social media audience. Seriously though, this place is off the hook, and we know why people flock here like seagulls to hot chips.

Sand is king at Whitehaven, and the reason it's so blinding is that it's made of almost 98 per cent silica – a mysterious geographical phenomenon that scientists can't explain. It's unique. None of the neighbouring beaches is anywhere near as glorious; most of them are made of broken coral. In fact, the closest contender for white sand is Fraser Island, whose silica content reaches only 60 per cent. An advantage of Whitehaven's whiteness is that the sand is so bright it reflects the sun and feels cool to walk on in the heat of the day. If you dig your toes in far enough it's actually cold. A disadvantage is that it's too cold for turtles to live and breed here. And for the final factoid on sand: it's illegal to remove it from Whitehaven Beach, and there is a $10,000 fine for anyone who does. They say if one person took a bottle of sand every day, in three years there'd be no beach left.

The most common way to access this incredible place is a daytrip via boat. Cruises leave daily from Airlie Beach, a tourist strip with little in the way of local vibes, but a high population of salty dogs. You'll arrive into Tongue Bay, from where you'll walk up to lookouts to do battle with other tourists vying for a view of Betty Beach below. Betty is where you'll swim in dazzling warm azure water. Depending on the time of year, you might be clad in a full-body stinger suit. Despite how unflattering you think they are for your beach pics, a stinger suit will allow you to swim in places where wearing sunscreen in the water is discouraged. From the beach, you'll be able to see over to Elk Island. Elk is rumoured to have the highest rate of death adders per square kilometre (which might be two, because it's a really small island – still scary though).

The best way to experience Whitehaven is to camp on Whitsunday Island for a few days. A ferry will drop you at the south end with all your gear and enough water for the duration of your stay. There are several camp sites available. All are highly sought after and allow walking between beaches, with exclusive access to Whitehaven outside of peak tourist times. Permits are essential.

Every day the tides around the Whitsundays change, and every day the sand moves. This means that every day the photos taken here will show slightly different swirls of blues, greens and whites. And though it's hard to imagine that you'll be so blown away by a place you've seen a thousand pictures of, rest assured, you will.

NEARBY

CHANCE TRAIL
Whitsunday Island

From Chance Bay a 3.6-kilometre one-way walking track will take you to Whitehaven Beach. Part of the Ngaro Sea Trail (one of Queensland's Great Walks), this section offers a secluded forest path to lofty peaks, perfect white-sand beaches and turquoise waters. And if you're camping at Chance Beach, you'll have uninterrupted access to it all.

SAWMILL BEACH CAMP
Whitsunday Island

Dugong Beach at Cid Harbour is one of the spots you can be dropped at to camp on the island. The shaded camp site here is popular with locals, but a 2.5-kilometre walking track will take you on to an even more exclusive spot at Sawmill Beach. The path leads you up through rainforest to views out over the beaches. You'll want to stay deserted on this island longer than Tom Hanks in *Castaway*.

THE SHED BAR
Nomads Airlie Beach,
354 Shute Harbour Rd

When in Airlie Beach, it's important to just embrace the tourist vibes, and the Shed might be the best place to do this. Located out the back of Nomads hostel, this open-air bar is known for good music and a friendly atmosphere. On any given day you will find a good intersection of locals and travellers swapping notes over a cold beer after a day out on the water.

LAKE

◔ **Best time to visit**
March to December. It's pretty much perfect year-round, but summer can bring of heavy rain and high temperatures.

◭ **How to get there**
From the main ferry terminal at River Heads (about 28km south of Hervey Bay) ferries take you to Kingfisher Resort or Wanggoolba Creek on Fraser's west coast. A direct, inland 4WD track runs from Kingfisher to Lake Wabby Lookout, then it's a short, steep hike to the lake. Drive across the island to Eurong, and turn left at the beach. Lake Wabby carpark is a further 8km drive to the north. From this trailhead, it's also a short, steep walk to the lake.

⊖ **Access**
Difficult. Hervey Bay is the main hub for accessing Fraser Island, but you can get a ferry from Inskip/Rainbow Beach. A 4WD is essential (for 4WD advice, see p. xi). All permits and fees must be purchased and displayed before arrival; sort these at Hervey Bay Visitor Info-Centre. Vehicle rental companies can organise all associated ferry, permit and camping fees.

⑤ **Cost of entry** Ferry return per person $58, per vehicle $110–200; vehicle access permit $48.20 (all subject to change)

☺ **Kid friendly** Yes

⊗ **Dog friendly** No

◠ **Water temperature** Warmish

◷ **Open** 24 hours

⊕ **Facilities** Toilets (at trailheads)

◉ **Must bring**
Tide charts and map of 4WD tracks. There is little phone service and you can't rely on it. Dust bin and brush to keep the car tidy.

LOCAL KNOWLEDGE

Saltwater is tough on cars so it's best to not drive on the beach within 2 hours of high tide. Also, never drive at night-time: dark 'coffee' rocks are almost impossible to see until you are on top of them.

Lake Wabby

A SHIMMERING OASIS IN A SEA OF SAND.

When we told people that we were writing a book about swimming, no name came up more frequently than Fraser Island. For two people who had never been, it felt like we were really getting our noses rubbed in it. Friends whom we thought had never travelled interstate suddenly dredged up childhood memories of white sand and clear water. Stories emerged of riding motorbikes naked on East Beach, training for triathlons in Lake McKenzie and burying a rental car at sea. Everyone loved Fraser, but nobody could agree which swimming hole was the very best. So we had to visit them all.

Needless to say, expectations were pretty high as we rolled off the barge. Our rental car, a gelded Suzuki Jimny, whizzed along like a child's toy. By the time we bogged ourselves, unstuck ourselves, and bogged ourselves again, we felt like we were really having the full experience. We quickly realised that despite being on an island (the world's largest sand island, to be precise), the best swimming would not be found at the beach. Fraser's top spots are in its perched lakes and spring-fed creeks scattered along the island's sandy spine. The beach is primarily a highway and the ocean an ever-looming threat – sharky, rippy and with tides that are constantly trying to pull you in. Apparently a couple of cars get written off here each month.

Our search eventually took us into the high sand blows to find Lake Wabby, where we immediately fell in love with this green gem surrounded by rolling dunes. It is hard to imagine that there would be any life up here, let alone an incredibly hospitable crescent of fresh water. This swim is the polar bear of our book – a uniquely threatened specimen that probably won't exist in 100 years. Prevailing easterly winds sweep across the island, causing the slow westward migration of Lake Wabby's dunes (in fact, all of Fraser Island is slowly moving closer to the mainland). The sand is gradually filling in this emerald lake, so every moment we spend here is precious.

Rainwater filters through the sand, suffusing Wabby with some of Australia's cleanest water. You can taste its sweetness on your lips and we couldn't help but take a couple of sips while swimming (we can't recommend you do this, of course, but we threw caution to the wind). As you move from the bank, the dune tapers away, quickly disappearing into the depths below. At 11.4 metres, this is the island's deepest lake. We spent the day watching clouds track across the sky, having the same conversation with other visitors: 'Isn't this the best!?' People coming and going, kids tumbling down the sand dunes or skidding along on bodyboards.

When our days on Fraser Island came to an end, we felt a great contentment knowing we had finally shared in this special place. Our trusted rental vehicle, now screeching and hissing like a feral cat, clawed its way back onto the barge. We collapsed into our seats and each raised a glass of $3 savvy b from the kiosk. 'Until next time,' we toasted.

LAKE MCKENZIE
Fraser Island

Probably Fraser Island's most legendary swimming spot, Lake McKenzie is busy with visitors, even on a bad day. The huge body of immaculate water spans 1200 metres by 930 metres. It is a perched lake, which means the surface lies considerably higher than nearby bodies of water. It also has bright white 60-per-cent silica sand, which is why the water here is clear, blue and so damn pretty.

ELI CREEK
Fraser Island

The largest sand island in the world has many swimming options. A float down Eli Creek with its gentle current is a popular one for swimmers of all levels. Some bring inflatable doughnuts. Once you get to the end (a few hundred metres), take the boardwalk back to the jump-in point and do it all again.

BAKERY IN EURONG
Fraser Island

The only bakery on the island, and therefore the best. After a couple of days spent trudging through sand, it seems like the best bakery in the world. Nothing out of the norm here – pies, sandwiches and cream-filled, iced sugary buns of various shapes and sizes. It does boast a $2 cinnamon doughnut though, which is the best bargain you'll find until you get back on the ferry (for $3 glasses of wine).

BEACH

Best time to visit
There is literally no bad time to visit. Avoid school holidays if you don't like to share.

How to get there
Park at Noosa National Park carpark or walk in from town. Follow the path 2km to the bay, which lies between Tea Tree Bay and Winch Cove. A short, steep track leads down to the beach.

Access
Easy. Paved path through Noosa National Park.

Cost of entry Free

Kid friendly Yes

Dog friendly No

Water temperature Cool

Open 24 hours

Facilities
Toilets, beach shower, cafe (all at trailhead)

Must bring
Sunglasses – the white sand can be glary.

LOCAL KNOWLEDGE

People often use the small rocks on Granite Beach to write things in the sand, like 'Hi Mum' or 'Wish you were here' or 'Places We Swim Rulz'. You can get a good photo from the track above.

Granite Bay

NOOSA NATIONAL PARK

ETERNAL SUNSHINE ON A SPOTLESS BAY.

We used to visit Noosa in the school holidays when we were kids. Back then, the main street had a handful of low-rise accommodation, one swimwear shop and one ice-cream shop. The air smelt like waffle cones, and tasted like salty salad rolls and sunscreen. We have a nostalgic feeling for the place. And though quite a few things have changed in this popular holiday town since the '90s, the national park is not one of them.

Noosa Main Beach may be famous for big crowds, gentle surf and a guy in a buggy that drives up and down the beach selling colourful frozen ice cones, but we like to find the more secluded spots. Follow the road as it weaves on under the cool rainforest canopy towards the national park. You will pass Little Cove, a tiny beach with longboarders and swimmers enjoying the protected waters. Leave your wheels when you reach the carpark; you're on foot from here.

The thing we love about Noosa National Park is that you can walk from end to end in one day (a rare thing in a country well covered by huge nature reserves). This path has a constant flow of walkers, runners and surfers carrying boards in. You get a sense that this national park is a real community asset. You could probably do the scenic coastal walk from the entry point to Sunshine Beach (10.8 kilometres return) in a morning, but why not take the day; pack lunch and stop at all the pretty beaches along the way.

Granite Bay is our favourite spot for a swim. It's the second of a series of protected, north-facing bays in the national park and, being that bit further in, it doesn't get as many people as popular Tea Tree Bay (the first). The beach is reached by a steep descent from the track, bordered by giant granite boulders and smaller, smooth rocks that collect on the fringes of the beach. A large rocky inlet on the south side provides some shaded spots for a few sunsmart beachgoers. The waves here lap calmly at the water's edge, providing easy entry and small waves to bodysurf right on to the sand – this is some kind of paradise.

Continue walking on towards Hell's Gate, past Winch and Picnic coves, stopping for a dip at Fairy Pool, a tiny rock pool that fills in at high tide. If you're lucky, you might spot some bodacious babes posing on the rocks with a selfie stick while you swim. Try not to disturb them and continue on your way after a plunge. Popular nude beach Alexandria Bay is the last stop along the scenic walk, a stretch of open beach where bare bottoms congregate at the southern end. Some say this is Queensland's favourite nude beach. Bathe unclad at 'ABay' before you continue on to pass Lion Head and hit Sunshine Beach, a surf beach that bookends the walk, where you'll turn around for the return journey (unless you prefer the bus back).

Though the region has seen a lot more foot traffic since we were here last, it's nice to know the best parts remain as good as we remember.

NEARBY

MASSIMO
75 Hastings St, Noosa Heads

After a walk through the national park, you deserve a treat. Locals and tourists queue here for creamy house-made gelato in traditional Italian flavours. This place has become a bit of an institution on Hastings Street, and its reputation is well earned. Make sure you get yours in a waffle cone.

LOCALE
62 Hastings St, Noosa Heads

A newcomer to the local strip, located at the base of the infamous 200-stair trail, Locale serves modern Italian food in a plush corner setting. There's a focus on local produce here, so don't be surprised to see Mooloolaba prawns, Fraser Island crab and Bangalow pork in various dishes. Since you're near the sea, order the squid-ink handkerchief pasta without a second thought.

VILLAGE BICYCLE
6/16 Sunshine Beach Rd, Noosa Heads

Just up the hill in Noosa Heads, Village Bicycle is a neighbourhood bar and restaurant serving food late into the night. With a surfy, dive-bar feel, this lo-fi haunt stands out (in a good way) in this bouji holiday town. It serves local beer on tap, American beers in bottles and cans, and booze-appropriate food like tacos, poutine and burgers from the kitchen.

BEACH

◔ **Best time to visit**
From June to December for the best underwater visibility, but there is no bad time to visit.

⊘ **How to get there**
Tangalooma Island Resort passenger ferry service for daytrippers and hotel guests departs Pinkenba (220 Holt St). Moreton Island Adventures operates a vehicle barge and passenger ferry from Port of Brisbane (14 Howard Smith Dr). Both can be booked online.

⊖ **Access**
Ferry or private boat only. Tracks on the island are all sand 4WD, but you can get around comfortably on foot to most major destinations and easily swim to the wrecks.

$ **Cost of entry** Adults $70-plus (return), depending on which ferry you take and if you bring a car.

☺ **Kid friendly** Yes

⊗ **Dog friendly** No

⌒ **Water temperature** Warm

🕐 **Open** 24 hours (note: night swimming is not recommended)

⊕ **Facilities**
Toilets, picnic tables, camping (book online), restaurants (Tangalooma Island Resort guests/visitors only)

🤿 **Must bring**
Snorkel, mask and fins, for obvious reasons. Goggles will be enough if you are hard pressed.

LOCAL KNOWLEDGE

Camping on Moreton Island is the best value and easiest way take it all in. The Wrecks campground is about 50 metres back from the snorkeling site and even has a wi-fi hotspot.

Tangalooma Wrecks

MORETON ISLAND

FIFTEEN SHIPS, THOUSANDS OF FISH, 20 METRES FROM THE SHORE.

What's that thing they say about one person's trash? The Queensland government thought little of the outcome when they decommissioned and sunk 15 vessels off the western shore of Moreton Island. The intention was to create a breakwater and safe harbour for boats, which is exactly what they accomplished. However, the unintended result was wildly more successful. Coral, requiring a hard surface on which to adhere, found an unlikely ally in the steel hulls, and rapidly began to populate the wrecks. With the coral, came small fish, which led to larger fish, groper, turtles, wobbegong sharks and stingrays. The ships have transformed into a thriving reef ecosystem and are now home to some of Australia's most interesting and accessible snorkelling.

A 75-minute ferry from Brisbane will land you on the world's third largest sand island, with the world's largest coastal sand mountain. If you are having trouble keeping track of the superlatives, so are we. In our opinion, they were reaching a little too far to rank this place on its sandiness, though there is certainly a lot of it. Like any tropical island, Moreton possesses postcard beaches. Like any tropical Australian beach, it is a classic scene complete with endless tinnies and inflatable sea creatures. The real attractions, however, are in the water.

A deep, narrow gutter separates the beach from 600 metres of continuous wreck. Depending on the tide, the current will sweep you along the channel and past the ships at a steady pace. Observe which direction people are drifting before jumping in. If you don't get to see enough on one pass, simply walk back to the start and jump in for another lap. It's about as easy as snorkelling gets; you don't even need flippers.

Use common sense while exploring and keep in mind that you are swimming among ageing, rusted metal. Huge mechanised cogs tower above the water; giant sand-mining bucket loaders are frozen mid-rotation; and tight schools of tropical fish swirl around barnacle-encrusted propellers – always close but somehow never within reach. Every angle and depth offers a new revelation. It feels like you're discovering the *Titanic*. Surely, if you find the right opening or window, there will be a double staircase and ballroom. Is that a car with a handprint on the window?

NEARBY

BLUE LAGOON
Moreton Island

The purest sand-filtered water can be found at this huge lake on the eastern side of Moreton Island. A popular swimming spot, accessible by 4WD only, it is also the island's water source. Some say this is the freshest water they've tasted, filled by the fresh, underground watertable that comes up through the sand.

MT TEMPEST
Moreton Island

Tempest is considered to be the highest coastal sand mountain in the world, reaching an impressive 285 metres above sea level. It's a steep climb through the sand, but these dunes are also one of the most impressive features on the island, and reveal sweeping 360-degree views over a sandy desert landscape from the top.

THE GUTTER BAR
21 Kooringal Espl, Kooringal, Moreton Island

Located on the southern tip of the island in Kooringal, the Gutter Bar is less feral than it sounds, which is good as it's the best bar on the island. It's only open until 6pm on weekends (4pm weekdays), so you've got to get in early for schooners and screenings of daytime footy games (the crowd can get rowdy).

POOL

🌓 **Best time to visit**
Weekdays after work

◭ **How to get there**
400 Gregory Tce, Spring Hill

⊖ **Access**
Easy. Central location and abundant
free parking.

⑨ **Cost of entry** Adults $5.50, kids $4

☺ **Kid friendly** Yes

⊛ **Dog friendly** No

⌾ **Water temperature** Heated; a warm mix
of salt and chlorinated water.

🕐 **Open** Mon–Thurs 5am–8pm, Fri 5am–
6pm, Sat–Sun 7am–6pm, public holidays
9am–5pm (closed Christmas Day and
Good Friday)

⊕ **Facilities**
Toilets, hot showers, cafe

🅐 **Must bring**
Money for an ice-cream

LOCAL KNOWLEDGE

An underwater observation room sits
below the pool deck, giving viewers an
exclusive vantage over swimmers in the
water, like looking out at them from a
submarine window. Unfortunately this
room is not currently open to the public,
but look out for the portal window
underwater on the north side of the
lap pool.

Centenary Pool

BRISBANE

A CULTURALLY SIGNIFICANT OUTDOOR PUBLIC POOL
IN THE HEART OF BRISBANE THAT HAS A *JETSONS* FEEL
ABOUT IT.

Few public pools make the cut for the best places to swim in Australia (in this book anyway). Not because we didn't check them out, nor because there aren't hundreds of great ones all over the country. Largely it's because they're all quite similar, most failing to offer something particularly distinctive to set them apart. The best swimming spots generally fall into one of three (or all three) categories – they must be either culturally significant, crazy beautiful or unique. Somehow, we believe this entirely human-built inner-city swimming spot ticks all those boxes.

The Centenary Pool complex is important for a number of reasons. Contrary to popular belief, its name has very little to do with its age; rather it was named during the centenary of Brisbane. The iconic structure, opened in 1959 and now heritage listed, was designed by renowned Queensland architect James Birrell. The project gave Brisbane its first 50-metre pool and high diving board, and remains one of the city's principal aqua-sports centres. But it was the innovative concept to house a fine-dining restaurant in the cantilevered building that raised the pool's status above that of mere sports facility – giving swimmers a place to splash out after their swim and dine with water views. These days, the structure has traded in white tablecloths for sweat towels, and is now home to the health club and gym.

Centenary Pool is operated by the Rackley family, who run the biggest learn-to-swim program in Australia. It's a swimming empire and the complex here is world class. The Olympic-size pool can be divided into two 25-metre sections for swimming classes and training at peak times. There is a wading area for kids and a multi-tiered diving pool, with boards at 1, 3, 5, and 10 metres. The top level has been out of action for more than a year now, but kids bounce off the lower springboards, while others creep along the 5-metre platform with trepidation, like they're walking the plank of a pirate ship.

Though its Modernist design still feels modern today – like something out of *The Jetsons* – Centenary Pool has had a few upgrades, and is now one of those rare pools you could comfortably stay at all day. In fact we spent and an entire afternoon going back and forth from the shaded seating to the water, before herds of kids arrived from school – a colourful mini Olympic team in training. Like many public spaces in urban areas, this one is full of life, and at times feels like the epicentre of the community.

NEARBY

SPRING HILL BATHS
14 Torrington St, Spring Hill,
Brisbane

Built in 1860, the Spring Hill Baths are
Australia's oldest original in-ground
pool, which means its design has not
been altered since it was built. This
might explain its obscure length: 23
yards (21 metres). With grandstand
seating and colourful private
changing rooms that border the pool
like English seaside beach boxes, the
building is a heritage-listed icon and
utterly charming. Despite its age and
classic stylings, the baths do have
some modern features, including a
semi open-air roof, making the space
feel both outdoors and sheltered.

QAGOMA
Stanley Pl, Southbank, Brisbane

When we first visited Queensland
Art Gallery | Gallery of Modern Art
(GOMA) we were blown away. This
is one of the best contemporary art
galleries in the country, and most of
the collection is free. Blockbuster
exhibitions celebrate expansive works
by Patricia Piccinini, Cai Guo-Quiang,
Yayoi Kasuma, Gerhard Richter and
Tracey Moffatt, and there are shows
by local artists such as Noel McKenna,
with his idiosyncratic maps.

GAUGE
77–79 Grey St, South Brisbane

Just across the road from GOMA,
and an ideal spot for lunch, Gauge
is a small, sophisticated cafe with
an inventive menu, and some of the
most impressive cafe-style food
we've eaten in Brisbane. The space is
filled mostly by one large, communal
table, and an open kitchen looks
out onto diners eating dishes such
as blood tacos or prawns splashed
with sesame milk. Gauge also serves
Supreme coffee, and opens for dinner
a few nights a week.

WATERFALL ROCK POOL

◖ **Best time to visit**
The water is surprisingly cold, so it is best to visit during those epic, hot, sticky summer days from November to March.

◬ **How to get there**
Springbrook plateau is 24km from Mudgeeraba or 36km from Nerang. Exit the Pacific Mtwy at Mudgeeraba (exit 79 from the north, exit 80 from the south) and follow Gold Coast–Springbrook Rd. Follow signs to Springbrook National Park.

⊖ **Access**
Easy. Parking at trailheads. Well-defined walking tracks.

$ **Cost of entry** Free

☺ **Kid friendly** Yes

⊗ **Dog friendly** No

◠ **Water temperature** Refreshing

🕐 **Open** 24 hours

⊕ **Facilities**
Toilets, picnic area, BBQ (all at trailhead)

🍴 **Must bring**
Your best chat if you're doing the long hike.

LOCAL KNOWLEDGE

Springbrook National Park is home to Australia's largest population of glow worms. Check out the night tours at Natural Bridge where the little larvae light up like stars in the dark.

Twin Falls

SPRINGBROOK NATIONAL PARK,
GOLD COAST HINTERLAND

WATERFALLS AND ROCK-POOL CASCADES NESTLED IN A COOL MULTI-STOREY RAINFOREST.

This is not the Gold Coast that you think you know. It certainly wasn't what we had in our minds. The entire hinterland, extending from Coffs Harbour up through the Sunshine Coast, is one of the most ancient and diverse wilderness areas in the country. This landscape inspired the classic movie *Fern Gully* and is the last remnant of rainforests that once covered the entire Gondwana supercontinent (Australia, Antarctica, India, and parts of Africa and South America). You could spend a lifetime hiking the region's volcanic peaks and swimming in pure spring water among tropical waterfalls and streams. All this within 30 kilometres of Surfers Paradise.

Despite its proximity to some of the busiest places in the country, Twin Falls and Springbrook National Park remains one of the least utilised wilderness areas in Queensland (probably for the better). It's not so much that it is a secret, just that the prevailing culture is so dominated by the beach that no one ever thinks to turn their head to the western horizon. Those that do discover that the fringe of coastal chaos quickly dissolves into suburban blocks, and then into hobby farms. Literally within 10 kilometres inland you are surrounded by dense, sleepy, primordial rainforest. The road climbs high into the volcanic plateau, through the hamlet of Springbrook to the Tallanbana picnic area, the jumping-off point for some of our favourite swims.

Twin Falls is a 1-kilometre walk down from the carpark, passing a couple of small waterfalls along the way. As the name suggests, the flow plunges in two dramatic sections. The pool below is a wide, deep oval, surrounded by flat boulders. Green is the overwhelming colour, with life bursting from every conceivable surface. Maidenhair ferns hang from the cliff-face, iridescent green moss covers the rocks, and ancient tree ferns tower overhead, drinking the mist of the falls. You can't help but be transformed into an amphibian here, moving back and forth between the pool and the rocks, watching a steady flow of people come and go.

Although you could happily spend a day here, massaging your back under the waterfall, we love to venture deeper into the canyon along the Warrie circuit track. The 17-kilometre distance scares most people away, so you are all but guaranteed to have it to yourself (averagely fit, active people should allow about 5 hours with swims). The loop is essentially a wet hike, passing under the cool rainforest canopy past seven waterfalls. At the midpoint, Meeting of the Waters, there are endless rock pools filling the valley floor – all of which demand a nudie swim. We couldn't help ourselves. Complete the circuit with a view of Surfers Paradise at Canyon Lookout. It's hard to believe two such contrasting environments can exist in the same place, but we are grateful to have both options.

COUGAL CASCADES
Springbrook National Park

A fragment of the national park only 21 kilometres' drive from Currumbin Beach. Follow Currumbin Creek Road up a beautiful valley until it dead-ends at the Cougal Cascades carpark. Walk the creek as far as you can; there are rock pools the whole way. Locals claim the morning session, so wait until 9am as a courtesy.

DANCING WATERS CAFE
33 Forestry Rd, Springbrook

A quaint cottage cafe with leafy views right next to the Purlingbrook Falls lookout and walking tracks. This vegetarian cafe offers a wholesome seasonal menu with veggie, vegan and gluten-free meals, such as hearty bowls of soup, toasties, burritos, nachos and house-made scones and cakes.

THE LOST FAWN CAFE
2319 Springbrook Rd, Springbrook

Nestled in the shadow of the forest, this is another local spot for breakfast and lunch. The classic big breakfast is a strong start before a long hike, as is the stack of fluffy blueberry pancakes with ice-cream and maple syrup; or drop in for a burger and a milkshake for lunch. On Sunday evenings there's live music and dinner.

Aqua English Instructor

SARAH SCARCE

Sarah Scarce never knew how popular her project would be when she launched Aqua English in 2006, a program to teach refugees and others speaking English as a second language (ESL) to swim. She certainly never expected that people would be bribing her with traditional African tea, cake and curry to get into her classes.

Sarah is an immigration lawyer who started Aqua English after she found that the primary victims of drowning fatalities and injuries around January were ESL speakers. So she partnered with the Brisbane and Gold Coast city councils to see what they could do. The program now receives permanent funding throughout the year to run classes at public pools around Brisbane and the Gold Coast for just the cost of pool entry for students.

Aqua English targets refugees and new arrivals into Australia, getting them swimming and helping them with the language spoken around the water. Things as simple as reading and understanding signs at the pool can be really foreign to a lot of people. Being able to have a conversation with a lifeguard, understanding their role, or simply having the confidence to come into a public pool in the first instance, paying the pool entry and starting that conversation, can be challenging. Aqua English provides a platform that introduces students to the pool, with the hope that after eight weeks they will be able to start coming by themselves and enjoy it.

We met Sarah before one of her classes at the Yeronga Park Pool in Brisbane one Saturday morning in January to chat about the program.

Since 2006, Aqua English has had 25,000 people swim with the program.

WE'RE AN ISLAND NATION AND WE HAVE A HUGE BEACH CULTURE, SO IT'S IMPORTANT THAT EVERYONE UNDERSTANDS HOW WE SPEAK AROUND THE WATER.

Q. Is the program something you initiated?
A. Yes. My mum is an English-language teacher and my background is in immigration law, so we're always drawn towards helping ESL speakers, migrants and refugees.

Q. What does the program involve?
A. We ask for 6 hours per person, and we get them to float, hop in the pool safely and identify the signs, develop some movement for about 5 metres and, if we're lucky, tread water. With 8 to 10 hours we need to get them treading water, which is integral, because when you see the 'swim between the flags' sign at the beach, it says put your hand up for help, but you can't do that when you're floating. You have to be able to tread water, so we're trying to fill in the gaps for people.

Q. What are the backgrounds of the majority of people that come here?
A. Majority outreach has been to women, so it sits at 70 per cent women, 30 per cent men. It wasn't deliberately targeted towards women, but when we broke down the stats, they are primary caregivers, so they are the ones most likely to have the children with them. They need to know how to keep watch and adequately supervise. Some of our communities have an average of about five to seven children per family, whereas the Australian average is 2.3, so that's a lot of supervision for one person who can't swim. We've had people from probably 35 to 40 different cultures – Afghani, Iraqi, Iranian, Persian, African, Sudanese, Somalian, Ethiopian, Burundian, Rohingya, Burmese, Thai, Vietnamese – we have a big outreach.

Q. What's the age group here?
A. For this group today we've targeted adults deliberately, so we say 16-plus, but we do make concessions if we've got mothers and daughters who want to have a go. Our oldest is 96, but our youngest has been six.

Q. Are you able to measure the impact of the program?
A. When we target one mum we know that mum is going to go back to her five children and will teach them and get them involved in swimming lessons, and then she will eventually drag her husband down to the water by his ears and get him to do swimming lessons. So that one person we teach at least outreaches to two, and then they can adequately supervise. But it's always been very popular. When I started at Yeronga, I asked one of our partners – IWAA (formerly Iraqi Women's Association of Queensland (IWAQ)) – to bring some ladies down to the pool. On the first day 25 ladies came down, which was my capacity. After that, if anyone was sick, other ladies would find out and try to slot in, or a lot of them would start baking. I wanted to accommodate them, but I didn't have the space, so they were trying to barter their way in with all this food.

Q. What were they making?
A. Oh, we had rice; the Africans do traditional coffee or tea; then we had cake, injera (traditional fermented bread), curries. I never had to worry about packing lunch.

Q. How do you moderate cultural differences like modesty and dress in the water?
A. It's difficult. To get some women in the water initially, I got my mother-in-law to sew curtains and we would set them up around the indoor pool to make things private. It was a method of breaking down a barrier, to get them into the water and feeling comfortable, until we could transition them to Islamic or modest swimwear, and then get them out in public. At the time when Islamic swimwear came to the market it was unattainable: at $260 a garment, it wasn't affordable for most people. We wanted people to get into the water, but they couldn't get in without something on and they couldn't wear clothes because they'd sink. So we did six months of this curtained area and that got them into the water, and then we transitioned them, taking down the curtain slowly – now it's not a problem. Once they feel comfortable and make that connection with the water, it's very hard to stop them from swimming.

Q. Why do you think swimming is so central to Australian culture?
A. We're an island nation and we have a huge beach culture, so it's important that everyone understands how we speak around the water, what we wear, what we do and why we embrace it so much. We explain this to our students. In Queensland, in particular, we have so many pools; every second backyard has a pool. Even if you don't want to swim, there's no way in hell you can keep your kids out of the water, especially growing up in Brisbane. There's a fine line between having to embrace swimming, and wanting to embrace it. I come from Tasmania originally and we still have a water culture down there, even though it's freezing. It's just the way it is in Australia.

Find out more about Aqua English at http://aquaenglish.com.au

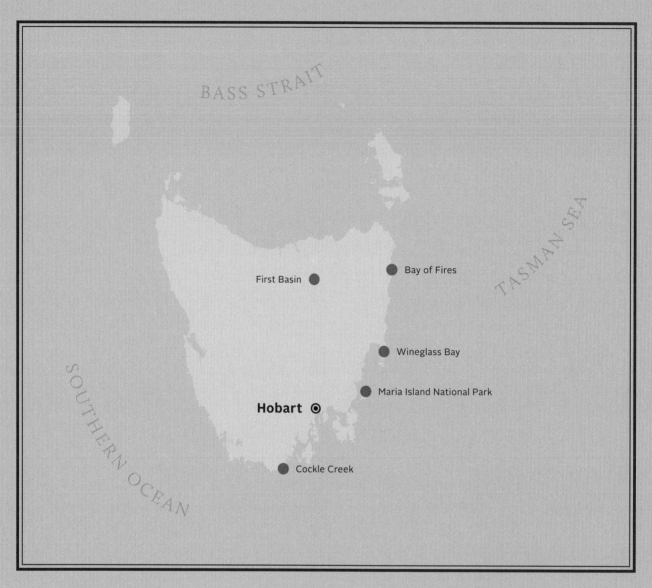

BASS STRAIT

TASMAN SEA

First Basin

Bay of Fires

Wineglass Bay

Maria Island National Park

Hobart ◉

SOUTHERN OCEAN

Cockle Creek

When to visit

December to May

Favourite swim

WINEGLASS BAY
(*see* p. 179)

Yes, we know this seems too obvious.
But it really is that great.

Road-trip advice

Bringing your own car is by far the easiest, best and most affordable way to visit Tasmania. The state has abundant free camping and great infrastructure for independent travellers. Be mindful that the *Spirit of Tasmania* ferry fills up months in advance. Book as early as possible, especially if you have a high vehicle.

A national-parks pass is essential: a Holiday pass is valid for eight weeks ($60 per vehicle or $30 per person/motorbike) or there's an Annual pass available ($96 per vehicle, $76.40 concession) giving access to all parks.

Best meal

SUMMER KITCHEN BAKERY
(*see* p. 183)

Tasmania

There is something about Tasmania that is immediately relaxing and comfortable.

Every time we arrive here, we experience a profound feeling of ease. A suspension of pretense and an elevation of authenticity. Despite the cool climate, or perhaps because of it, the island is home to the warmest people. Locals always seem to have time for a chat and are sincerely eager to share their favourite places. They brim with pride at Tassie's natural beauty and are justified in their near unanimous belief that it is the best state. You can take a deep dive into its fine food culture or live quite comfortably on flathead and apples alone. Tasmania is a pleasure to explore and small enough that you never seem to be far from a great swim.

We searched the state from coast to coast, top to bottom, east to west. From alpine lakes to conjoined islands, to serpentine rivers, to towering dams – every place is perfect, on a good day. However, consistency is what we strive for and the right conditions are all the more important here. As many would guess, the water is cold. Furthermore, where Victoria has mastered four seasons in one day, Tasmania has refined that art to one hour, so the curation process was all the more important.

We processed our field data using our patented algorithm: western Tassie – lush, rainy, wild. Central Tassie – mini New Zealand, mountainous, snowy. East coast – dry, sunny, predictable. Our computation yielded a strong east-coast bias. Thanks to the rain shadow cast by the Central Highlands, weather fronts that roar onto the west coast are often toothless and depleted by the time they reach the east, so you can have confidence that almost any month of the year will produce stunning days and perfect swims there.

If you like white sand and perfectly clear water, this is the place for you. If you like going to the beach but not sharing it with other people, this is the place for you. If you like the immune-boosting power of cold water, this is the place for you. Tasmania may not be the biggest nor most celebrated state but it has a reputation for distinguished quality, and its swims are no exception.

Bay of Fires

NORTH-EAST COAST

A PROTECTED BAY OF
GLISTENING BEACHES WITH
THE SOLITUDE OF A DESERTED
ISLAND. #HEAVEN

TASMANIA

BEACH

Best time to visit
February and March is when the water is at its warmest.

How to get there
The beach is well signed from St Helens. Follow Binalong Bay Rd (C850) 10km to a junction. Turn left on Gardens Rd to enter Bay of Fires Conservation Area. Choose from many beach turn-offs along the way (it's 6km to Cosy Corner). Or continue straight to Binalong Bay township and beach (2.5km).

Access
Easy. There is abundant parking along the bay and walks are short to the beach. Rock scrambling difficulty may vary.

Cost of entry Free

Kid friendly Yes

Dog friendly Yes. Dogs are allowed on the beach here but there are some time restrictions. Check signs before unleashing your hound.

Water temperature Cold

Open 24 hours

Facilities
Toilets

Must bring
Rubbish bags – there are no bins here. Carry out what you bring in.

LOCAL KNOWLEDGE

This region is home to some of the freshest, most abundant crustaceans in the state. Make sure you tap into this bounty while you're here.

We are of the opinion that Tasmania is home to the best beaches in Australia, and though it might be hard for some to reconcile, going north isn't always the answer to our sandy desires. We take a trip to Tassie annually each March – some say the best time of year to visit, after the rush and before it gets too cold – and each time we discover more to love about this state. It is at once a forgotten land and a celebration of remote beauty. It is also a place where you can fully relinquish the demands of phone reception. It's amazing to think this place is the same size as the entire country of Sri Lanka. Only the population is about 40 times smaller, which leaves wide open expanses of beach for just a few cool-water swimmers.

The Bay of Fires (larapuna) is a favourite holiday destination for visitors and locals alike. Beach houses and shacks are dotted up the coast from Binalong and St Helens to The Gardens, where the road ends at a cattle station. No doubt sleepy places to live for most of the year, these fishing towns swell in the summer, as Tasmanians make their way to the coast – their version of Victoria's Lorne or Apollo Bay.

Binalong Beach is arguably one of the country's most beautiful town beaches. We wonder how locals could ever be impressed by another stretch of sand. This water is comparable to iconic beaches in Queensland and WA, but has none of the scary sea creatures. It does have a chill though, something that motions swimmers into wetsuits for most of the year.

From Binalong Bay, take Gardens Road into Bay of Fires Conservation Area and to more brilliant beaches: Eden, Jeanneret, Swimcart and – our pick – Cosy Corner. Each stop has free camp sites with a 30-day maximum stay, so there's always a healthy number of caravans and motorhomes pitched up by the water – white beacons along the coast. Some visitors fish off the rocks while others clamber over the giant lichen-covered granite. In fact, it was the red lichen that carpets the rocks that we first thought the iconic bay was named after. We later found out the name Bay of Fires is derived from early sailors' observations of the dunes lit up by the fires of local Pakana people.

Swimmers can take the opportunity to plunge into refreshing, clear water, and relish in the magnificence of the surrounds. In our minds, this is something you cannot miss. Encounters with sea life are possible too. This region is home to Australia's best seafood – think crayfish, crabs and scallops in abundance just off the rocks. And with water temperatures usually a few degrees warmer than neighbouring Freycinet, we'd be surprised if it wasn't also the swimming capital of Tasmania.

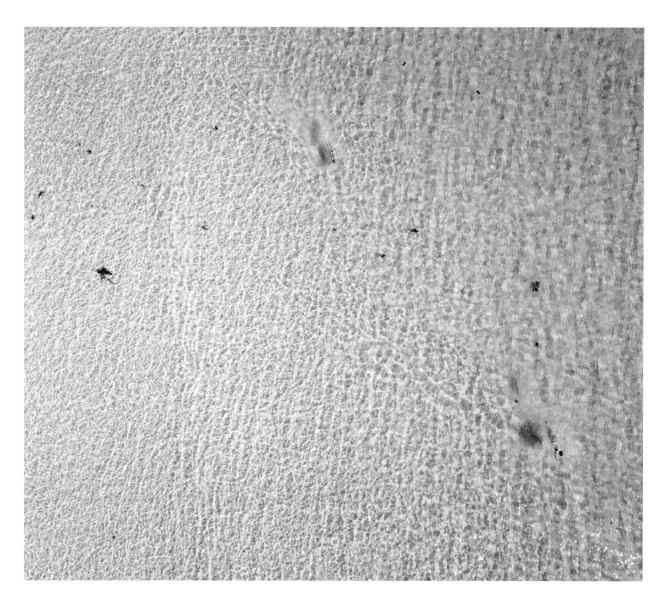

NEARBY

ST HELENS BAKERY
8 Cecilia St, St Helens

Because this region is known for its quality seafood, it might seem sacrilegious to put scallops in a pie and curry them. But no-frills town bakeries like St Helens' are as important to any Australian road trip as bringing your swimsuit. Don't miss this culinary delight.

PYENGANA DAIRY COMPANY (THE TASMANIA FOOD CO)
St Columba Falls Rd, Pyengana

This may not be your first encounter with Pyengana cheese in Tasmania; it's stocked in stores around the state. It is made by a fourth-generation dairy farmer known for his rich, creamy unhomogenised milk and cloth-bound cheddar. Visiting the dairy is like a cellar-door experience for cheese – sample different seasonal cheeses and pick up a few to take with you.

BAY OF FIRES LODGE WALK

A four-day hike though the Mt William National Park, exploring the stunning Bay of Fires coastline. Guided tours include accommodation in luxury tents and lodges along the way, catered meals and days filled with hiking, kayaking and swimming. Adventure meets luxe. Bookings are essential.

POOL   **GORGE**

☽ Best time to visit
From December to March (the water
is warmest February to March).

⌂ Address
74–90 Basin Rd, West Launceston;
74 Gorge Rd, Trevallyn

⊖ Access
Easy. Carparks on Basin Rd and Gorge Rd
($5 for eight hours). Alternatively, walk
up the gorge from Kings Bridge.

$ Cost of entry Free

☺ Kid friendly Yes

⊗ Dog friendly No

⌒ Water temperature Cold

◷ Open 24 hours (pool open from October
to Easter only)

⊕ Facilities
Cafe, restaurant, toilets, hot showers

⊚ Must bring
Baby oil to lather on your body for
warmth when swimming in the river
(and to blend in with the locals).

LOCAL KNOWLEDGE

The Basin has inspired many myths
about its depth: some locals say it is a
bottomless pit; a volcanic plug; or that
a submarine sent in to find its bottom
during the 1960s ran out of cable before
accomplishing this feat. However,
measurements in 2011 found the
maximum depth is 36 metres.

First Basin

CATARACT GORGE, LAUNCESTON

A PICTURESQUE GORGE WITH A 1930S LIDO-STYLE POOL,
A NATURAL RIVER BASIN AND A CHAIRLIFT SAILING
OVERHEAD.

First Basin in Cataract Gorge was our first stop after arriving into
Devonport on the *Spirit of Tasmania*. It was hard to believe that
we were going to be uncovering anything new right in the middle of
Launceston, but it turns out Australia's third-oldest city is home to a
unique natural land formation on its fringes.

Arriving at Cataract Gorge had us feeling like we'd just stumbled
upon a summer alpine holiday village, with its lido-style pool, natural
water basin and a weir with rocks to bask on and jump off, plus a two-
seater chairlift sailing overhead. Your first glance will likely be from
above, where you look out towards the gorge, as far as a suspension
bridge in the distance. In the foreground below is the bright-blue
50-metre pool, with a backdrop of the South Esk River running
between rocky gorge walls, hiking trails and landscaped gardens. It's
bloody beautiful, and rather quaint.

To see the place in its fullest, do the loop walk that takes you from
the pool, over the suspension bridge, past the Basin Cafe (where you'll
probably meet some resident peacocks), down through the gorge along
the flat path, then across Kings Bridge at the road and up the zigzag
path back to the Gorge Restaurant. The return journey will get your
heart ticking, so stop at the lookouts for a breather and take in the
painting-like views.

By then, you'll be warm enough for a swim. The pool in the basin
may appear to be the shallowest in Tasmania, with a minimum depth
of 0.2 metres, but it does get deeper. Half the pool is for wading; the
other half – a large, open area (up to 1.5 metres deep) – is for laps.
Tiered concrete-step seating winds round the sides, and beyond that
are rolling grassy parklands. You can imagine hundreds of visitors
gathering here on busy summer weekends.

The river running through the gorge is also great for swimming.
A group of locals swim daily in the afternoons when the sun is on the
water (roughly between 4.30pm and 5pm). They chat at the banks,
covering themselves with baby oil before plunging into the dark water,
cutting laps across the middle, which spans 187 metres. They tell us
the oil helps to keep their muscles warm and prevent cramping, but in
summer we think they might also be working on their tans.

Sunsets in Launceston are legendary, so stay a little later if you can.
Or watch from a kayak as you paddle downstream and spill out into
the Tamar River; it'll be too cold to swim here when the sun goes down.

NEARBY

SAINT JOHN CRAFT BEER BAR
133 St John St, Launceston

A beloved gathering place and bar with a huge variety of beer, wine, cider and spirits: there's a constantly changing selection of 14 craft brews on tap (international, Australian and Tasmanian) and even more in bottles. At lunch you can BYO food, or order something from the food van out the back.

STILLWATER
2 Bridge Rd, Launceston

The stalwart of elegant casual dining in Launceston. The restaurant, housed in a renovated flour mill at the edge of the Tamar River, offers an all-day menu with a focus on Tasmanian producers. Think berries laced through desserts in summer, Southern Ocean seafood such as snapper and abalone in main dishes, and local wines to match. In 2018 the space that was the providore and gallery was transformed into boutique accommodation.

WINES FOR JOANIE
163 Glendale St, Sidmouth

Just outside of Launceston in the Tamar Valley, this 56-hectare farm and vineyard is run by a Queensland couple who moved to Tasmania for a quieter rural lifestyle and the love of wine. On the property behind an old apple-packing shed they've opened a cellar door serving pinot noir, pinot gris, chardonnay and sparkling. It's as charming as it sounds.

Wineglass Bay

FREYCINET NATIONAL PARK

THE JEWEL IN THE CROWN
OF TASSIE SWIMS AND A
FIERCE COMPETITOR FOR OUR
NATIONAL TREASURE.

TASMANIA

BEACH

Best time to visit
November to May

How to get there
Turn off the Tasman Hwy between Swansea and Bicheno at Coles Bay Rd, following signs to Freycinet National Park. Pass through Coles Bay along the well-signed road to the Wineglass Bay/ Mt Amos carpark.

Access
Moderate. Park at the trailhead and walk about 2.5km over a saddle and down the other side to the beach. The trail is fairly steep, albeit very short.

Cost of entry National-park pass required (check fees at www.parks.tas.gov.au).

Kid friendly Yes

Dog friendly No

Water temperature Cool to cold

Open 24 hours

Facilities
Toilets at trailhead carpark; no facilities at Wineglass Bay beach.

Must bring
A thick towel. The water is colder than it looks.

LOCAL KNOWLEDGE

Great beaches are not to be confused with those that are popular with locals. This is a famed tourist destination rather than a local swimming spot, but one that is celebrated by all for its grandiose beauty.

The Freycinet Peninsula is the epicentre of our long-standing love affair with Tassie's east coast. No matter how many times we visit, we are overwhelmed by a sense of awe and discovery. Wineglass Bay is an enormous, sheltered beach possessing all the attributes of a perfect place to swim – white sand, clear water and an amphitheatre of granite mountains. Despite being one of the state's most visited places, tourism hardly scratches the surface.

We've come to know the area much better since our friend Zac moved from Melbourne to Swansea, giving us a little needed excuse to make the pilgrimage a couple of times each year. Through him we have had access to the tight little community of farmers, fishers, winemakers, swimmers and general legends who together comprise the region's few year-round residents. More importantly, Zac offers an inside edge on when (autumn) and where (can't say) to find the best wild mushrooms and blackberries.

While the locals often roll their eyes at our boundless enthusiasm for Wineglass Bay, preferring more-accessible and low-key haunts like Honeymoon Bay or Bicheno's Safety Beach (Waubs Beach), Zac is a recent enough migrant to not yet be jaded by its popularity. It's become our small tradition to camp at Friendly Beaches and spend a few days hiking, swimming and generally frolicking around Wineglass Bay.

Looking at an aerial snapshot, you could quite reasonably think you were on Queensland's famous Whitehaven Beach – at least until you get in the water. But what you lose in water temperature, you make up for in solitude. A couple of lazy cruises venture into the bay, but none of them dumps hordes on the beach. The only way to get there is to walk, and that means passing through the Freycinet Peninsula's patented Tourist Filtration System (TFS).

It's a short, steep walk from the busy carpark to the saddle and lookout, where most visitors tend to congregate. This is the first stage of the TFS. Satisfied with a good view, many hikers will turn back before ever reaching the beach itself. Those that continue the steep descent down to the water rarely venture any further than a few metres from the trail access point – TFS stage two. This leaves kilometres of virgin white sand and a sheltered cove at the southernmost tip. Only the keenest will make it this far, but the effort is rewarded with a private piece of paradise.

NEARBY

MT AMOS
Freycinet National Park

A 4-kilometre hike/scramble up Mt Amos leaves from the Wineglass Bay carpark. This strenuous climb will take you to the summit (450 metres) for what is without a doubt the best 360-degree views over Wineglass Bay and the rest of the park. You'll feel on top of the world!

HONEYMOON BAY
Freycinet National Park

There is definitely something romantic about this aptly named bay between the visitors centre and the Wineglass Bay carpark, with its clear, calm water, protected swimming and giant boulders for lovers to laze on. Mussels fringe the water's edge, so enter by diving over them.

THE GULCH
25 Esplanade, Bicheno

The Gulch may be Bicheno's next best attraction after its beaches. About 30 to 40 minutes' drive north of Freycinet, this sleepy coastal fishing town is home to the best fish and chips in the country. Place your order at the open window and dine on the catch of the day out the back while watching the town's fishing fleet pull in.

BEACH   **CREEK**

○ **Best time to visit**
December to March, when the water
is at its warmest and the weather is
most predictable.

⌂ **How to get there**
Turn off Huon Hwy 2km north of
Southport at Hastings Cave Rd. In 4km
the road will pass the Hastings Cave turn-
off and become Lune River Rd. The road
continues changing names as you travel
south, but there are no real turns; just
keep driving until it dead-ends at Cockle
Creek/Recherche Bay (about 24km).

⊖ **Access**
Easy. The last 10km is unsealed,
so be careful in the rain. Parking and
camping available all along the road
at Recherche Bay.

$ **Cost of entry** National-park entry fees
apply beyond the Cockle Creek bridge.

☺ **Kid friendly** Yes

⊗ **Dog friendly** Yes, on leash. But you
cannot take them across the Cockle
Creek bridge or into the national park.

◠ **Water temperature** Cold

◷ **Open** 24 hours

⊕ **Facilities**
Pit toilets, untreated tank water

◍ **Must bring**
A fuel or gas stove for cooking.
No fires allowed.

LOCAL KNOWLEDGE

Cockle Creek is the furthest point
south you can drive in Australia and
was once a settlement with more than
2000 residents. Now there are about 10
permanent residents (not including the
local echidna colony).

Cockle Creek

SHELTERED BAY AND TIDAL LAGOON AT THE END OF
THE EARTH.

If you want insight into what Tasmania may have looked like before farming, forestry, mining and hydro, this is the place. Cockle Creek is the entry to Southwest National Park and the Tasmanian Wilderness World Heritage Area, which comprises about 20 per cent of the island. Much of this region is only accessible by foot, helicopter or boat, and that isolation has made it a stronghold for some of our most threatened species. This remote settlement is the last stop on Australia's southernmost road, the furthest point of the most forgotten state, and truly seems like the end of the earth. Standing here, you are closer to Antarctica than to Cairns. This makes it the perfect place to unplug, think, walk, observe and, of course, to swim.

The fierce winds known as the roaring forties travel virtually unabated to deliver the cleanest air in the world and non-stop weather to this part of Tasmania. Clouds race and bump and push their way across the sky. We've seen Cockle Creek go from 16°C with horizontal rain to 30°C, and back again. All within 24 hours. The sky is always putting on a show down here, but on a sunny day, or a sunny hour, you cannot help but be drawn into the astonishingly clear water.

The sheltered natural harbour of Recherche Bay is an oasis of calm in this wild land. Few waves ever penetrate it and those daring enough to take the cold plunge will have kilometres of white-sand beach all to themselves. Our top spot, however, is in the tidal inlet. Because the water is relatively shallow here, knee- to head-depth, it is dramatically warmer than anywhere else. Reliable pools are formed around the pylons of the single-lane bridge, and while you are here you may as well grab some lunch: oysters populate the intertidal rocks and, true to name, there are about 1000 cockles per metre in the mud (unfortunately, harvesting is prohibited).

A few rustic shackies line the bay, which we suspect enjoy some of the lowest occupancy rates in the country. Most visitors will find themselves camping, as there are no fees, provided that you respect the one month limit. While we didn't stay a full term, it was easy to let the days slip by. When the sun was out we would mermaid in the creek and hike through mossy forests. When the weather turned it would provide the perfect excuse to cook long meals and read our books. Cockle Creek was the remedy for a sickness we didn't know we had. It's a place to be immersed in ancient life and healing water. The perfect antidote to city life.

NEARBY

SOUTH CAPE BAY
Southwest National Park

Having driven our surfboards all around Tasmania and barely used them, we heard there was a chance for a wave 7 kilometres into the national park at South Cape Bay. While the surf-check was fruitless, the walk was extraordinary. Passing through meadows, fern-filled gullies and mossy forests of blackwoods to the coffee coloured rocks of South Cape gave a delightful taste of the famous six-day (85 kilometre) Southwest Track from Melaleuca to Cockle Creek.

SUMMER KITCHEN BAKERY
21 Marguerite St, Ranelagh

Now, we know we talk about bakeries a lot, but this one was truly something special. We might even go so far as to say the best of our trip. It's a super-cute country larder selling house-made bread, pastry, jams and relish, and good coffee. Get the wallaby and potato pie and follow it straight up with a slice of spelt carrot cake or a currant-and-almond-stuffed scroll (like an escargot). Everything we ate here was fantastic. Closed Mondays.

WILLIE SMITH'S APPLE SHED
2064 Huon Hwy, Grove

Roadside farm gates could be mistaken for apple-vending machines around the Huon Valley, which is how you know the fruit is abundant. Willie Smith's organic cider is made on the Smith family farm, where they have been growing apples since 1888. Now you can sample it in their rustic barn, open daily for food and drink, with live music on Sundays.

BEACH

◐ **Best time to visit**
December to March, when it's warmest.

⊘ **How to get there**
Ferries depart from Triabunna five times daily from September to April and three times daily from May to August (no service Tuesdays and Thursdays in winter). Confirm times and current prices with Encounter Maria Island (www.encountermaria.com.au).

⊖ **Access**
Ferry or private boat. All trails on Maria Island are very well maintained and signposted.

$ **Cost of entry**
National-park pass required (check fees at www.parks.tas.gov.au).

☺ **Kid friendly** Yes

⊗ **Dog friendly** No

◠ **Water temperature** Cold. Helped by a nip of whisky before the first plunge. After that, you're fine.

◷ **Open** 24 hours

⊕ **Facilities**
Toilets, rainwater tanks and bad-weather shelter (all campsites); showers (Darlington only).

◉ **Must bring**
Food, water, a head torch and $1 coins for the hot shower

LOCAL KNOWLEDGE

The island's name is pronounced Ma-*rye*-ya, like Mariah Carey.

Maria Island National Park

EAST COAST

A MOUNTAINOUS ISLAND OFF THE EAST COAST, WITH AN ABUNDANCE OF SECRET BEACHES AND COVES.

It was no coincidence that we saved Tasmania for last on our trip around the country – it was always going to be a high note to end on. We invited some friends down to join us for our final weekend off the mainland, and headed to Maria Island. Just over an hour out of Hobart, it is an ideal spot for camping close to the city. We promised our companions an adventurous few days of hiking and swimming, and were excited to have some company joining us in the water.

A half-hour ferry to the island leaves from the town of Triabunna several times a day. As a bumpy swell rose high into the distance, the scent of seasickness welcomed visitors to the open ocean. But we were on solid land again before we knew it, a robust northerly wind blowing in over the port of Darlington. Deep, clear water softened this arrival – we could tell the island was going to reveal beautiful swimming spots, just as soon as the clouds parted.

Like many places in Tasmania, Maria Island began as a convict penitentiary, became a pastoral settlement and is now a World Heritage site. Well before all of this, the Puthikwilayti people were custodians of the land (for about 40,000 years), giving the island a past rich in both Indigenous and colonial history.

There are no shops or cars on this far-flung island – the ultimate respite – and most people who stay overnight bring in all food and water needed to camp at one of three sites: Darlington, French's Farm and Encampment Cove. All are basic, but a $1 coin will buy you a luxurious hot shower at Darlington, just the treatment you need after a day of hiking and swimming in glacial waters.

You can leave the world behind you, hiking or riding bikes around an unpopulated isle of sweeping bays, rugged cliffs, open woodlands and rolling hills, your journey punctuated by encounters with copious Australian wildlife. It's a one-stop shop for sightings of docile wombats, pademelons, potoroos and the odd Tasmanian devil hopping around at night.

We took the coastal route round to the Painted Cliffs, past Return Point to Point Lesueur and over to an isthmus connecting the north and south sections of the island – each of these spots brought us incredible clear, calm water, perfect for a dip mid-hike. Our favourites were the protected bays on the west side – Chinamans and Shoal – which are sheltered in most conditions.

Continuing on the Haunted Bay Lookout track takes you down the spit, past the wilder waters of Riedle Bay (good for a bodysurf depending on the swell) to the southern region. Like most of Maria, you'll almost certainly have it all to yourself. This is an island off an island, off an island, and the perfect adventure to celebrate the end of an epic swimming mission.

NEARBY

MONA
65 Main Rd, Berriedale

No trip to Tasmania is complete without a stop at the Museum of Old and New Art, owned by millionaire entrepreneur and proud Hobart resident David Walsh. Set on the banks of the Derwent River, MONA is one of the country's best contemporary art galleries and has brought the city the crowds and credibility it deserves. A visit is life-changing.

THE AGRARIAN KITCHEN EATERY & STORE
11a The Avenue, New Norfolk

A cooking school and farm that has since expanded to a slick country restaurant in the town's old mental asylum. Seasonal produce is celebrated here, with a community of growers, farmers and fishers supplying the restaurant. Dishes are simple, delicate, wholesome and organic. A place to celebrate with friends over a large lamb shank and some local pinot. Make sure to order all of the deserts.

MT WELLINGTON

It's hard to ignore the looming presence of Mt Wellington when you visit Hobart. Trails and tracks weave up and around woodland forest to an exposed, windswept peak (1200 metres). It's a steep hike that takes a couple of hours, but well worth it for the views (if you don't find yourself in clouds). Start at Fern Tree Tavern (680 Huon Rd, Fern Tree), where you'll return for a stout at the end, and stop in at the Lost Freight, a shipping container in the middle carpark serving coffee and Monte Carlos.

Olympian and Ocean Swimmer

SHANE GOULD

Early one morning in March, we meet one of Australia's greatest ever female swimmers, Shane Gould, at her home beach in Bicheno. During Shane's brief but prodigious swimming career, she won three gold medals in world record times at the Munich Olympics in 1972, at the age of 15, and then retired from competitive swimming less than two years later. She has since dedicated much of her life to studying, practising, observing and teaching swimming.

Each morning just after dawn, she swims at Waubs Beach with the Bicheno Coffee Club Wild Ocean Swimmers. As the name suggests, they're as much about the coffee and chats as they are about the laps. It's a still morning, without a ripple of swell in the water. At this time of year, it's the warmest the water gets (up to 20°C), but most of the group swim in wetsuits with silicone caps. When it gets colder (11°C/12°C in August), they add balaclavas, gloves and booties.

Swims last from 20 minutes to an hour, and there's an understanding to never swim alone. There are varying levels of ability and inclination to swim, talk and plunge. Steve and his sea-dog Smooch paddle in a kayak alongside most days.

After the swim they all sit on the deck of the surf club in the sun, sipping from thermoses of hot ginger tea or coffee. If they're lucky, someone brings a treat after testing a new recipe at home – a pumpkin scone experiment or Phil Tuck's fruitcake are favourites, but Jeanne's apricot scones with apricot coulis also freshen up a salty mouth.

When she's not swimming, Shane is working with her husband Milton on the Shane Gould Swimming Project, providing swimming and water safety programs in Fiji and Australia. When we meet her, she is neck-deep in the finishing touches of her latest thesis, a cultural study of swimming in Australia.

I WAS SCARED, SO I'D SWIM CLOSE TO THE BEACH WHERE I COULD TOUCH THE BOTTOM WITH MY HANDS.

Q. Tell us about the importance of having daily experiences with nature.
A. I just feel good going out into nature, and I think a lot of people do too. I think it's healthy. As human beings we need nature and I have chosen places to live that are good for the soul, good for physicality. This place [Bicheno] helps me to think. The bonus is to meet crazy people like this [points to Pam who is sitting next to her in a wetsuit and a fluffy hat].

Q. What brought you to Bicheno?
A. I'm a climate-change refugee ... [laughs] a menopause refugee. I was having hot flushes.

Q. Where else have you lived?
A. I was in WA, then Sydney for a couple of years. Then Launceston for two years, then we missed the ocean so we came down here.

Q. Where in WA?
A. Margaret River. I was there for about 32 years. I moved there when I was very young, just newly married, and had four children there. Before the wineries, it was a run-down dairy area. When people discovered it had really good surf, the town got a bit of momentum. People started growing wine and horticultural products, and the economy changed and tourists came and built properties. Suddenly, it was the Margaret River you know today.

Q. How does having a place to swim or a public pool affect the community?
A. Like runners, musicians or artists, swimmers tend to congregate together. For me it meant forming a new group of friends. When I first started ocean swimming in Margaret River, at Prevelly, I was scared, so I'd swim close to the beach where I could touch the bottom with my hands. I'd been a surfer for years, but I'd never swum in the ocean.

This is going to be our sixth winter swimming here [in Bicheno]. We've become familiar with the animals and the seasonal cycles. We get whales, dolphins, and sometimes stingrays. There are schools of fish. We get crabs molting and migrating, and then octopuses chasing them. You see so many different things.

Q. How has your relationship with swimming changed throughout your life?
A. I grew up in Fiji for about seven years as a kid (age three to nine) so outdoor, natural swimming is what I'm inclined towards. But when I moved back to Australia, for seven or eight years I was competing and training in pools, so that became my mindset for swimming. We had family holidays at the beach and we were always bodysurfing; but the pool was where you swam [laps]. It wasn't until I got involved with ocean swimming that it gave different meaning and contexts to what swimming could be. I just love the feeling of water on my body, the exertion and the rhythm of the stroke, the exhale and inhale, and the vistas.

Q. You've lived in some of the most beautiful places in Australia. How does the landscape and water shape the people?
A. 'Why are Australians so associated with the water?' is the fundamental question in my thesis, and it's got nothing to do with being close to the coast. The weather is pleasant; there's a lot of space; our cities were built on land where there are really nice accessible beaches and inlets. Yet England, Germany and Sweden are similar; [the people there] love swimming too – there are loads of shallow lakes that get warm in the summer. They have fantastic coastlines around the Baltic and all their spa swimming. And so Australians are not the only swimmers. It's a shared human experience; it's just that the Australian environment is exotic.

Q. Have you found attitudes to swimming are different inland compared to the coast?
A. The word 'swimming' is so broad. When people are on the river, they are *on* the river not *in* the river. They are on boogie boards and doughnuts and waterskiing. But what I've noticed is that most people who go to the beach are just in the water, getting thumped by the waves, or standing, plunging and soaking up the energy of the ocean. I call them 'dry-heads', because they are swimming vertically.

You really have to commit yourself to swim horizontally. But their experience is still swimming because they are interacting with the water. They might have their feet off the bottom for periods of time and be suspended and have that lovely feeling of weightlessness that you can only get in the water or up in space.

Q. Do you swim every day?
A. Most days. Sometimes it changes, but it's a good way to start the day. It's nice to come out and engage with people and catch up and hear about things they are dealing with or have a laugh and share the beauty and experience. It's good for the body and mind, and the social side gets massaged and fed.

Index

A

Addiscot Beach, Point Addis Vic. 44–5
Adels Grove Qld 148, 149
Adels Grove Campground, Adels Grove Qld 149
Aireys Inlet Vic. 45
Aireys Pub, Aireys Inlet Vic. 45
Airlie Beach Qld 156, 157
Albert + Nikola, Dunsborough WA 107
Alexandria Bay, Noosa NP Qld 160
Alice Springs NT 118, 119
Alice Springs Aquatic and Leisure
    Centre NT 118–19
Alma Bay, Magnetic Island Qld 154
Alpha Box & Dice, McLaren Vale SA 75
Alpine Hotel, The, Cooma NSW 33
Amalia Gorge, El Questro Wilderness
    Park WA 98
Andrew 'Boy' Charlton Pool, Sydney NSW 18–19
Angelsea Vic. 44, 45
Angourie NSW 8
Angourie Blue Pool, Angourie NSW 8
Apollo Restaurant, The, Potts Point NSW 21
Aqua English 168–9
Aragunnu, Wapengo NSW 35
Art is an Option, Dargan NSW 31
Arthur Bay, Magnetic Island Qld 153–5

B

Babinda Boulders Qld xiv, 151
Badenoch's Deli, Moorak SA 78
Bakery in Eurong, Fraser Island Qld 159
Balding Bay, Magnetic Island Qld 154
Barrk Malam Bushwalk, Kakadu NP NT 133
Basin, The, Rottnest Island WA 104–5
Bay of Fires Tas. 173–5
Bay of Fires Lodge Walk Tas. 175
Beach Break, Marion Bay SA 71
beach safety 37
Bell Gorge, The Kimberley WA 92–3
Bermagui Blue Pool NSW 34–5
Bermagui NSW 34, 35
Berriedale Tas. 185
Berry Springs NT 135, 137
Betty Beach, Whitsunday Island Qld 156
Bicheno Tas. 180, 181, 186–7
Bills Old-fashioned Cakes and Pies,
    Lithgow NSW 31
Binalong Beach Tas. 174
Bitter Springs, Mataranka, Elsey NP NT 122–3
Bitter Springs Cabins and Camping,
    Mataranka NT 123
Black Rock Vic. 50–1
Blinman Pools, Flinders Ranges SA 68–9
Blue Door Kiosk, Merewether NSW 13
Blue Lagoon, Moreton Island Qld 163
Blue Waterholes, High Plains NSW 33
boating WA 105
Bogey Hole, The, Newcastle NSW 13
Bondi NSW 21
Bondi Beach NSW 20, 21
Bondi Icebergs, Bondi Beach NSW 20–1
Bondi to Bronte ocean swim NSW 37
Boodjamulla (Lawn Hill) NP Qld 147–9
Boston Brewing Co, Hay WA 111
Brisbane Qld 162, 164–5
Broken Head NSW 4–5

Bronte Beach NSW 36
Broome WA 90, 91
Brunswick Heads NSW 3
Buley Rockhole, Litchfield NP NT 137
Bundjalung NP NSW 8
Bushrangers Bay, near Cape Schanck Vic. 53–5

C

Cabana Cabarita, Cabarita NSW 3
Cabarita NSW 2, 3
Cabarita Beach NSW 2–3
Cable Beach WA 90
Cape Le Grand NP WA 112
Cape Leveque, Dampier Peninsula WA 90–1
Cape Naturaliste WA 106–7
Cape Range NP WA 99–101
Cape Schanck Vic. 53–5
Caporn, Trevor and Adele 115
Captain Moonlite, Anglesea Vic. 60–1
Castle Rock, Cape Naturaliste WA 106–7
Cataract Gorge, Launceston Tas. 176–7
Centenary Pool, Brisbane Qld 164–5
Cerberus Beach House, The, Half Moon Bay Vic. 51
Champagne Pools, El Questro Wilderness Park WA
    89
Chance Trail, Whitsunday Island Qld 157
Charlton, Andrew Murray 'Boy' 18
Childers Cove, Mepunga Vic. 42–3
Chinamans Bay, Maria Island Tas. 184
Clarence Dam, Dargans Creek Reserve NSW 29–31
cliff-jumping/rock-jumping
    NSW 8, 26, 30
    NT 132
    SA 74, 78, 81
    Vic. 40
clothing optional beaches 44, 112, 160
Clovelly Beach NSW 23–5
Clovelly NSW 24
Cockle Creek Tas. 182–3
Coles Bay Tas. 180
Colonel's Son, The, Black Rock Vic. 51
Connell, Scott 86
Coogee NSW 24
Cooma NSW 33
Cornish Kitchen, The, Moonta SA 71
Cosy Corner Beach Tas. 174
Cottesloe WA 102, 103
Cottesloe Beach WA 102–3
Cottesloe Beach Hotel, Cottesloe WA 103
Cougal Cascades, Springbrook NP Qld 167
Crazy Acre Mango Farm and Cafe,
    Berry Springs NT 137
crocodile safety 140–3
Cronulla NSW 27
Curl Curl NSW 16

D

Da Orazia Pizza + Porchetta, Bondi NSW 21
Dalhousie Homestead, Witjira NP SA 67
Dalhousie Springs, Witjira NP SA 65–7
Daly Waters NT 123
Daly Waters Pub, The, Daly Waters NT 123
Dampier Peninsula WA 90–1
Dancing Waters Cafe, Springbrook Qld 167
Dargan NSW 31

Dargans Creek Reserve NSW 29–31
Darlington, Maria Island Tas. 184
Darwin NT 138–9
Davey Mac's, Black Rock Vic. 51
Denmark WA 110, 111
Derby WA 93
diving
    Qld 154
    SA 78
Downtown Espresso Bar, Esperance WA 113
Dunsborough WA 106, 107

E

Eagle Bay WA 107
Eagle Bay Brewing Co, Eagle Bay WA 107
Eden Beach Tas. 174
El Questro Gorge, The Kimberley WA 88–9
El Questro Station, El Questro Wilderness Park WA
    88, 89
El Questro Wilderness Park WA 87, 88, 89
Elephant Cove, William Bay NP WA 109–11
Eli Creek, Fraser Island Qld 158
Elk Island Qld 156
Ellery Creek Big Hole, Namatjira NT 119
Elsey NP NT 122–3
Emma Gorge, The Kimberley WA 85–7
Emma Gorge Resort WA 86
Esperance WA 112–13
Exmouth WA 100, 101
Eyre Peninsula SA 72–3

F

Fern Pool, Dales Gorge, Karijini NP WA 96
Figure Eight Pools, Royal NP NSW 27
Fingal Vic. 55
Finnerty, Emma 36–7
First Basin, Cataract Gorge,
    Launceston Tas. 176–7
Fish Creek Vic. 59
fishing
    NSW 4, 26
    SA 72
    WA 90, 105
Fitzroy Vic. 49
Fitzroy Pool, Fitzroy Vic. 47–9
Fleurieu Peninsula SA 74–5
Flinders Island Tas. xiv
Flinders Ranges SA 68–9
Florence Bay, Magnetic Island Qld 154
Florence Falls, Litchfield NP NT 137
Flour and Stone, Woolloomooloo NSW 21
food trucks, Casuarina Drive, Nightcliff NT 138
Forest Hill Winery, Denmark WA 111
Fraser Island Qld 158–9
free bush-camping, Parachilna Gorge Rd SA 69
Fremantle WA 105
Fresh Fish Place, The, Port Lincoln SA 73
Freshwater NSW 16
Freshwater Creek Vic. 45
Freshwater Creek General Store,
    Freshwater Creek Vic. 45
freshwater crocodiles 141–3
Freycinet NP Tas. 179–81
Froth Craft Restaurant / Microbrewery,
    Exmouth WA 101

G

Gauge, South Brisbane Qld 165
Geoffrey Bay, Magnetic Island Qld 154
Geographe Bay WA 106
Gerega, Remy 102
Germanchis, Matt 60–1
Ghan NT 67
Gibb River Road WA 86, 88, 92
Giro Osteria, Cronulla NSW 27
Glen Helen Gorge, Tjoritja/West MacDonnell NP NT 120–1
Glen Helen Homestead, West MacDonnell Ranges NT 120, 121
GOMA, Southbank, Brisbane Qld 165
Goods, The, Alice Springs NT 119
gorges
    NT 119, 120–1, 127, 131, 132–3
    Qld 147–9
    Tas. 176–7
    WA 85–9, 92–3, 95–7
Gould, Shane 186–7
Gourmet Gecko, Lightning Ridge NSW 10
Granite Bay, Noosa NP NSW 160–1
Graze, Warrnambool Vic. 43
Greens Pool, William Bay NP WA 109–11
Gregory Downs Hotel, Gregory Qld 149
Gregory Qld 148, 149
Gregory River Qld 148
Grotto, The, Wyndham WA 87
Grove Tas. 183
Groves, Jackson 80–1
Gulch, The, Bicheno Tas. 181
Gunlom Falls, Kakadu NP 129–31
Gusto on the Beach, Curl Curl NSW 16
Gutter Bar, The, Moreton Island Qld 163

H

Halcyon House, Cabarita NSW 3
Half Moon Bay, Black Rock Vic. 50–1
Hamersley Gorge, Karijini NP WA 95–7
Harliquin Takeaway & Convenience Store, Lightning Ridge NSW 10
Harvest, Newrybar Village NSW 5
Hay WA 111
Helensburg NSW 27
Hellfire Bay, Esperance WA 112
Heysen Trail SA 69
High Plains NSW 33
Hobart Tas. 185
Honeymoon Bay, Freycinet NP Tas. 180, 181
Horseshoe Bay, Magnetic Island Qld 154
Horseshoe Bay Fish and Chips, Horseshoe Bay, Magnetic Island Qld 154
Hotel Rottnest, Rottnest Island WA 105

I

Il Lido Canteen, Cottesloe WA 103
Innes NP SA 70–1

J

James Price Point, Dampier Peninsula WA 91
Jarrangbarnmi (Koolpin Gorge), Kakadu NP NT 131

Jatbula Trail NT 127
Jeanneret Beach Tas. 174
Jim Jim Falls, Kakadu NP NT xiv, 133
John Hayes Rockhole, Trephina Gorge NT 119
Junk, Steve 110

K

Kakadu NT 130, 131
Kakadu NP NT xiv, 129–33
Karijini Eco Retreat, Karijini NP WA 96
Karijini NP WA 95–7
Katherine Gorge, Nitmiluk NP NT 127
kayaking Tas. 175, 176
Kermits Pool, Hancock Gorge, Karijini NP WA 96
Kermond's Hamburgers, Warrnambool Vic. 43
Kimberley, The WA 85–9, 92–3
King Leopold Ranges WA 92, 93
Kingfisher Resort, Fraser Island Qld 158
Kooljaman, Dampier Peninsula WA 90
Kosciuszko NP NSW 32–3
Kulgera Road House, Ghan NT 67
Kyneton Vic. 40, 41

L

lagoons
    NSW 26–7
    SA 77–9
Lake Argyle Resort WA 87
Lake McKenzie, Fraser Island Qld 158, 159
Lake Wabby, Fraser Island Qld 158–9
Langley Vic. 40–1
Launceston Tas. 176–7
Lawn Hill, Boodjamulla (Lawn Hill) NP Qld 147–9
Lawn Hill Gorge, Boodjamulla (Lawn Hill) NP Qld 147–9
Lazy Lizard Tavern and Caravan Park, Pine Creek NT 131
Leliyn (Edith Falls), Nitmiluk NP NT 125–7
Lennox Head NSW 5
Leonard's Mill, Second Valley SA 75
Lightning Ridge NSW 10–11
Lightning Ridge Bore Bath, Lightning Ridge NSW 10–11
Lightning Ridge District Bowling Club, Lightning Ridge NSW 10
Litchfield Helicopter Flights, Litchfield NP NT 135
Litchfield NP NT 134–7
Lithgow NSW 31
Little Blue Lake, Mt Gambier SA 77–9
Little Waterloo Bay, Wilsons Promontory NP Vic. 57–9
Locale, Noosa Heads Qld 161
Lombadina WA 91
Long Time No Sea, Baragga Bay NSW 35
Lost Fawn Cafe, The, Springbrook Qld 167
Lucky Bay, Esperance WA 112
Lucky Bay Cafe, Nightcliff NT 138

M

McGain's Nursery, Cafe and Foodstore, Anglesea Vic. 45
McLaren Vale SA 74, 75
Magnetic Island Qld 153–5

Maguk, Kakadu NP NT 132–3
Manning Gorge, Derby WA 93
Margaret River WA 107, 187
Maria Island NP Tas. 184–5
Marion Bay SA 71
Marlin Bar, Horseshoe Bay, Magnetic Island Qld 154
Massimo, Noosa Heads Qld 161
Mataranka NT 122–3
Mataranka Thermal Pool, Elsey NP NT 123
Meeniyan Vic. 59
Melbourne Vic. 47–9
Merewether NSW 12, 13
Merewether Ocean Baths, Merewether NSW 12–13
Mile End Bagels, Fitzroy Vic. 49
Millner NT 138
Mimosa Rocks NP NSW 34
Mister Jones & Honorbread, Bermagui NSW 35
Mitchell Plateau WA 93
MONA, Berriedale Tas. 185
Moonta SA 71
Moorak SA 78
Moo's at Meeniyan, Meeniyan Vic. 59
Moreton Island Qld 162–3
Motor Car Falls, Kakadu NP NT 131
Mount Amos, Freycinet NP Tas. 181
Mount Dare, Witjira NP SA 67
Mount Gambier SA 77–9
Mount Kosciuszko Summit Hike, Thredbo NSW 33
Mount Schank SA 78
Mount Tempest, Moreton Island Qld 163
Mount Vic Flicks, Mount Victoria NSW 31
Mount Victoria NSW 31
Mount Wellington Tas. 185
Mount William NP Tas. 175
Mrs Jones, Denmark WA 111
Mrs Jones the Baker, Freshwater NSW 16
Muchacha Mexican Kitchen, North Curl Curl NSW 16
Mudgeeraba Qld 166
Murnanes Beach, near Warrnambool Vic. 42

N

Namatjira NT 119
Napier Quarter, Fitzroy Vic. 49
Nelly Bay, Magnetic Island Qld 154
New Norfolk Tas. 185
Newcastle NSW 12–13
Newrybar Village NSW 5
Nightcliff Pool, Nightcliff WA 138–9
Ningaloo Reef WA 99–101
Nitmiluk NP NT 125–6
Noosa Heads Qld 161
Noosa NP Qld 160–1
Norries Head NSW 2
North Bondi NSW 21
North Curl Curl NSW 16
North Curl Curl Beach NSW 15–17
nudie beaches 44, 112, 160

O

Ocean Blues, Esperance WA 113
ocean pools
    NSW 8–9, 12–13, 15–17, 23–5, 34–5
    SA 72–3
Ok Pie Shop, Mt Gambier SA 78

Old Shanghai at Fremantle Markets, Fremantle WA 105
Ormiston Gorge, West MacDonnell Ranges NT 121

P

Pacific Hotel, Yamba NSW 8
Paddock Coffee Shop, The, Fish Creek Vic. 59
Parachilna Gorge Road, free bush-camping SA 69
Parachilna SA 69
Parakeet Bay, Rottnest Island WA 104
Parap Market, Millner NT 138
Parker Point, Rottnest Island WA 104
Peninsula Hot Springs, Fingal Vic. 55
Perth WA 102–3
Pine Creek NT 131
Pinkemba, Moreton Island Qld 162
Pizzeria Trieste, Port Lincoln SA 73
Point Addis Vic. 44–5
Point Lesueur, Maria Island Tas. 184
Point Roadnight Beach, Anglesea Vic. 44
Polperro, Red Hill Vic. 55
Pondalowie Bay, York Peninsula SA 71
pools
    NSW 18–19, 20–1, 32–3
    NT 118–19, 138–9
    Qld 164–5
    Tas. 176–7
    Vic. 47–9
Port Lincoln SA 72, 73
Port Lincoln NP SA 73
Port Lincoln Swimming Enclosure SA 72–3
Port Willunga SA 75
Potts Point NSW 19
Prairie Hotel, The, Parachilna SA 69
Punamii-unpii (Mitchell Falls), Mitchell Plateau, WA 93
Pyengana Dairy Company, Pyengana Tas. 175

Q

QAGOMA, Southbank, Brisbane Qld 165

R

Ranelagh Tas. 183
Rapid Creek Market, Millner NT 138
Recherche Archipelago WA 112
Recherche Bay Tas. 182
Red Bank Gorge, West MacDonnell Ranges NT 121
Red Hill Vic. 55
Red Spoon, Cottesloe WA 103
Refuge Cove, Wilsons Promontory NP Vic. 58
Remote Aboriginal Swimming Pools Project (Remote Pools) 114–15
Riedle Bay, Maria Island Tas. 184
rips 37
rock pools
    Qld 166–7
    SA 68–9
    Vic. 53–5
    WA 87, 88–9, 95–7, 109–11
Rottnest Island WA 104–5
Rottnest Island Bakery, Rottnest Island WA 105
Royal George Hotel, The, Kyneton Vic. 41
Royal NP NSW 26
Rustico at Hay Shed Hill, Margaret River WA 107

S

St Andrews Beach Brewery, Fingal Vic. 55
St Helens Tas. 174, 175
St Helens Bakery, St Helens Tas. 175
Saint John Craft Beer Bar, Launceston Tas. 177
saltwater crocodiles 140–3
Sandy Cove, near Warrnambool Vic. 42
Sawmill Beach Camp, Whitsunday Island Qld 157
Scarce, Sarah 168–9
Scottie's, Newcastle NSW 13
Seal Rocks NSW xiv
Sealers Cove, Wilsons Promontory NP Vic. 58
Second Valley, Fleurieu Peninsula SA 74–5
Shed Bar, The, Airlie Beach Qld 157
Shell Beach Rock Pool, Innes NP SA 70–1
Shelter, Lennox Head NSW 5
shipwrecks
    Qld 154, 162–3
    Vic. 50
Shoal Bay, Maria Island Tas. 184
Short Order Local, The, Exmouth WA 101
Shuk, North Bondi NSW 21
Sidmouth Tas. 177
Sleaford Bay, Port Lincoln NP SA 73
Smoking Gun Bagels, Woolloomooloo NSW 21
snorkelling
    NSW 26
    Qld 162
    SA 70, 74
    WA 100, 104
Source Dining, Kyneton Vic. 41
South Brisbane Qld 165
South Cape Bay, Southwest NP Tas. 185
South Glory Cave, Yarrangobilly NSW 32
Southbank, Brisbane Qld 165
Southwest NP Tas. 182, 183
Soy, Bondi Beach NSW 21
Spring Hill Qld 164, 165
Spring Hill Baths, Spring Hill Qld 165
Springbrook Qld 167
Springbrook NP Qld 166–7
Sri Venkateswara Canteen, Helensburgh NSW 27
Standard Dave Pizza, Warrnambool Vic. 43
Star of Greece, Port Willunga SA 75
Stillwater, Launceston Tas. 177
Strickland Bay, Rottnest Island WA 104
Suffolk Park NSW 5
Summer Kitchen Bakery, Ranelagh Tas. 183
Sunshine Beach, Noosa NP Qld 160
surfing
    NSW 2, 4, 16
    Qld 160
    SA 72
    Vic. 44
    WA 104
Swansea Tas. 180
Sweet Kiss Cake Shop, Clovelly NSW 24
Sweetwater Pool, Nitmiluk NP NT 126, 127
Swimcart Beach Tas. 174
Sydney NSW 18–21, 23–5

T

Tan, Eugene 20
Tangalooma Wrecks, Moreton Island Qld 162–3
Tasmanian Wilderness World Heritage Area Tas. 182
Taylors St Quarter, Esperance WA 113

Telegraph Saddle, Wilsons Promontory NP Vic. 58
The Agrarian Kitchen Eatery & Store, New Norfolk Tas. 185
The Alpine Hotel, Cooma NSW 33
The Apollo Restaurant, Potts Point NSW 21
The Basin, Rottnest Island WA 104–5
The Bogey Hole, Newcastle NSW 13
The Cerberus Beach House, Half Moon Bay Vic. 51
The Colonel's Son, Black Rock Vic. 51
The Cornish Kitchen, Moonta SA 71
The Daly Waters Pub, Daly Waters NT 123
The Fresh Fish Place, Port Lincoln 73
The Goods, Alice Springs NT 119
The Grotto, Wyndham WA 87
The Gulch, Bicheno Tas. 181
The Gutter Bar, Moreton Island Qld 163
The Kimberley WA 85–9, 92
The Lost Fawn Cafe, Springbrook Qld 167
The Paddock Coffee Shop, Fish Creek Vic. 59
The Prairie Hotel, Parachilna SA 69
The Royal George Hotel, Kyneton Vic. 41
The Shed Bar, Airlie Beach Qld 157
The Short Order Local, Exmouth WA 101
The Trentham Collective, Trentham Vic. 41
thermal springs
    NSW 10–11, 32–3
    NT 122–3
    SA 65–7
Thredbo NSW 33
Tidal River Vic. 58, 59
Tjaynera (Sandy Creek) Falls, Litchfield NP NT 136–7
Tjoritja/West MacDonnell NP NT 120–1
Tongue Beach, Whitsunday Island Qld 156
Tophat Coffee Merchants, Clovelly NSW 24
Townsville Qld 154
Trentham Vic. 40, 41
Trentham Collective, The, Trentham Vic. 41
Trephina Gorge NT 11c 9
Triabunna Tas. 184
Tunnel Creek, King Leopold Ranges WA 93
Turpins Falls, Langley Vic. 40–1
Turquoise Bay, Cape Range NP WA 99–101
Twin Falls, Kakadu NP NT 133
Twin Falls, Springbrook NP Qld 166–7

U

Ubirr rock art site, Kakadu NP NT 133
Upper Gorge walk, Boodjamulla NP Qld 149

V

Viet Rose, Fitzroy Vic. 49
Village Bicycle, Noosa Heads Qld 161
Vivonne Bay, Kangaroo Island SA xiv
volunteer lifesavers 36–7

W

Walker Creek, Litchfield NP NT 135
Wanggoolba Creek, Fraser Island Qld 158
Wangi Falls, Litchfield NP NT 134–5
Wapengo NSW 35
Warrnambool Vic. 42–3
waterfalls
    NT 125–7, 129–31, 133–7
    Qld 166–7

Vic. 40–1
WA 85–9, 93
Wattamolla Beach, Royal NP NSW 26–7
Waubs Beach, Bicheno Tas. 180, 186
West Beach, Esperance WA 112–13
West MacDonnell Ranges NT 120–1
Whale Tour with Live Ningaloo, Exmouth WA 101
whale-watching WA 106
Whitehaven Beach, Whitsunday Island Qld 156–7
Whites Beach, Broken Head NSW 4–5
Whitsunday Island Qld 156–7
William Bay NP WA 109–11
Willie Smith's Apple Shed, Grove Tas. 183
Wilsons Promontory NP Vic. 57–9
Wineglass Bay, Freycinet NP Tas. 179–81
Wines for Joanie, Sidmouth Tas. 177
Witjira NP SA 65–7
Woerle, Stuart 140–1
Woolloomooloo NSW 19
Woolloomooloo Bay NSW 18
Wylie's Baths, Coogee NSW 24
Wyndham WA 87

Y

Yamba NSW 8
Yamba Cinema, Yamba NSW 8
Yamba Main Beach NSW 7–9
Yarrongobilly NSW 32
Yarrongobilly Thermal Pool NSW 32–3
Yellow Flower, Suffolk Park NSW 5
Yorke Peninsula SA 70–1
Yuraygir NP NSW 8

Z

Zebedee Springs, El Questro Wilderness Park WA 87

Acknowledgements

Publishing a book is like having a child – you conceive it, you nurture it, you spend a lot of money on it and you release it into the world with the hope that it won't embarrass you. Best case scenario, it does really well and pays for your early retirement.

It took a village to raise this book-child and so it only seems fitting that they should share the credit and/or blame. Thank you to all of the great people at Hardie Grant Books. To name a few – Melissa Kayser and Astrid Browne for giving us an excuse to explore Australia. Megan Cuthbert for her work as editor, project manager, and master juggler. Evi O for making the book beautiful. Susan Paterson for distilling our ramblings into a fragrant cologne. Olivia Fleetwood, Monica Svarc, Sallie Butler and Kasi Collins for getting *Places We Swim* into all of the right hands.

Thank you to our photo contributors – Remy Gerega, Nikki To, Eugene Tan (Aquabumps), Jackson Groves, Alex Kydd, Kate Berry, and Michelle Rowse.

Thank you to all of the people that shared their time and expertise with us, including Stuart Woerle, Scotty Connell, Greg Tate, Bernie Egan, Trevor and Adele Caporn, Liam Carmody, Steve Junk, Matt Germanchis, Gemma Gange, Sarah Scarce, Emma Finnerty and Shane Gould.

It wouldn't have been possible to make this book without the advice, inspiration, and free accommodation from the following people: Paul and Michelle Rowse, the Kelly family + Bobbie, Syme family, Mason/Sklovsky family, Doney family, Snowdon family, Anny and Miles, Romy and Gus, Sam, Nush, Kate Fenn, Cassie and Dan, Jack, Mat, Susie, Moose and PRC.

Thank you to everyone that we met along the way that gave us directions or took us to a local spot.

Thank you to our mechanic, Dave Bell.

Finally, thank you (our beloved reader) for buying our book and also buying a second copy as a gift.

Published in 2018 by Hardie Grant Travel,
a division of Hardie Grant Publishing

Hardie Grant Travel (Melbourne)
Building 1, 658 Church Street
Richmond, Victoria 3121

Hardie Grant Travel (Sydney)
Level 7, 45 Jones Street
Ultimo, NSW 2007

www.hardiegrant.com/au/travel

Explore Australia is an imprint of
Hardie Grant Travel

A catalogue record for this
book is available from the
National Library of Australia

Places We Swim
ISBN 9781741175660

10 9 8 7 6 5 4 3 2 1

Publisher
Melissa Kayser

Project editor
Megan Cuthbert

Editor
Susan Paterson

Proofreader
Alison Proietto

Design
Evi-O.Studio

Typesetting
Kerry Cooke, Eggplant Communications

Index
Max McMaster

Prepress
Kerry Cooke and Splitting Image Colour Studio

Printed and bound in China by LEO Paper Group

Photo credits

All images are © Dillon Seitchik-Reardon, except for the
following images:

Back cover – Nikki To, Bondi Icebergs

Title page – Nikki To, Bondi Icebergs

Page iv – Eugene Tan of aquabumps.com, Bondi Beach

Page viii – Caroline Clements (top left), south-west
Tasmania

Page xiii – Michelle Rowse, Boodjamulla (Lawn Hill)
National Park

Page xiii – Peter Lik, Tourism and Events Queensland,
Alexandria Bay

Page xv – Jackson Groves, Babinda Boulders

Page 21 – Nikki To, Bondi Icebergs

Pages 22–3 & 25 – Remy Gerega, Clovelly Beach

Page 41 – Kate Berry (left), Turpins Falls

Page 75 – Jackson Groves, Second Valley

Page 80 – Jackson Groves, Uluru

Page 101 – Alex Kydd, Turquoise Bay

Page 103 – Remy Gerega, Cottesloe Beach

Page 147 - Paul Rowse, Boodjamulla (Lawn Hill)
National Park

Page 159 – Jesse Smith (top) and Matt Ralmondo (centre),
Tourism and Events Queensland, Fraser Island

Page 181 - Caroline Clements, Wineglass Bay